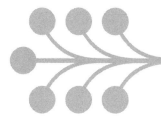

Working Well with Babies

Comprehensive Competencies
for Educators of Infants and Toddlers

Claire D. Vallotton, PhD, Holly E. Brophy-Herb, PhD,
Lori Roggman, PhD, and Rachel Chazan-Cohen, PhD

Redleaf Press®
www.redleafpress.org
800-423-8309

Published by Redleaf Press
10 Yorkton Court
St. Paul, MN 55117
www.redleafpress.org

First edition 2021
Cover design by Renee Hammes
Interior design by Louise OFarrell
Typeset in Adobe Chaparral Pro
Interior photos by iStock.com/sturti (page 53), iStock.com/FatCamera
    (pages 138–139), and iStock.com/SDI Productions (page 162).
Printed in the United States of America
28 27 26 25 24 23 22 21   1 2 3 4 5 6 7 8

Library of Congress Cataloging-in-Publication Data
Names: Vallotton, Clare D., author. | Brophy-Herb, Holly E., author. |
    Chazan-Cohen, Rachel, author. | Roggman, Lori A., author.
Title: Working well with babies : comprehensive competencies for educators
    of infants and toddlers / Clare D. Vallotton, Holly E. Brophy-Herb,
    Rachel Chazan-Cohen and Lori Roggman.
Description: First edition. | St. Paul, MN : Redleaf Press, 2021. |
    Includes bibliographical references. | Summary: "Working Well with
    Babies describes the comprehensive competencies (including the
    knowledge, dispositions, and skills) that educators of infants and
    toddlers must have to provide optimal support for infants and toddlers.
    Designed as a learning resource for both in-service and pre-service
    infant/toddler practitioners, this text details the nine competency
    dimensions of infant/toddler educators developed by the Collaborative
    for Understanding the Pedagogy of Infant/Toddler Development (CUPID)"—
    Provided by publisher.
Identifiers: LCCN 2021001529 (print) | LCCN 2021001530 (ebook) | ISBN
    9781605545509 (paperback) | ISBN 9781605545516 (ebook)
Subjects: LCSH: Early childhood education. | Child development.
Classification: LCC LB1139.23 .V35 2021 (print) | LCC LB1139.23 (ebook) |
    DDC 372.21—dc23
LC record available at https://lccn.loc.gov/2021001529
LC ebook record available at https://lccn.loc.gov/2021001530

Printed on acid-free paper

To our children who helped us appreciate the profound wonder of infancy and toddlerhood and the tremendous challenges and joys of being caregivers and educators:

Colette Eron Marie Vallotton
Isabelle Catherine Herb
Sophia Rose Herb
Rae Jean Sailor
Mark William Sailor
Eve Chazan Cohen
Arlo David Chazan Cohen

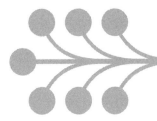

CONTENTS

ACKNOWLEDGMENTS

The authors of this book are sincerely grateful to the many individuals who have supported its development. First, we wish to acknowledge the Collaborative for Understanding the Pedagogy of Infant/Toddler Development (CUPID). CUPID is a group of more than fifty scientists and educators of infant-toddler development, care, and education working to better prepare and support the infant-toddler workforce by improving teaching and training of preservice and in-service practitioners. You can learn more at cupidconsortium.org. Our ultimate goal is to support the highest quality practice in the field of infant-toddler care and education; this book contributes by providing research- and standards-based resources for teaching and training. The many members of CUPID have contributed to the formation and organization of the ideas in this book, inspiring us through their research, teaching, and advocacy for the field of infant-toddler care and education. Several CUPID members have contributed directly to the writing and editing of this book:

- Jean Ispa, who helped write the chapters Educators of Infants and Toddlers, and Guiding Infant and Toddler Behavior

- Gina Cook, who helped write the chapters Educators of Infants and Toddlers, and Reflective Practice

- Kalli Decker, who helped write the chapter Supporting Development and Learning

- Maria Fusaro, who helped write the chapter Supporting Development and Learning

- Carla Peterson, who helped write the chapter Including Infants and Toddlers with Additional Support Needs and Their Families

- Julia Torquati, who helped write the chapter Leadership, Mentoring, and Coaching

We have great admiration and appreciation for our colleagues who are practitioners in the field of infant-toddler education, from whom we draw inspiration and with whom we exchange ideas that inform both research and practice. Finally, we are so grateful to the dedicated educators, generous families, and ever-exploring infants and toddlers at the Michigan State University Child Development Laboratories who let us observe and document their work and learning to provide examples and images for this book.

CHAPTER 1

Educators of Infants and Toddlers

—with Gina Cook and Jean Ispa

The science of child development paints a clear and critical picture: how well a child is doing at age three is a good predictor for how that child will do in school and even later in life. Our earliest experiences lay the foundation for how we will learn and interact with others. By age three, children already show great variation in the complexity of their brains, in the number of words they know, and in the ways they establish relationships with adults and peers. These differences are in part based on the characteristics the children were born with, but they also depend to a large degree on the children's experiences with the adults in their world.

There is growing recognition that the first three years of life are a distinct developmental period. As babies (children under three years) undergo rapid brain development, they are highly reliant on relationships with adults and highly responsive to environmental quality. During this critical growth period, the majority of infants (babies under eighteen months) and toddlers (babies between eighteen months and three years) in the United States spend time in out-of-home care each day, and at least one-third of those children are enrolled in center-based care. In fact, 40 percent of children in out-of-home care spend thirty-five hours or more per week in child care placements, clocking in more than eighteen hundred hours per year in care settings. Think of how differently this care and educational experience adds up for a child who has a highly qualified educator, compared to a child with an adult who meets their basic needs but does not have the **skills**, **knowledge**, or **disposition** to truly support their development.

These earliest years provide a unique opportunity for adults to have a long-term impact on children's future outcomes across a range of developmental domains. Research by economist James Heckman (2008) underscores the long-term societal economic advantages of investing in high-quality early childhood programming for babies and young children. No wonder, then, that families (people with whom a child has an ongoing relationship defined by family roles, regardless of biological or legal relationship), educators, and policy makers have been paying more attention to the quality of infant and toddler care and education. For several decades, the preschool period (ages three to four) was seen as the time to make children "ready for school." Today the infant-toddler period is the new frontier of school readiness. Educators and researchers are making efforts to professionalize the early care and education workforce, define **learning** objectives for infants and toddlers, and provide guidance in **best practices** to support school readiness beginning in infancy. For example, whereas in 2010 only thirty-one states reported having early learning guidelines (ELG) specifically for infants and toddlers, by 2013 forty-five states had such guidelines and twenty-eight states had specific certifications for infant-toddler care providers. This has led to increasing demands for professional degrees or certifications for practitioners working with infants and toddlers.

As we focus on this age group, we must guard against simply pushing frameworks developed for older children down to the infant and toddler years. In fact, new ways of conceptualizing infant-toddler outcomes and best practices could be pushed up to benefit the care and education of preschoolers. Many preschool frameworks were developed with an eye toward integrating them with elementary school guidelines, but instead preschoolers would benefit from practices used with younger children that encourage more attention to relationships and quality interactions, connections among developmental domains, exploration, and play.

In this book, we use the terms *educator* and *practitioner* interchangeably to reflect professionals working with infants, toddlers, and their families. Many titles are applied to those who work with young children and families. This book refers to *practitioners* as those who work with babies and families in any professional context, and the term *educator* for those who intentionally support others' development and learning, including educators of infants and toddlers, regardless of their professional title. We use the term *baby* to reinforce the idea that infants and toddlers under three are vulnerable and reliant on their relationships with adults, even after they start to walk and talk. This book can be used by the practitioner who is eager to learn more about quality infant-toddler care and education and wants to develop as a professional, or it can be used as a course textbook for a student planning to work with infants, toddlers, and their families. While the book primarily addresses those who work in group care settings (center-based and family child care), figure 1.1 shows how we understand the overlapping roles within the infant-toddler workforce, including those of infant-toddler educators, home visitors (professionals who work with parents or families in the context of the family's home) or family educators (professionals who

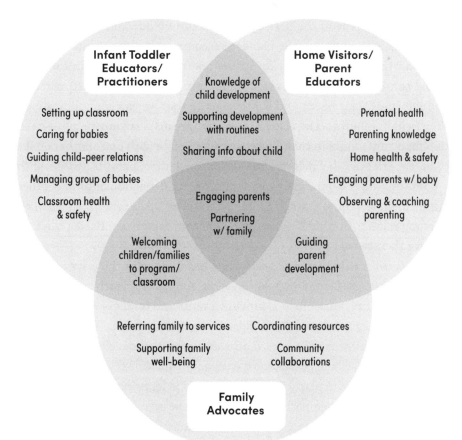

Infant Toddler Educators/ Practitioners

Setting up classroom

Caring for babies

Guiding child-peer relations

Managing group of babies

Classroom health & safety

Knowledge of child development

Supporting development with routines

Sharing info about child

Home Visitors/ Parent Educators

Prenatal health

Parenting knowledge

Home health & safety

Engaging parents w/ baby

Observing & coaching parenting

Engaging parents

Partnering w/ family

Welcoming children/families to program/ classroom

Guiding parent development

Referring family to services

Supporting family well-being

Coordinating resources

Community collaborations

Family Advocates

Figure 1.1. Overlapping Roles and Competencies for Infant-Toddler Professionals

provide education to families about children, parenting, and family life), and family advocates, and the shared and unique **competencies** needed for each role. The book will focus on developing these competencies—the knowledge, dispositions, and skills—that help infant-toddler educators support child well-being through direct care.

Why Focus on Infants and Toddlers? Brains, Dependency, and Relationships

Why do educators need specific skills to work with infants and toddlers? What is so special about this age, anyway? One answer is brains! The human brain grows more in the first three years of life than it will during the rest of the lifespan. This rapid growth makes the brain especially open to influences from experience. Young children (between birth and age eight years) are especially vulnerable to negative experiences but also exceptionally open to the benefits of positive experiences. Development during this period sets the stage for development and learning in preschool, elementary school, and life in general.

The second reason the first three years are unique and require special skills from educators is that babies are completely dependent upon the adults in their lives not only for safety and basic care, but also for emotional connection and cognitive stimulation. They rely on us to perceive and interpret their needs and subtle cues so that we can communicate on their behalf. Infants—and also toddlers who are just learning to talk—need the important adults in their lives to communicate with one another about their experiences, behaviors, and needs, including parents (those with a parenting role, regardless of biological or legal relationship) and other family members, other caregivers (any adult who takes care of babies in an ongoing relationship), educators, and other professionals. Babies can't do this for themselves.

The third reason this is a special time has to do with the ways in which babies' brains are shaped by relationships. As you will learn in chapter 3, consistent, caring relationships provide infants and toddlers with the sense of security they need to fully explore their environments. Exploration is important because it promotes motor and cognitive development. Moreover, babies' emotional connections with adults provide crucial stimulation for their brains, particularly the areas involved in learning about others (for example, developing empathy), developing their sense of themselves (self-worth), and expressing and regulating emotions. These are essential skills for getting along in the world.

Because of the vulnerability and opportunity of the first three years—the fast growth of the brain, the total dependence on adults, and the critical role of relationships—infant-toddler educators need unique competencies based on knowledge, dispositions, and skills, to accomplish high-quality work.

Babies Get Lost in the Field of Early Childhood Education

Another reason we focus on the competencies of infant-toddler educators is that there are few relevant sets of standards for this age level set by departments of education or accrediting agencies. Most standards for early child educator competencies either focus on teachers working with preschool-age children or are very broad, covering the whole early childhood period from birth to age eight years old. Covering such a broad age range often means the competencies most related to infants and toddlers get short shrift.

Babies—and their educators—get lost in early childhood education for reasons like these:

1 "Education" is assumed to start at five years old, and "early education" is assumed to start at three years old.

2 Educational services for children five years and older are paid for by the public, but educational services for children under five are paid for by families unless children are in early special education or other intervention programs (like those for families living in poverty).

3 Work with infants and toddlers has been seen as low-skill work (hence the ubiquitous term *babysitting*) and as primarily women's work.

4 Many professionals who work with babies and their families—including medical professionals, public health workers, and social workers—are not trained in child development or early education.

In this book, we argue that working with babies and their families involves both care and education, and it is one of the most complex and challenging jobs in our society. While this book is focused on infant-toddler educators who work in group care settings, these competencies also extend to those who work as home visitors—and in fact, these same skills are foundational for many professional roles involving work with and for babies and families.

How We Think about Babies and Their Educators

Our conceptual framework, or our way of thinking about infant-toddler care and education, is both developmental and contextual—that is, it is based on the science of child development and emphasizes how development is influenced by the many contexts of young children's lives. It is based on three beliefs: First, the first three years comprise a unique and important period in human development. Second, early development requires responsive caregiving relationships. Third, infants and toddlers learn best through active engagement and by exploring their physical and social world. These beliefs are backed by the theories and research that underlie the field's current thinking on best practices for educating and caring for infants and toddlers.

Relationships are the primary and essential context of early development, according to developmental theorists. Psychologist Urie Bronfenbrenner (2005) represented the centrality of the caregiving relationship by putting it at the core of his bull's-eye diagram of the embedded contexts of early development, and Arnold Sameroff (2009) referred to life in infancy as "we-ness" rather than "I-ness." These relationships are themselves embedded in community, cultural, and societal contexts that influence goals for children's development. They permeate the ways in which caregivers and families promote those developmental goals in their everyday routines, playful interactions, and other experiences that help infants learn about the world.

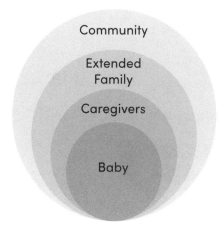

Figure 1.2. Important Relationship Contexts for Development

Attachment theory emphasizes infants' close relationships with parents and other caregivers as a crucial foundation for building confidence to explore, learn, and interact with others. Renowned attachment theorists John Bowlby (1982) and Mary Ainsworth (1979) viewed attachment—or the unique bond between a baby and caregiver (parents or others)—as the source of lifelong love and emotional well-being. Babies' sense of security in this relationship gives them the confidence to explore their worlds. This sensoriomotor exploration in infancy is the origin of human intelligence, as seen by Jean Piaget, a famous psychologist who advanced our understanding of infants' and young children's cognitive development. We will share other examples of the importance of relationships in chapter 3 and talk about the important things babies learn and how they learn them in chapter 6.

Abundant research across many **cultures** shows that babies who are securely attached to their caregivers are more likely to explore new environments, develop good communication skills, and regulate their emotions and behavior than babies with insecure attachments. These skills will help them later in forming positive relationships with peers, succeeding in school, and eventually becoming responsible adults who have stable romantic relationships and warm, responsive relationships with their own children. Although children deprived of responsive care in the earliest years can be helped if they receive such care later, development is much smoother if it is provided by caregivers (including child care providers as well as family members) from the earliest days of life. Responsive caregivers support babies' exploration and guide their understanding of how relationships work and how the world works. This is why caregivers and early educators are so important to babies' development, and it is why we have written this book.

The Structure of This Book and How to Use It

This book focuses on you—the practitioner who works, or will work, with infants, toddlers, and their families. We have organized the book around the competencies needed to engage in high-quality, developmentally supportive infant and toddler programming, and we guide the reader through building these competencies. These competencies can be aligned with other national competency frameworks for early child educators, and used to set goals for **professional development**.

As seen in figure 1.3, we focus on three types of competencies—knowledge, dispositions, and skills—in nine different domains (see figure 1.4 on page 7 for competency domains). That is, we describe what you need to know, what attitudes and values promote high-quality early care and education, and what to do to become the most effective infant-toddler practitioner you can be.

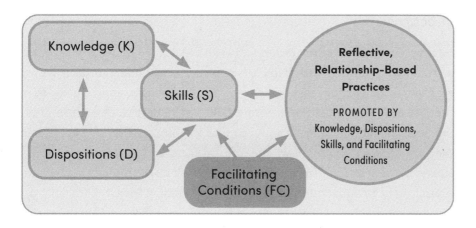

Figure 1.3. How Competencies Influence Practices

As we describe in figure 1.3, knowledge, dispositions, and skills all influence our practices with infants, toddlers, and families. Notice the two-way arrow between knowledge and dispositions, showing how they influence each other. Our dispositions—that is, our beliefs, attitudes, and values—may lead us to be more or less receptive to new knowledge and skills. Likewise, our dispositions may change as we gain new knowledge or skills. Both knowledge and dispositions contribute to the acquisition of new skills. There is also a two-way arrow between skills and practices. As we apply skills in practice, those skills get stronger and we can more easily apply them in different contexts. As you read each chapter, you will notice that when we discuss skills, we will also describe the reflective, **relationship-based practices** associated with those skills. **Reflective practices** and relationship-based practices are essential for high-quality work with children and families; you will learn more about these qualities in chapters 2 and 3. Finally, note that figure 1.3 also includes **facilitating conditions** that are necessary to enable practitioners to exercise their skills. For example, access to ongoing professional development and paid time for **curriculum** planning are facilitating conditions that allow educators to develop and implement high-quality experiences in the classroom.

Knowledge

This book provides the core knowledge you need to work well with infants, toddlers, and families. Based on the science of child development, care, and education, we focus on the things you need to understand deeply to be the most effective practitioner you can be. The science of child development continually expands, so there is more and more to know about infants, toddlers, and their families, and far more than we can fit in this book! Therefore, we point to other sources for more comprehensive knowledge in some areas. If you read this book thoroughly, at the end you will have the core knowledge you need to inform your beliefs, attitudes, and values, and to build your skills.

Dispositions

Infant mental health scholars Jeree Pawl and Maria St. John (1998) remind us that when working with babies, *how we are* is as important as *what we do*. *How we are* is about dispositions—attitudes, beliefs, and values—that support or hinder practitioners from doing their best work with infants, toddlers, and families. Beliefs and attitudes are informed by knowledge, but they are different from knowing empirical facts and are more emotional and personal in nature. They shape how we do what we do and bring out our commitment to doing our best. For example, we may *know* that picking up a crying baby is the quickest way to stop crying and that it will support the baby's emotion-regulation skills but still harbor a feeling that picking up a baby each time they cry will spoil them. We may also know our legal and ethical responsibilities to accommodate infants and toddlers with **additional support needs**, but this is separate from valuing the contributions of each child's uniqueness to the community of young learners. Many of the dispositions we describe in this book are those that research shows are related to high-quality practice and positive child outcomes, and others are part of the ethics and values of early childhood professional associations. While this book cannot give you dispositions in the way it can give you knowledge, each chapter describes relevant dispositions, and the Reflect Back, Think Ahead sections invite you to reflect on your own dispositions and how they affect your work.

Skills

We describe skills as what you must be able to do to implement high-quality reflective practices with infants, toddlers, and families. Skills involve being able to apply your knowledge and adapt it to specific situations. How will this book help you build skills to promote high-quality practices? Learning theorist John Dewey (1933) said famously, "We do not learn from experience . . . we learn from reflecting on experience" (78). In the Professional Learning Guide (PLG [see page 11]) that accompanies this book, we provide specific ways for you to self-assess, reflect, practice, and develop your competencies. The guide will invite you to assess your own competencies and reflect on your practices to build awareness of yourself and others while challenging you to set goals and find opportunities to practice the skills you want to develop.

Facilitating Conditions

Finally, we describe the facilitating conditions that promote educators' skills and reflective, relationship-based practices. Facilitating conditions exist within programs (child care center, early child education setting), rather than within the individual practitioner. Without the necessary facilitating conditions, educators may have the skills to plan and engage in high-quality experiences, but they will not be able to apply them in practice with babies, nor further develop those skills. Facilitating conditions are often the program policies and administrative supports that promote educators' capacities to develop and use their skills to engage in effective, high-quality reflective practices. Establishing facilitating conditions is the responsibility of program **directors**, **supervisors**, and other leaders, though individual practitioners can advocate for changes that will support their high-quality practice. Facilitating conditions are described near the beginning of each chapter so that **leaders** (administrators, directors, supervisors, and **coaches**) can easily find them to understand what they must do to support educators of infants and toddlers to provide the highest quality experiences for babies. In handout 1.1, Facilitating Conditions Checklist, program administrators will find a checklist for evaluating the status of facilitating conditions in their programs and setting goals for establishing the facilitating conditions that educators of infants and toddlers need to develop and use their competencies.

www.redleafpress.org/wwb/1-1.pdf

Nine Competency Domains

The nine competency domains crucial for working as an infant-toddler educator are related to one another in important ways, as seen in figure 1.4. Reflective practice starts at the left. It is represented as a large arrow behind the other competencies because this is the starting place, and it requires ongoing attention to allow you to intentionally develop other competencies. **Professionalism** is depicted along the bottom of the figure because as

Figure 1.4. Nine Domains of Comprehensive Competencies for the Infant-Toddler Workforce

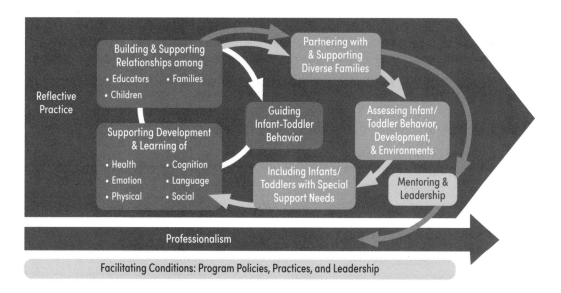

www.redleafpress.org/wwb/1-2.pdf

you learn about and develop the other competencies, you will grow as a professional by building knowledge of the field and being able to describe it to others. The inner circle (white arrow) represents the three central aspects of daily work with infants and toddlers: building and supporting relationships are the necessary foundation for effectively guiding infant-toddler behavior, which is a central part of supporting development and learning. The middle circle (light gray arrows) represents work that must intentionally involve families, including **assessing** infants and toddlers (and sometimes family/home environments) and working with families to include babies with additional support needs. The outer circle (medium gray arrows) reflects work with other adults, which is still founded in relationships with families but goes further to develop mentoring relationships with other adults (families, colleagues) as it relies on and builds skills in professionalism. Finally, the facilitating conditions described at the bottom of the figure underscore the fact that no one can do this important work alone. Policies, program practices and resources, and leadership make it harder or easier—and sometimes possible or impossible—to do your best work by using your competencies. Find the full list and description of all competencies and facilitating conditions in each domain in handout 1.2. Comprehensive Competencies List.

Abbreviations for the competency domains

- Competencies for Supporting Reflective Practice (RFP)
- Competencies for Building and Supporting Relationships (REL)
- Competencies for Partnering with and Supporting Diverse Families (FAM)
- Competencies for Guiding Infant-Toddler Behavior (GDB)
- Competencies for Supporting Development and Learning (DVL)
- Competencies for Assessing Behavior, Development, and Environments (ABD)
- Competencies for Including Infants and Toddlers with Additional Support Needs and Their Families (INC)
- Competencies for Leadership, Mentoring, and Coaching (LED)
- Competencies for Professionalism (PRO)

Abbreviations for knowledge, dispositions, skills, and facilitating conditions

- Knowledge (K)
- Dispositions (D)
- Skills (S)
- Facilitating Conditions (FC)

Organization of Chapters

The order of chapters within this book is intentional to support practitioners in building their own competencies as professionals. Thus, the chapters are not organized based on what you need to know first to work with babies but rather on what you need to know first to become a professional in the field of infant-toddler education, following figure 1.4. Within each chapter, we begin with an overview of the competency dimension and its importance to infant and toddler programming. We describe the facilitating conditions for building and exercising the competencies in that chapter. Then we address the knowledge, dispositions, and skills needed to provide high-quality infant and toddler care and education.

Throughout this book, you will be invited to engage in **reflection** on yourself as a learner and a practitioner. The capacity to engage in self-reflection is critical to our own personal growth and our growth as professionals. Self-reflection brings increased awareness and understanding of self and others, helping us to act with intentionality and flexibility in our work. As you read each chapter addressing each of the nine competency areas, think about a goal you will set for yourself in that area. In the last chapter of this book, we have included a brief self-assessment in which you can reflect on how your knowledge, dispositions, and skills have changed over the course of reading and thinking about the content in this book.

www.redleafpress.org/wwb/professional learningguide.pdf

Additional Material Available Online

Infant-toddler care and education are complex and make for a challenging job. This book attempts to be comprehensive in addressing the competencies needed by practitioners, but it cannot contain everything you need. Thus, we provide additional material online to extend what is offered in the book.

- Professional Learning Guide (PLG) to Competency Development: a workbook containing opportunities to self-assess, reflect on, practice, and develop your professional competencies related to each chapter in this book, including this one.

www.redleafpress.org/wwb/keyterms.pdf

- Key Terms: an alphabetical list of important concepts described throughout the book, with definitions.

- Resources and Further Readings: suggestions for further reading and additional resources related to the content of each chapter.

www.redleafpress.org/wwb/resources.pdf

Selected References

Ainsworth, Mary. 1979. "Infant-Mother Attachment." *American Psychologist* 34 (10): 932–37.

Bowlby, John. 1982. *Attachment and Loss*. Vol. 1. 2nd ed. New York: Basic Books.

Bronfenbrenner, Urie. 2005. *Making Human Beings Human: Bioecological Perspectives on Human Development*. Los Angeles: Sage.

Dewey, John. 1933. *How We Think: A Restatement of the Relation of Reflective Thinking to the Educative Process*. Chicago: Regnery.

Heckman, James J. 2008. "The Case for Investing in Disadvantaged Young Children." In *Big Ideas for Children: Investing in Our Nation's Future*, 49–58. Washington, DC: First Focus. https:/heckmanequation.org/assets/2017/01/Heckman20Investing20in20Young20Children.pdf.

Pawl, Jeree H., and Maria St. John. 1998. *How You Are Is as Important as What You Do . . . in Making a Positive Difference for Infants, Toddlers and Their Families*. Washington, DC: Zero to Three.

Sameroff, Arnold J. 2009. "Conceptual Issues in Studying the Development of Self-Regulation." In *Biopsychosocial Regulatory Processes in the Development of Childhood Behavioral Problems*, edited by Sheryl L. Olsen & Arnold J. Sameroff (1–18). Cambridge: Cambridge University Press.

CHAPTER 2

Reflective Practice

— with Gina Cook

Building a reflective practice means carefully observing the situations around us, then pausing to think about what we see and experience so we respond with intention, perhaps changing our practices. You can draw upon reflective practices spontaneously as a part of a general stance to your work, such as stopping to carefully consider the meaning of a baby's behavior before responding. You can also implement specific and systematic practices that enhance your work over time, such as methodically observing, documenting, and reflecting on babies' behaviors as they grow. The dispositions, knowledge, and skills that inform high-quality reflective practices are summarized in figure 2.1.

Why is reflective practice important? Reflection enables us to make meaning of our experiences and behaviors and to make intentional changes based on this learning. It allows us to develop thoughtful and supportive responses and to act with intention, rather than simply reacting based on assumptions or habit. When we respond thoughtfully and with intention, we can better build the relationships and provide individualized interactions and supports that are essential for babies' growth and learning.

Reflective practice helps you gain competencies over time. It gives you self-knowledge: what you know and what you need to know more about, what you believe and value and how that influences your work, and what you are comfortable and confident doing and the skills you'd like to gain. A reflective practice can help you better communicate what you do and why to parents and to others in the field of early child care and education, and it can help you decide what professional development opportunities to seek out.

How is reflective practice related to other competencies? Reflective practices, like relationships, undergird all competencies. The process of reflection enhances your relationships and work with infants, toddlers, and families. We hope this book serves as a tool for your reflective practice.

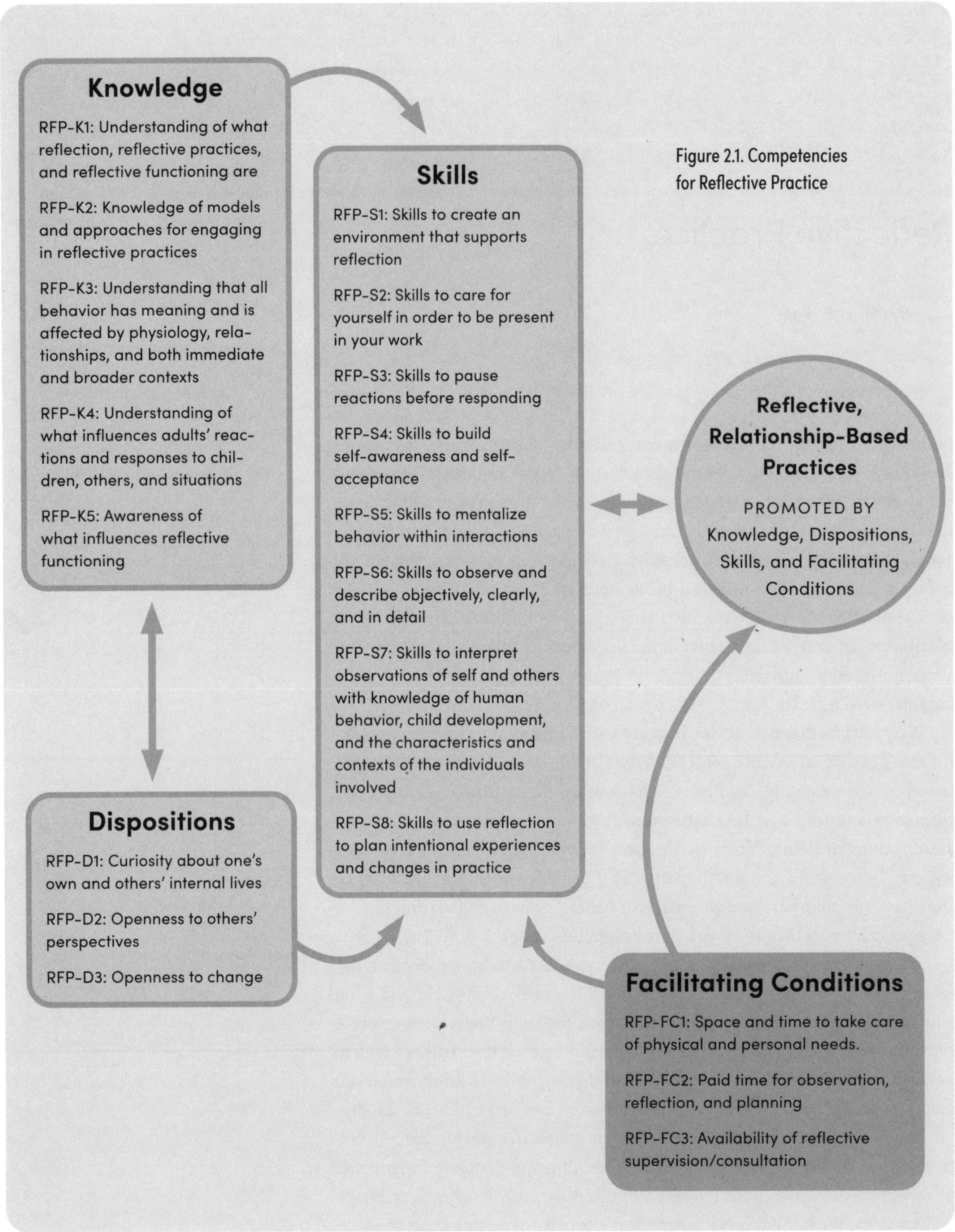

Knowledge

RFP-K1: Understanding of what reflection, reflective practices, and reflective functioning are

RFP-K2: Knowledge of models and approaches for engaging in reflective practices

RFP-K3: Understanding that all behavior has meaning and is affected by physiology, relationships, and both immediate and broader contexts

RFP-K4: Understanding of what influences adults' reactions and responses to children, others, and situations

RFP-K5: Awareness of what influences reflective functioning

Skills

RFP-S1: Skills to create an environment that supports reflection

RFP-S2: Skills to care for yourself in order to be present in your work

RFP-S3: Skills to pause reactions before responding

RFP-S4: Skills to build self-awareness and self-acceptance

RFP-S5: Skills to mentalize behavior within interactions

RFP-S6: Skills to observe and describe objectively, clearly, and in detail

RFP-S7: Skills to interpret observations of self and others with knowledge of human behavior, child development, and the characteristics and contexts of the individuals involved

RFP-S8: Skills to use reflection to plan intentional experiences and changes in practice

Figure 2.1. Competencies for Reflective Practice

Reflective, Relationship-Based Practices

PROMOTED BY Knowledge, Dispositions, Skills, and Facilitating Conditions

Dispositions

RFP-D1: Curiosity about one's own and others' internal lives

RFP-D2: Openness to others' perspectives

RFP-D3: Openness to change

Facilitating Conditions

RFP-FC1: Space and time to take care of physical and personal needs.

RFP-FC2: Paid time for observation, reflection, and planning

RFP-FC3: Availability of reflective supervision/consultation

In each chapter, we invite you to reflect on yourself (your thoughts, feelings, experiences, intentions) and the work you do with infants, toddlers, and families. This includes reflecting on the underlying meaning of others' behavior; on how our own experiences, thoughts, and feelings affect our understandings of others' behavior; and on how our actions affect others. Knowing yourself, the strengths you bring to the work, and which situations are challenging for you is essential knowledge in building relationships.

Facilitating conditions. High-quality infant and toddler programming requires support at the program administration level to allow practitioners to build their skills in reflective practice. At the most basic level, educators need the space and time to take care of their physical and personal needs (RFP-FC1). Specifically, resources to support basic human needs include an adult space for breaks, a restroom with adult-sized facilities, a space for breastfeeding educators to pump their breastmilk, spaces to store, heat, and eat lunches/meals, and adequate staffing to allow educators to take restroom and meal breaks. With the demands of infant and toddler caregiving, it can be surprisingly easy for educators to feel that they cannot leave the classroom for toileting breaks, for example. A variety of studies, such as those by researcher Kyong-Ah Kwon (2019), have found that early childhood educators, especially infant and toddler educators, experience more physical stressors and more health-related issues than those in other **professions**. This is largely because of the physical demands of caring for young children and the restricted time for personal care.

Second, administrators must provide paid time for educators' **observation**, reflection, and planning of their work with infants, toddlers, and families (RFP-FC2), with at least weekly planning time included in their work schedules. The planning time should be of sufficient length to allow for review and reflection on observations, as well as discussion and planning with coeducators. Third, administrators should ensure access to ongoing **coaching** or **reflective supervision**/consultation on a monthly or bimonthly basis (RFP-FC3). The individual or group meetings with a facilitator trained in **infant mental health** allow educators to reflect on their experiences and process their thoughts and feelings. New insights from these sessions often lead to more individualized, reflective, and high-quality interactions with babies and others.

Knowledge

Engaging in reflective practices with infants, toddlers, and families is an intentional act that takes forethought, planning, and practice, just as any new skill does. Before educators can use reflective practices, they must first understand what reflection is, what the processes for reflective practice are

(RFP-K1), and what models and approaches allow for the use of reflective practices in early care and education (RFP-K2). Reflective practices also rely on the understanding that all behavior (our own, infants', and even parents') has some meaning and expresses needs, and thus the work of reflection is to thoughtfully interpret those meanings and needs (RFP-K3). Reflective practitioners must understand that our own reactions and responses often reflect our beliefs about infants and toddlers and are heavily influenced by our prior experiences (RFP-K4). Given this, it is important that educators understand what influences their **reflective functioning** (RFP-K5).

Understanding reflection, reflective practices, and reflective functioning (RFP-K1)

Reflection is a process of working to better understand yourself and others that leads to awareness and an understanding of one's own reactions, experiences, beliefs, values, and theories of development, as well as those of others. Observation of self and others is a first step in reflection; it is an intentional practice of watching and listening to systematically gather detailed information. Your reflection on these observations makes them meaningful. Observing babies' characteristics and interactions (with yourself and others), then reflecting on those observations, allows you to identify babies' unique strengths, challenges, and needs. You get to know the patterns of interactions and qualities of relationships they have with you, their families, and others. With this knowledge, we are able to be intentional in supporting babies' development by individualizing interactions in ways that are well aligned with each baby and family. In turn, individualized interactions through observation and reflections strengthen relationships.

Reflective practices are characterized by a stance of wondering rather than a stance of assumptions. Broadly speaking, educators who assume a reflective approach are curious about others' internal experiences, including others' thoughts, feelings, desires and goals. Their interactions are done with forethought and intention and with attention to others. Educators who engage in reflective practices do so in a continuous process that involves ongoing observation, interpretation of observed behaviors and interactions, and analysis relative to children's growth and developmental needs. They use their conclusions to guide their interactions with babies and families and to individualize their experiences.

Sometimes the process of observing and reflecting is done methodically, such as when educators formally document **emerging skills** and then intentionally provide experiences to scaffold them. (We will talk more about this process in chapter 6 on supporting development and learning.) At other times, reflective practices occur informally in everyday moments.

For example, imagine a toddler becoming intensely upset when a parent leaves after the morning arrival. An educator utilizing a reflective stance wonders how the experience of adjusting to a new child care experience feels for the toddler and for the parent. The educator is aware of their own responses, such as whether they are comfortable with the toddler's distress or becoming anxious themselves. They consider the toddler's **temperament** and strategies used at home to comfort the child. The educator observes the toddler's cues to help determine how to respond. The educator uses this information to respond with respect and sensitivity in ways individualized to this particular child. Rather than giving a hurried response that **dismisses** the toddler's feelings to alleviate their own distress ("You're fine. Mom will be back"), the educator can acknowledge and validate the toddler's feelings and experiences and offer comfort in a way that works for the child ("You're crying. You look so sad. Your mom left and you miss her. Mom said your blankie helps you feel better when you are sad. Would you like your blankie while I hold you?").

Reflective functioning refers to one's capacity to consider **mental states** such as thoughts, feelings, intentions, goals, and desires in ourselves and in others, and to consider how these mental states affect our own and others' behavior. Reflective functioning can be enhanced over time through reflective practice.

Knowledge of models and approaches for engaging in reflective practices (RFP-K2)

Graham Gibbs (1988) developed a self-reflective cycle to help people reflect on their experiences and learn from them. The model has also been applied to early childhood educators. Figure 2.2 outlines the Gibbs model, which essentially guides educators to **notice and describe** all aspects of a situation. For example, this would include where and when the situation occurred, what the adult did, what the child did, what happened next, and how it ended. Educators then **reflect** to identify their own and others' thoughts and feelings—what was the educator thinking and feeling before, during, and after the interaction? What might the child have been thinking and feeling? All emotions are acceptable; the key is to identify the emotion and consider why it was evoked. It is important to consider why we felt a particular emotion and how our own experiences and needs may have contributed. (We will discuss **triggers** for strong emotions in the next sections—RFP-K3 and RFP-K4.) We suggest that educators also notice and describe their physiological reactions, such as changes in heart rate, breathing, and body tension, that reflect stressful experiences. The third step is to **evaluate** what happened, thinking about what worked well—and not

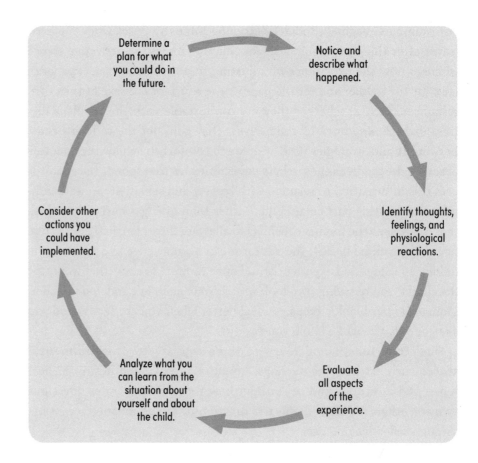

Figure 2.2. Adaptation of the Gibbs Self-Reflective Model

so well. Fourth, the educator **analyzes** what new information or understandings can be gained from the situation. The fifth step is to **draw conclusions** about effective strategies. The final step is to **determine a plan** of action for the future. For example, perhaps the cycle of reflection yielded new insights about particular ways a baby needs to be supported. Such models of self-reflection help educators recognize and challenge inaccurate assumptions they might hold, consider multiple perspectives, and identify new approaches.

Understanding that all behavior has meaning and is affected by physiology, relationships, and context (RFP-K3)

All behavior has meaning. Even if a behavior is unintentional, it comes from somewhere, and it has something to tell us. **Internal states**—such as physical needs, desires, feelings, thoughts, intentions, and beliefs—powerfully influence the way a baby behaves and responds. Babies' internal states and the resulting behavior can be influenced by a baby's temperament, stress, or illness, or by external factors such as caregiver behaviors, the physical environment, and the social environment, including who is in the room and how they are interacting with each other. (We describe the primary influences on behavior at greater length in chapter 5, Guiding Infant and Toddler Behavior.) Adults' behaviors too are influenced by physiology. For example, parents with unresolved trauma show different brain activity in reaction to caregiving prompts as compared to parents without unresolved trauma.

Detecting what is behind the behavior. Infants' internal states can be understood by carefully observing their eye movements, facial expressions, body posture and movements, breathing patterns, and levels of activity. For example, a relaxed baby who feels calm and secure will have slower and smoother limb movements with more relaxed muscle tone. A baby who is tense, overwhelmed, stressed, or anxious may show tighter muscle tone with stiffer limbs and jerkier movements. Reading babies' body language gives us a window into their mental states.

Another way to understand infants' mental states is to observe the context and gather clues about what the baby might be responding to. For example, some infants are very sensitive to environmental stimuli, such as bright lights, which make the baby feel agitated and behave in a fussy manner. Or perhaps someone the baby has never met has entered the room. Reflective practice means observing behavior and context and wondering what is behind the behavior. Ultimately, we cannot always know for sure what babies' behaviors mean, but our interpretations become more accurate as we get to know individual babies better and as our own skills in observing and reflecting develop. Later in this chapter, you'll learn a cycle of four questions to ask yourself about a baby's behavior before responding (except in urgent, dangerous situations, of course!).

Understanding what influences adults' reactions to children and situations (RFP-K4)

To fully engage in reflective practice, you must be able to reflect on the reasons for adults' reactions to babies, as well as on babies' behaviors. Most importantly this includes reflecting on yourself and your own actions and reactions, but it can also include reflecting on the behaviors of colleagues and parents.

Relationship history. Adults' prior relationships are powerful influences on their interactions with babies. Our earliest relationships with our parents and other caregivers inform our expectations surrounding relationships. Through secure relationships in early childhood, we come to view ourselves as valuable, capable partners. When relationships are not secure, we may come to view emotional closeness as something to avoid, or even feel emotionally threatened. This discomfort or fear can make it difficult to build relationships with babies and families. Work from attachment researchers such as Inge Bretherton (1990) has shown us that we tend to carry these templates into adulthood unless we reflect carefully on our prior experiences and how we may or may not want to repeat relationship behaviors that are familiar to us.

Emotional triggers. To varying extents, every individual comes to adulthood with positive and negative experiences we have internalized from our earliest relationships. These early experiences—and how we react to them emotionally—are built into the foundations of our brains. When something in the present reminds us of these experiences, we can become triggered. Triggers include words; situations; sensory experiences like smells, sights, and sounds; and other environmental characteristics that evoke a sense of psychological or physical threat. We feel threatened when our basic psychological needs for things like a sense of autonomy, competence and connection to others (such as feelings of acceptance, love, and respect)—feel compromised. So a trigger that evokes negative feelings such as shame, disapproval, rejection, dismissal, or contempt can make us feel psychologically threatened. For instance, an educator who was punished as a child for showing anger may have internalized a message that anger is something to avoid and have feelings of shame or rage associated with expressions of anger. Then, when a toddler angrily shouts "No!" to that educator, they may react strongly if they feel disrespected or challenged, particularly if the educator was punished for showing behaviors perceived as defiance in their own family growing up. Similarly, a program director who provides performance evaluation information to an educator in a punitive, embarrassing way can trigger a strong defensive reaction, particularly if that person has experienced shame or embarrassment related to **punishment**. A parent who has experienced physical abuse may react hostilely when their baby pulls their hair too hard. Each of our triggers are uniquely our own, and no one else knows what they are.

Self-reflection. Observation and self-reflection are powerful tools that enable us to recognize our triggers. Eventually we can learn to step back before we react when a triggering behavior occurs. It is important for educators to reflect on their strong reactions to identify triggers and come to understand why the trigger elicits a strong reaction in light of our past experiences. This awareness helps us have empathy for ourselves when we react in a way that does not reflect our best selves. Knowledge of infant and toddler behavior, and knowledge of parenting and family systems, also help us to see babies' and families' behaviors from a developmental perspective, reducing the likelihood that their behaviors will trigger us. Over time, this growing awareness also allows us to anticipate and prevent situations in which we might become triggered. We learn to repair our interactions and relationships when we do react in ways that may hurt others.

Awareness of what influences reflective functioning (RFP-K5)

Reflective functioning refers to our capacity to think about our own and others' mental states with interest and curiosity and to understand our own and others' behaviors as reflecting mental states. Each adult's ability and willingness to do this varies. It can be quite hard to do! If you are unable to identify your own mental states, it is difficult to recognize a child's mental state and then link that mental state to their behavior. Our current well-being and mental health, our previous traumatic experiences or **adverse childhood experiences** (ACEs), and our own attachment insecurities can get in the way of recognizing our own or others' mental states.

Well-being. Our capacity to engage in reflective practice can be influenced by our immediate needs and states. For example, physical wellness, hunger, and fatigue play a role in how much emotional and physical energy we have for observing and reflecting. Mental health, particularly anxiety and depression, influences reflective practices, as do work-related stresses. Infant and toddler educators report greater work stress than do educators of older children. Given the great emotional labor and physical demands of caring for infants and toddlers, this is not surprising. In the skills section, we will describe self-care practices that can enhance your well-being and support your reflective functioning.

Adverse childhood experiences and trauma. Adverse childhood experiences (ACEs) can include experiencing maltreatment, witnessing violence, being separated from a parent for a long time, living in a home with alcohol or drug abuse, or feeling unloved, and they are linked to a variety of negative outcomes for adults. ACEs may reflect trauma immediate to the family (such as maltreatment or domestic violence) or to the community (for example, witnessing violence in the neighborhood) or characterize trauma related to national and global events such as war, famine, and pandemics, including the 2020 COVID-19 global pandemic. Adults who experienced more ACEs report more problems in both mental and physical health. They also have more challenges in positive parenting, and the effects of childhood adversity can carry on from one generation to the next (e.g., Lomanowska and colleagues 2017). ACEs can hamper a caregiver's ability to provide sensitive and responsive care to their baby, and a caregiver's own history of trauma predicts the number of ACEs their children will experience. In fact, researcher Sohye Kim and colleagues (2014) found that mothers with prior trauma that was unresolved showed dampened brain activity when looking at photos of their babies in distress as compared to mothers without trauma. Being exposed to trauma negatively affects a child's brain development and their ability to **mentalize**—the capacity to understand one's own and others' internal thoughts, emotions, and intentions. An inability to mentalize in childhood can limit a person's capacity for reflective functioning as an adult, resulting in trauma that is passed down through generations. Some studies, such as work by Maria Muzik and colleagues (2015), suggest that increasing a caregiver's capacity for reflective functioning may help reduce the effects of their early adverse experiences. By fostering an adult's ability to understand their own emotions and reactions, and those of the children they care for, we may be able to increase positive, responsive caregiving behaviors and disrupt the intergenerational transmission of harmful experiences and interactions.

Attachment insecurity. Children with secure attachments may have more opportunities to practice mentalization within their relationships. Children with secure attachment relationships have warm, predictable, sensitive caregivers who are attuned to babies' cues and try to understand babies' perspectives and read their mental states. Thus, caregivers are modeling what it is to read and understand another's mind, and babies are experiencing what it is like to be understood. Over time, this may help children acquire mentalization skills themselves. On the other hand, an insecure attachment can decrease a person's ability to mentalize in childhood and is associated with impaired reflective functioning in adulthood.

Though many things can hinder reflective functioning and disrupt reflective practices, adults can learn the skills of observation and engage in these practices intentionally. Practicing these skills builds adults' capacities. We will describe these skills and practices further later in this chapter.

Dispositions

Curiosity about our own and others' internal lives (RFP-D1) and openness to new ideas and perspectives (RFP-D2) are the critical dispositions that allow us to more readily reflect on our own and others' experiences. Seeing from others' perspectives is central to empathizing with children and their families, and it helps us become more open to changing our views on something, even our deep-seated beliefs (RFP-D3).

Curiosity about your own and others' internal lives (RFP-D1)

In so many ways, reflective practice is characterized by a sense of curiosity and wonder. Reflective educators are curious about babies' experiences and their own reactions and responses. Such curiosity signifies a willingness to reflect thoughtfully on your own beliefs and their origins, as well as your reactions to **challenging behaviors** and situations. You wonder about how the baby feels and experiences everyday moments and how these feelings and experiences influence their development.

Openness to others' perspectives (RFP-D2)

This disposition involves a willingness to reflect thoughtfully on children's (and families' and colleagues') behaviors and perspectives, including what drives their reactions to you. In the field of infant and early childhood mental health, pioneered by psychoanalytic therapist Selma Fraiberg and colleagues (2003), practitioners are encouraged to ask, "What about the baby?" meaning that they should try to see the world from the baby's perspective, wonder about the baby's experiences, and be curious about what the baby might be feeling, thinking, and needing. Curiosity and openness are at the core of wondering, "What about the baby?" When you are in the midst of a trying situation or a hard time in your life, perspective taking and any reflective practice can be more difficult. Studies show that those who are drawn to human service fields, such as working with infants and toddlers, are more likely to have had difficult childhood experiences than professionals in other fields (Esaki and Larkin 2013). However, professionals who have worked to understand the influences of those early experiences on their own lives and development are often empathic adults skilled in perspective taking.

Openness to change (RFP-D3)

Openness to change means having a willingness to challenge yourself, including your own assumptions about the nature of development and adults' roles or the meaning, purpose, or motivation behind child behavior. For example, perhaps an educator was raised with the idea that young children can be manipulative. An openness to change means that the educator is willing to rethink this assumption as they learn more about early development, babies' needs, and the ways in which unmet needs underlie behavior.

Openness to change is about your willingness to engage in reflection and to let those reflections guide changes in your own behavior. This openness is aided by an attitude of curiosity and by your own sense of security and confidence in who you are as a person and as a professional. There are people who are more or less open to change, and there are times in your life when you are more or less open to change. Many people are more open to change during the process of education and training as they look for new insights and build new skills.

Figure 2.3 describes the skills involved in reflective practices, which start with creating an environment that facilitates reflection (RFP-S1) and implementing self-care routines that allow educators to be present in their work (RFP-S2). Key skills needed to effectively reflect during interactions include pausing before reacting (RFP-S3), becoming self-aware and accepting your own reactions (RFP-S4), and then accepting the mental states of others that underlie their behavior (RFP-S5). Finally, reflective practice requires ongoing, objective observations (RFP-S6) and interpretations of those observations to understand oneself and others (RFP-S7), allowing practitioners to plan and change their interactions with intention (RFP-S8).

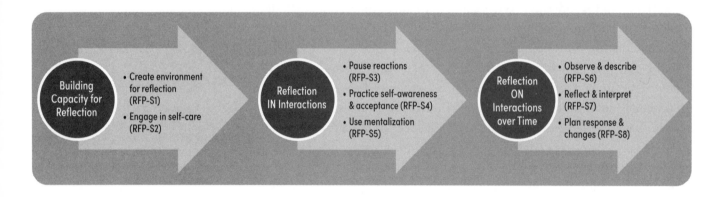

Figure 2.3. Contexts and Skills to Build Reflective Functioning and Reflective Practices

Creating an environment that supports reflection (RFP-S1)

Reflection relies on intentional observations of infants and toddlers, taken on a regular basis (usually weekly). Program budgets should include materials to support the educators' reflections, such as notepads and pens for writing **anecdotal records** or **running records**, cameras for taking photos or videos of babies interacting, and storage spaces for such documentation. With some simple organization—such as filing observations by date, by child, or by domain—educators can create a method for compiling rich information that can contribute to their cycle of reflective practice.

STRATEGIES ——————————————————

※ Create a plan for collecting and organizing thoughts, reflections, and observations throughout the day, such as keeping a notebook and pen in the classroom. In resources available through the National Association for the Education of Young Children (NAEYC), Bates and colleagues (2019) suggest strategies such as focusing on particular children each day (such as your **primary caregiving** group) and using colored index cards for notes with colors reflecting a domain area or daily focus. Revisit your reflections and observations during weekly planning time.

✳ Keep observation collection tools (such as pen and paper, a camera, or a tablet with camera) in easy to access locations in the classroom. Try keeping a pen-and-notebook set or sticky notes in each classroom area (book area, block area, house corner, and so on) or use voice-to-text apps to record observations efficiently.

Ms. Jessica keeps her camera and note cards accessible to record babies' work and development.

Caring for yourself so you can be present in your work (RFP-S2)

Building internal resources and habits for caring for yourself is absolutely necessary, both because you are important as an individual and because caring for yourself helps you engage in reflective practices. Interactions between babies and their caregivers are the primary context of babies' development. The quality of those interactions depends heavily upon the caregivers' well-being. Working with infants and toddlers is physically demanding, emotionally exhausting, and cognitively challenging; thus, work-related stress among early childhood educators is particularly high. Likewise, reflecting intentionally and thoughtfully on babies' behaviors requires the mental space and other internal resources that good self-care can facilitate.

Getting enough sleep, eating healthfully, and taking time to engage in relaxing activities outside of work are all important elements of self-care, as well as doing things you love and spending time with people who make you feel loved. Developing positive strategies for coping with stress is also critical. Caring for yourself is essential if you are to be fully available for babies and their families. Finally, as we noted earlier, part of the facilitating conditions that administrators provide is to ensure that educators have personal and physical care breaks during the day (RFP-FC1). It can be very easy to miss breaks in the ongoing demands of caring for infants and toddlers.

STRATEGIES

* Make a list for yourself of activities or people that help you feel calm, happy, and like your best self; make sure these are incorporated into your life each week.

* Create a simple sleep routine, such as listening to calming music or reading for a few minutes before bed. If possible, use your sleeping space only for sleep and not for work. Try to avoid using your phone, computer, or other screens in the hour before you plan to sleep.

* Keep a gratitude journal or simply start the day by thinking about one thing, however small or great, for which you are grateful. A wealth of research shows that people who practice gratitude report greater feelings of well-being.

* Develop habits of caring for yourself at work, which might include taking brief breaks, communicating additional needs to your coeducators and supervisors, and engaging in **mindfulness** practices (described below).

Pausing reactions before responding (RFP-S3)

Pausing in the moment, before you react, is a first step to a reflective response. Pausing is a **self-regulation** skill that takes practice to develop. When you pause to notice thoughts and feelings in the moment (more in RFP-S4), you can respond thoughtfully rather than merely reacting in habitual ways. Pausing, reflecting, and *then* responding is a key reflective practice that promotes relationships and high-quality care for infants and toddlers. It also models for babies (and others) the self-regulated behavior you want them to develop. There are countless opportunities throughout the day to pause and respond thoughtfully instead of reacting without intention. For example, daily arrival and departure times can be emotionally challenging for everyone. Pausing to notice your own thoughts and feelings, as well as the feelings and needs of the baby and parent, can guide you to respond compassionately, supporting the parent-baby relationship and the educator-family relationship.

Consider this drop-off situation. Baby Xavier is screaming as his mother, Juanita, prepares to go, and Juanita pauses at the door with a worried look on her face. Teacher Will could react quickly and dismiss the mother's concern, saying, "He'll be fine. Go ahead and go." Juanita would go, but she might worry about Xavier all day and have trouble concentrating at work. Instead, Will could pause to notice the mother's feelings as well as his own, and then decide how to respond with intention. For example, he might choose to acknowledge the mother's feelings and offer comfort: "I can see you are worried. It's hard to say goodbye. I'm going to be right here to help Xavier feel better at school. I'll be able to tell you all about his day when I see you later." Juanita would leave feeling reassured about Xavier's well-being, and she would gain trust in Will.

Pausing also enables you to consciously become aware of and suspend your assumptions about a situation. For example, imagine doing a home visit with a new family and arriving at the home for the first time to see discarded food on the floor and trash overflowing the garbage can. Taking a moment to notice your own reactions allows you to note assumptions you might be making about the family and then choose to suspend those assumptions to get to the know the family and their particular strengths and needs.

STRATEGIES

- ❈ Find times in your work with others when you feel like you're on autopilot, then consciously bring your attention to your own internal states. As you train yourself to become more aware, you will be less likely to operate without intention.

- ❈ Take a few deep breaths when you feel stressed and overwhelmed. Deep breathing lowers your heart rate and helps you feel calmer.

- ❈ Consider identifying moments of anxiety or stress as part of your end-of-day reflections. Over time, you will begin to see patterns in what kinds of events are most challenging and in what contexts.

- ❈ Throughout the day, ask yourself questions such as *Why did I react that way? What am I feeling right now? Was my reaction really about this situation or something else?* Over time, you will notice patterns—what you react to and when, how you feel, and what your reactions are really about. This awareness will help you see others more accurately as well because your view will not be clouded by your own reactions.

✳ Practice identifying your emotions outside of work too. If you're feeling angry while stuck in traffic, think about what's driving your anger. Often there are secondary emotions behind what we are feeling in the moment. For example, feeling angry at traffic might be more about a neglected need earlier in the day, such as feeling disrespected or undervalued or physically depleted.

Building self-awareness and self-acceptance (RFP-S4)

Self-awareness and self-acceptance are key foundations of reflective practice. You need to be aware of your own physical and emotional states in the moment when they are happening if you are to understand your own reactions to people and situations. This understanding is foundational for learning to respond to situations, not just react to them. Physical internal states include being tired, hungry, in pain, or needing to go to the bathroom. Emotional internal states can encompass the whole range of emotions, but in infant-toddler work they commonly include challenging emotions such as feeling stressed, anxious, overwhelmed, uncertain, frustrated, angry, and sad, as well as neutral and positive emotions such as surprise, curiosity, joy, and excitement. Self-awareness begins with pausing intentionally at moments during the day to observe our own physical and mental states (see RFP-S3). This awareness is an important aspect of mindfulness, the practice of noticing thoughts, feelings, and sensations in the moment and accepting them without judgment. For example, if Teacher Mia arrives at work feeling tense about an interaction that happened at home, she notices and acknowledges the tense feelings without criticizing herself, saying to herself, *I'm feeling tense all over my body, and a little anxious, which makes sense because I'm still worried about that argument at home this morning.* She avoids self-critical thoughts such as *It's silly for me to be upset about that.*

Engaging in reflective practices takes a good deal of focus and work. Mindfulness practices are tools that can help us become reflective by helping us learn to pause and become more self-aware and self-accepting. Mindfulness practices can also become a form of self-care, building internal resources that help educators cope with stress and regulate their emotions and reactions.

www.redleafpress.org/wwb/2-1.pdf

STRATEGIES ――――――――――――――――――――――――

✳ Infant-toddler educators can practice mindfulness throughout the workday, using these strategies to pause, calm, and become self-aware. See handout 2.1, Mindfulness for Educators.

❊ Using mindfulness practices in the classroom can help educators model for babies a calm, aware, and accepting presence. Educators can use simple practices together with toddlers to support their emotion regulation. See handout 2.2, Mindfulness for Babies.

Mentalizing behavior within interactions (RFP-S5)

At its heart, reflective practice is about understanding one's own and others' mental states. Working to accurately understand others' mental states and linking behavior with mental states is the art of **mentalizing**. For example, if a toddler is having a tantrum, an educator engaged in mentalization will focus less on the tantrum itself and more on understanding the unmet physical or emotional needs that led to the behaviors, such as wondering how overwhelmed the toddler might feel. Mentalization is typically reflected in how educators talk to infants and toddlers (and to families and colleagues). For instance, when mentalizing, educators reflect out loud, describing children's emotions ("You're smiling; you seem happy"), their thoughts ("Hmm, you're thinking about how to keep the blocks from falling over"), their intentions and goals ("It looks like you are trying to get up onto that trike"), or their desires and needs ("You want the red ball").

When we articulate another's mental state, our own awareness of that person's mental state, which may be quite different from our own, increases. That helps us respond accordingly. Articulating a child's mental states communicates to the child that their thoughts, feelings, goals, and needs are valuable. Over time, identifying mental states in an intentional way builds babies' knowledge and understanding of their own and others' emotions and other internal states, a skill that is linked to the child's later self-regulation and social-emotional skills. Research from scientists such as Ilaria Grazzani and colleagues (2016) shows that toddlers whose caregivers talk about their emotions in sensitive and appropriate ways use more emotion talk themselves, a skill that children need to fare well in many social contexts. In handout 2.3, Reflective Speech, we define and provide examples of specific ways of talking with infants and toddlers that are reflective. By reflecting out loud in our interactions, we create a habit and culture of reflection with those around us.

www.redleafpress.org/wwb/2-2.pdf

www.redleafpress.org/wwb/2-3.pdf

STRATEGIES ─────────────────────────

 ❊ While you are learning about different types of reflective talk, pick one or two types of talk to intentionally focus on each week.

※ Take a few minutes at the end of each day to think about your experiences and the children's experiences. Ponder how both joyful and challenging moments felt for you and how they felt for the baby. You can use the same strategy as you reflect on your interactions with families.

Observation and Reflection over Time

Once we have skills to pause, notice without judgment, and reflect in the moment, we can build skills in making careful and accurate observations. That is, we take these observation and reflection skills to a new level by using them intentionally and systematically over time, which lets us plan supports for babies' well-being and development. Here we describe the set of skills that work together in a cycle of observing (RFP-S6), reflecting (RFP-S7), and planning thoughtful responses (RFP-S8).

Figure 2.4 outlines a continuous process of reflecting on the child's experience to respond with compassion and support. This cycle mirrors the skills we have already discussed, first to pause and notice, then to become aware of your own and others' thoughts and feelings before finally determining how to respond. Here we show how this works over time, as you make multiple observations, reflect on them altogether, and plan responses to implement later. This demonstrates how reflective practices are both in-the-moment interaction skills and also skills that can guide your work with children more broadly and systematically.

Figure 2.4. Observe, Reflect, and Respond Cycle

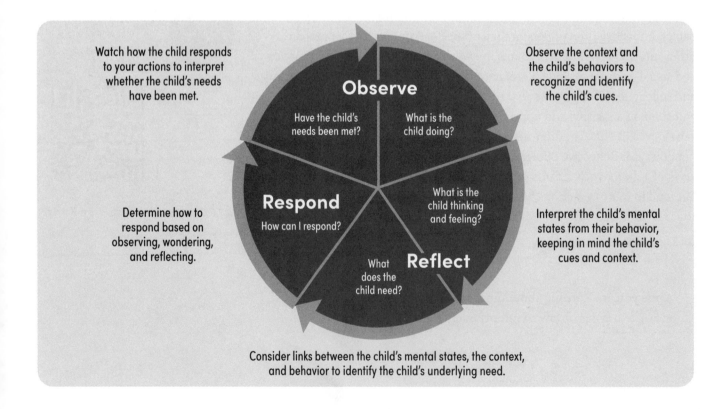

Watch how the child responds to your actions to interpret whether the child's needs have been met.

Observe the context and the child's behaviors to recognize and identify the child's cues.

Determine how to respond based on observing, wondering, and reflecting.

Observe
Have the child's needs been met?
What is the child doing?

Respond
How can I respond?
What is the child thinking and feeling?

What does the child need?
Reflect

Interpret the child's mental states from their behavior, keeping in mind the child's cues and context.

Consider links between the child's mental states, the context, and behavior to identify the child's underlying need.

Observing and describing objectively, clearly, and in detail (RFP-S6)

As we intentionally observe, we notice children's interests and efforts and see their capabilities. Observing objectively means noticing and describing behavior without assumptions, without attributing any meaning or particular intentions to them. We observe exactly what happened, including what the child is doing and saying, what the context/setting is, and who else is involved. We also observe their behaviors that give us clues to their internal states, such as their body posture, facial expressions, or what they are looking at. Then we also observe ourselves. We notice our physiological reactions, our emotions, our behaviors. These observations become the data we use in our reflections.

STRATEGIES

⁂ Take clear and detailed anecdotal records—written descriptions of meaningful moments that show the baby's behavior or development.

- Include information about the physical location, day, and time, and who was present.

- Give enough detail that a parent or colleague could understand what happened just from the anecdote, and enough information that you can interpret the baby's behavior and understand their development.

- Be objective and stick just to the facts of what the child said and did, saving your interpretations for later. You may not always have time to write down your interpretations in the moment. Try to jot down a few key words or brief descriptions that will help you remember your observations and thoughts. Return as soon as you can to more fully write the anecdotes and your interpretations.

Ms. Sweazy joins the toddlers at the table, writing anecdotal records about what they say while they mark in their journals.

Practice, practice, practice! As your observation skills improve, you will notice more details and make fewer assumptions, looking for all of the relevant information before responding. Table 2.1 provides examples of more and less detailed and more and less objective anecdotal records for the same event.

Table 2.1. Recording Clear, Detailed, and Objective Observations

	Less Objective *Notice the bolded words that indicate less objective descriptions.*	More Objective
Less Clear and Detailed	Jordan was **happily** pulling the caps off the pens and they all slipped out of his hands. He **got really upset** when he saw them on the ground.	Jordan was pulling caps off several markers when they slipped out of his hands. He looked at the markers on the floor, then yelled.
Clearer and More Detailed	On Wednesday, April 3, during morning free-play in the classroom, Jordan (23 months) was **interested in** using the markers at the art easel where **he saw** another child making art. He held some markers in his hands, **trying to** take the caps off and put them all on his fingers. There were too many things in his hands, **so** the markers all fell on the floor, **which upset** Jordan. He **got frustrated** and started to yell about his pens being on the floor.	On Wednesday, April 3, during morning free-play in the classroom, Jordan (23 months) stood at the art easel; one other child was nearby. J held four markers in his hands. He took the cap off of one and placed it on his fingertip. He took a second cap off, placing it on another fingertip. When he took the third cap off, the markers all fell out of his hands. J looked down at the floor; his eyebrows were furrowed, and he said loudly, "My pens on floor!"

Interpreting observations with knowledge of human behavior, child development, and the characteristics and contexts of the individuals involved (RFP-S7)

After making observations, the next step is to reflect on them and make interpretations, determining what they can tell you about the baby and about yourself. In these reflections, you consider what the baby might be feeling and thinking and how it relates to the context and behaviors you noticed. To interpret our observations, we draw on our knowledge of human behavior, child development, and the characteristics and contexts of the individuals involved. Reviewing and reflecting on observations can provoke new questions and help you plan future observations. In table 2.2, we consider what we can learn from the observation in table 2.1.

Table 2.2. Interpreting Observations

Observation	Interpretation	Notes and Questions
. . . during morning free-play in the classroom, Jordan stood at the art easel; one other child was nearby.	J is spending time in the art area near other children.	Does J spend a lot of time in the art area? Is he interested in making art?
He held four markers in his hands and took the cap off of one and placed it on his fingertip. He took a second cap off, placing it on another fingertip. When he took the cap off a third one, the markers all fell out of his hands onto the floor.	J engaged in systematic behavior and seemed to have a goal in mind. He has fine-motor skills and strength to take caps off of pens and put them on fingers. But he misjudged his ability to hold the pens in his hands and didn't anticipate what would happen. This behavior is not something I've seen other children do; I think Jordan came up with it on his own, using the material in a new and creative way.	
J looked down at the floor; his eyebrows were furrowed, and he said loudly, "My pens on floor!"	Jordan was frustrated that the pens fell. This tells me he had a goal in mind that he didn't reach. J is now using 4-word sentences, and he used the word "my" correctly!	Is J usually easily upset, or just when he is focused on a goal and something gets in his way?
My reaction: I was curious to see what Jordan would do with the pens once he got the caps on his hands. I felt sorry for him when he couldn't finish what he started, and I wanted to go help him do it. But I stopped myself so I could check with him about his feelings and what he wanted to do next.		Do I tend to jump in and help most children, or is it just this child? Or is it just when children are frustrated?

Review several observations together to learn about the child and yourself. What patterns are here? What do these tell me about the child? What am I learning about myself? For example, your observations over time might yield insights about the child and yourself: *Jordan is creative and pursues his own goals with persistence but gets easily frustrated when his goals are blocked. I tend to want to jump in and solve problems for children because I don't like to see them upset. But if I wait a minute, they often figure it out for themselves.* In short, writing and reviewing observations is a foundational part of reflective practice, which continually enhances your relationship with and ability to support individual babies and develops your own reflective skills over time.

✳ Use key words or abbreviations for emotional or other needs that drive babies' behaviors. Examples include "indep" to denote a need to strive for **independence**; "sep" to denote separation anxiety, and so on. Over time, you will begin to see common themes in the emotional needs that underlie behavior.

✳ Identify common developmental themes that underlie behaviors. Identifying the theme means you can better meet the developmental need in positive ways. For example, as infants become interested in cause-and-effect relationships, they may engage in a variety of behaviors, such as pushing food off a high chair tray, dumping baskets of toys, and even biting. You can use abbreviations for these too.

Using reflection to plan intentional experiences and changes in practice (RFP-S8)

With observation and reflection, educators form intentional responses that keep the baby's feelings, goals, intentions, **developmental skills**, and needs in mind. Such intentional responses build the educator-baby relationship and enable educators to more thoughtfully plan their support for babies' development. From the example above, an educator may plan a response for the next time Jordan is working hard on a difficult task. *Since Jordan had strong understanding of language, next time he's doing a difficult task I can help him with my words, but I will let him do the task physically on his own unless he asks for help.* With this kind of intention in the forefront of your mind, you are more likely to pause, observe, reflect, and respond thoughtfully next time you encounter a similar situation.

Finally, the last step in the cycle of observing, reflecting, and responding is to start over at the beginning by observing how the child responds to what you did. In our example, what did Jordan do when he encountered a frustrating task and the educator talked with him about his goals and feelings? Did that strategy work for him? You may find it helpful to write down your observations and conclusions in the last step of the cycle. As you become more familiar with the process, it may not be necessary to record your conclusions in writing; instead, it may be sufficient to identify and think about your final conclusions in your mind. Whether or not you write down this final observation, you have become more intentional about pausing, observing, and responding to this situation and can use the information you gain to continually enhance your work with this child.

Reflect Back, Think Ahead

Look back at the figure at the beginning of this chapter that shows the knowledge, dispositions, and skills involved in the Reflective Practice competency domain. Which of these competencies did you have when you began this chapter? Which competencies did you develop? Which competencies will you intentionally work on building next? Use the Reflective Practices chapter of the Professional Learning Guide (PLG [see page 11 for the QR code link]) that accompanies this book to support your own professional growth in this domain.

Selected References

Bates, Celeste C., Stephanie Madison Schenk, and Hayley J. Hoover. 2019. "Quick and Easy Notes: Practical Strategies for Busy Teachers." *Teaching Young Children* 13 (1). www.naeyc.org/resources/pubs/tyc/oct2019 /practical-strategies-teachers.

Bretherton, Inge. 1990. "Communication Patterns, Internal Working Models, and the Intergenerational Transmission of Attachment Relationships." *Infant Mental Health Journal* 11 (3): 237–52.

Brown, Kirk Warren, and Richard M. Ryan. 2003. "The Benefits of Being Present: Mindfulness and Its Role in Psychological Well-Being." *Journal of Personality and Social Psychology* 84 (4): 822–48.

Esaki, Nina, and Heather Larkin. 2013. "Prevalence of Adverse Childhood Experiences (ACEs) among Child Service Providers." *Families in Society: The Journal of Contemporary Social Services* 94 (1): 31–37.

Gibbs, Graham. 1988. *Learning by Doing: A Guide to Teaching and Learning Methods*. Oxford: Oxford Center for Staff and Learning Development, Oxford University.

Grazzani, Ilaria, Veronica Ornaghi, Alessia Agliati, and Elisa Brazzelli. 2016. "How to Foster Toddlers' Mental-State Talk, Emotion Understanding, and Prosocial Behavior: A Conversation-Based Intervention at Nursery School." *Infancy* 21 (2): 199–227.

Kim, Sohye, Peter Fonagy, Jon Allen, and Lane Strathearn. 2014. "Mothers' Unresolved Trauma Blunts Amygdala Response to Infant Distress." *Social Neuroscience* 9 (4): 352–63.

Kwon, Kyong-Ah. 2019. "Are Early Childhood Teachers Happy and Healthy?" Jeannine Rainbolt College of Education at the University of Oklahoma. www .ou.edu/education/bridges/fall-2019/early-childhood-teachers-happiness.

Kwon, Kyong-Ah, and Lieny Jeon. 2019. "Happy Teacher Project: Supporting Early Childhood Teachers' Physical, Psychological, and Professional Well-Being." Presentation at Child Care and Early Education Policy Research Consortium, Washington, DC.

Lomanowska, Anna M., Michel Boivin, Clyde Hertzman, and Alison Fleming. 2017. "Parenting Begets Parenting: A Neurobiological Perspective on Early Adversity and the Transmission of Parenting Styles across Generations." *Neuroscience* 342 (7): 120–39.

Muzik, Maria, Katherine L. Rosenblum, Emily A. Alfafara, Melisa M. Schuster, Nicole M. Miller, Rachel M. Waddell, and Emily Stanton Kohler. 2015. "Mom Power: Preliminary Outcomes of a Group Intervention to Improve Mental Health and Parenting among High-Risk Mothers." *Archives of Women's Mental Health* 18 (3): 507–21.

Slade, Arietta. 2005. "Parental Reflective Functioning: An Introduction." *Attachment & Human Development* 7 (3): 269–81.

Whitaker, Robert C., Brandon D. Becker, Allison N. Herman, and Rachel A. Gooze. 2013. "The Physical and Mental Health of Head Start Staff: The Pennsylvania Head Start Staff Wellness Survey, 2012." *Preventing Chronic Disease*, Centers for Disease Control and Prevention (CDC). www.cdc.gov/pcd/issues /2013/13_0171.htm.

CHAPTER 3

Building and Supporting Relationships

Relationships are the context in which infant and toddler development and learning occur. Thus, relationships are at the core of your work, including your relationships with everyone who influences babies and your work with them. Knowledge of early relationships and development also better equips us to explain our practices to others and advocate for high-quality infant-toddler care and education. The dispositions, knowledge, and skills that promote high-quality practices in building and supporting relationships are summarized in figure 3.1.

To effectively build and support all of the relationships that surround babies, we must understand the nature of babies' relationships, including how other relationships affect them, as well as the approaches, policies, and practices that support relationships. Some key relationships are shown in figure 3.2.

Why are building and supporting relationships important? Psychoanalyst and physician Donald Woods Winnicott (1964) wrote that babies do not exist alone; they exist in a relationship with others, such as parents and caregivers. Babies are always interacting, developing, and learning through their relationships with others. The baby-caregiver relationship exists within, and is influenced by, a set of other important relationships. The educator-family relationship is a critical model for babies as it typically involves the interactions between the most important people in their lives. Peer relationships give babies opportunities to practice the skills they need in a social environment. Relationships with your colleagues contribute to the quality of the work environment and set the tone for babies. Relationships between educators and supervisors/directors influence educators' well-being and practices.

In a positive relational environment, babies learn skills such as regulating themselves; engaging in helping behaviors; learning to express needs;

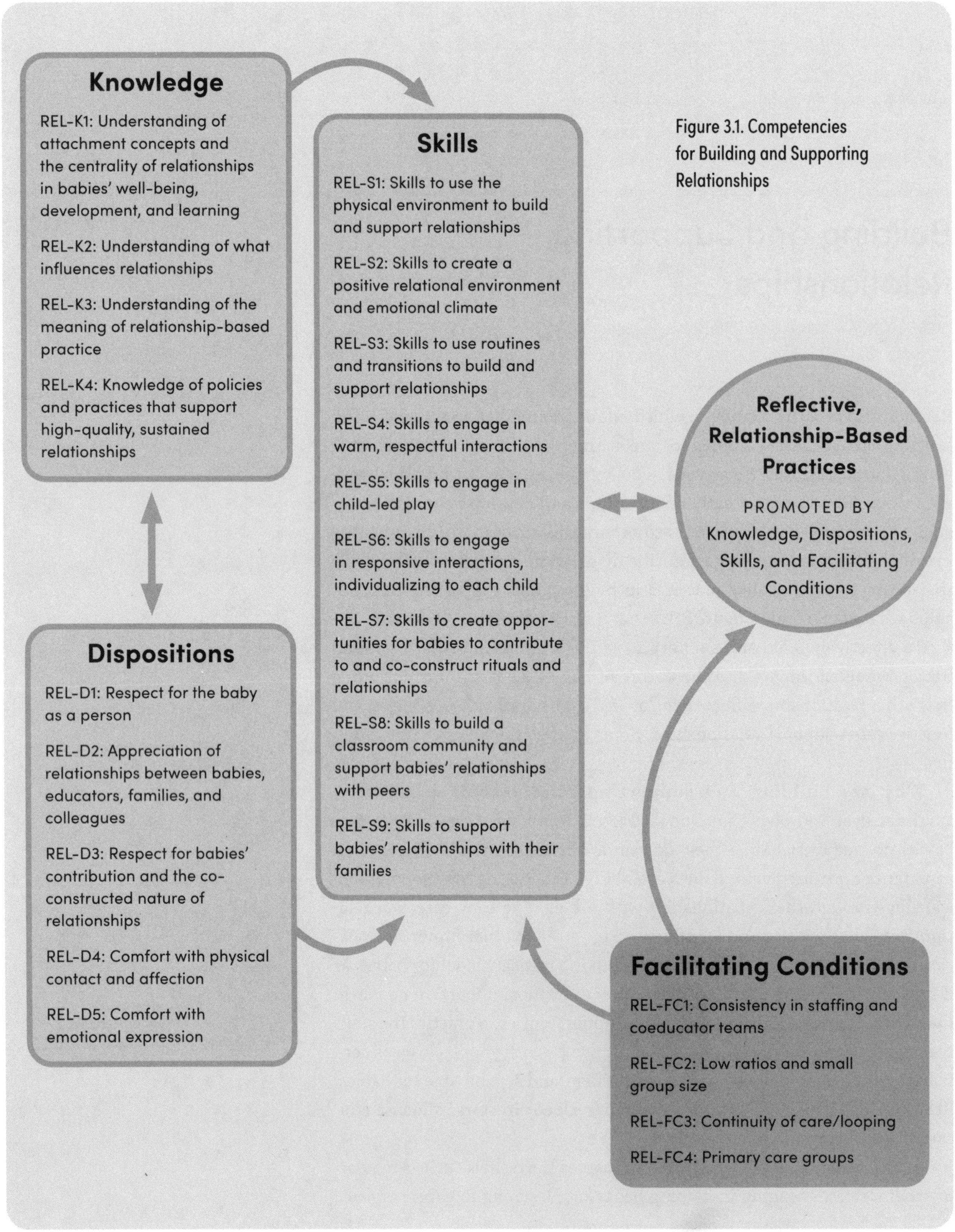

Knowledge

REL-K1: Understanding of attachment concepts and the centrality of relationships in babies' well-being, development, and learning

REL-K2: Understanding of what influences relationships

REL-K3: Understanding of the meaning of relationship-based practice

REL-K4: Knowledge of policies and practices that support high-quality, sustained relationships

Dispositions

REL-D1: Respect for the baby as a person

REL-D2: Appreciation of relationships between babies, educators, families, and colleagues

REL-D3: Respect for babies' contribution and the co-constructed nature of relationships

REL-D4: Comfort with physical contact and affection

REL-D5: Comfort with emotional expression

Skills

REL-S1: Skills to use the physical environment to build and support relationships

REL-S2: Skills to create a positive relational environment and emotional climate

REL-S3: Skills to use routines and transitions to build and support relationships

REL-S4: Skills to engage in warm, respectful interactions

REL-S5: Skills to engage in child-led play

REL-S6: Skills to engage in responsive interactions, individualizing to each child

REL-S7: Skills to create opportunities for babies to contribute to and co-construct rituals and relationships

REL-S8: Skills to build a classroom community and support babies' relationships with peers

REL-S9: Skills to support babies' relationships with their families

Figure 3.1. Competencies for Building and Supporting Relationships

Reflective, Relationship-Based Practices

PROMOTED BY Knowledge, Dispositions, Skills, and Facilitating Conditions

Facilitating Conditions

REL-FC1: Consistency in staffing and coeducator teams

REL-FC2: Low ratios and small group size

REL-FC3: Continuity of care/looping

REL-FC4: Primary care groups

and, eventually, managing conflicts. When relationships are safe, secure, warm, and sustained over time, babies, families, educators, and programs thrive. Just as reflective practices are at the heart of your development as a professional, relationships and relationship-based practices are at the heart of your work with each individual baby and family.

How are building and supporting relationships related to other competencies? Building relationships with babies and supporting their relationships with peers and families forms the bedrock of all aspects of early childhood programming. The next chapter is about working with families. Relationships are the foundation of guiding babies' behavior (chapter 5) and supporting their development and learning (chapter 6). Building relationships with colleagues is a part of professionalism (chapter 9) and enables mentoring and leadership (chapter 10).

Facilitating conditions. Program administrators can build high-quality relationships with infants, toddlers, and their families by implementing program policies that support consistency in staffing and coeducator teams (REL-FC1), small group size and appropriate educator-child ratios (REL-FC2), **continuity of care/looping** practices (REL-FC3), and primary care groups (REL-FC4). Although some practices, such as primary caregiving, can be within the control of individual coeducator teams, administrators have to create staffing schedules that make it possible. Likewise, administrators who support ongoing professional development opportunities and provide a supportive climate contribute to longevity and consistency in staffing and coeducator teams.

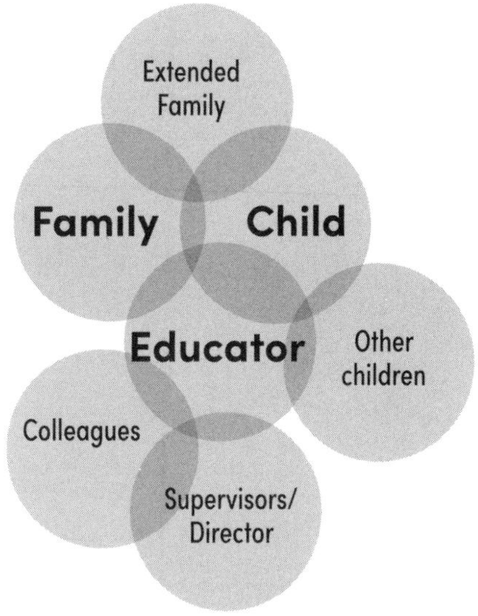

Figure 3.2. Central Relationships in Infant-Toddler Settings

Knowledge

Knowledge about attachment relationships (REL-K1), what influences relationship quality (REL-K2), and how to use this knowledge in daily interactions (REL-K3) provides a foundation from which relationship-based caregiving skills develop. In addition, knowledge of how program policies influence and facilitate relationship-based practices in the classroom (REL-K4), such as how to create and use primary caregiving groups, contributes to high-quality caregiving, though these also depend on the facilitating conditions (REL-FC2, FC3, FC4).

Understanding attachment concepts and the centrality of relationships to babies' well-being, development, and learning (REL-K1)

Humans are social beings who come into the world expecting to form and benefit from relationships. The attachment relationships we form in infancy shape our development and experience for our lifetimes.

Relationships and the human brain. Humans are hardwired for relationships. For instance, the prefrontal cortex in an infant's brain is activated when a parent and infant gaze at each other, but not when there is no shared eye contact between an infant and parent. The prefrontal cortex is in the frontal lobe, the part of your brain behind your forehead. Parts of the prefrontal cortex govern things like emotion regulation, emotional communication, decision-making, and flexibility in responses to people and the environment. Given the importance of these areas for successful interactions with others, the prefrontal cortex is sometimes called the "social brain."

Babies' brains are literally built by the interactions they have with others. Ongoing, repeated interactions over time form the connections between neurons (nerve cells in the brain), including those in the prefrontal cortex. When the baby experiences and participates in warm, sensitive relationships, the baby's brain is stimulated. It triggers a biochemical response that increases and strengthens connections and adds coating around the cells (myelin), which results in faster thinking and responding. If you look at the brain of a child who has experienced stable, secure relationships and the brain of a child who has experienced chronic stress and violence, you may see that gray matter volume differs between children who have and have not experienced trauma." Importantly, this is the foundation of the brain architecture that supports development and learning throughout a child's life. This is why we say that early educators and caregivers are brain builders.

In parallel, adults are also hardwired for relationships with young children. During parent-infant interactions, the parent's brain, specifically parts of the prefrontal cortex that are involved in empathy, mentalizing, and emotion regulation, are activated to help the parent engage in responsive caregiving. Babies and caregivers are connected brain to brain, and they influence one another as they interact and form relationships.

Attachment. Attachment theorist Mary Ainsworth (1979) describes attachment as an emotional bond between a baby and caregiver that lasts across time and space. Central attachment relationships form over the first year of life. As babies interact with those around them (parents, educators), they form an **internal working model** about relationships and the world around them. For instance, if a parent responds quickly and supportively to an infant's cries, the infant comes to view the world as a safe and predictable place (*I cry, and Daddy always comes to help me*) and to understand relationships as being safe and nurturing (*I can trust that* *someone will always come*). Babies with secure attachments see themselves as lovable, and they are empowered to explore and learn from the world with confidence. They develop new skills and learn new concepts quickly and easily. That is why attachment security in infancy and toddlerhood is associated with later academic and social success. Secure attachments continue to play an important role throughout the lifespan. For example, a recent research study (Dagan et al. 2018) found that adverse childhood experiences were associated with biological markers of health risks only for youth with insecure-dismissing attachment representations; there were no associations between prior trauma and health risks for youth with secure attachment styles. These results suggest that secure attachments help us weather the storm of adverse experiences.

On the other hand, babies with insecure relationships often understand the world, and others, as unpredictable. These babies may be less likely to explore the world around them, which can negatively affect their development and learning. Insecure relationships are associated with later depression and anxiety, as well as less positive academic and social outcomes. However, it is important to note that caregiving and infant behaviors that suggest secure and insecure relationships vary widely across cultures and are culture specific. When considering attachment relationships, it is critical to understand the cultural and familial contexts of behavior.

The nature of interactions. Whether due to caregivers' fatigue, stress, or distraction, there are moments when caregivers and babies get out of sync. Perhaps the caregiver misses the cue a baby gives and the baby becomes frustrated, or the baby is tired and less able to be soothed by the caregiver. These **ruptures**—mismatches or missed cues in interactions—may be minor or more significant. Fortunately, **repairs** often follow ruptures, when the caregiver realigns their mind and behavior with the child. For example, imagine that an educator is holding a baby who is gazing upward at a mobile. They visually explore the mobile for a few moments together, and then the educator tries to engage the baby's attention in a new toy. The baby fusses at being redirected. Here a rupture has occurred. The educator was ready to move on to a new object, but the baby wasn't. The educator repairs the rupture by accurately interpreting the baby's cues, saying, "You're still interested in the mobile" as they return their attention to it. This repair was made possible because of the caregiver's mentalization, interpreting the baby's internal mental states. This ability is supported through reflective practice and part of **reflection in interactions**. All relationships experience disruptions—in fact, it is pretty common. But it is through sensitive repairs that these interactions support secure relationships between babies and their caregivers. We provide some additional examples of ruptures and repairs in interactions in table 3.1.

Table 3.1 Rupture and Repair in Interactions

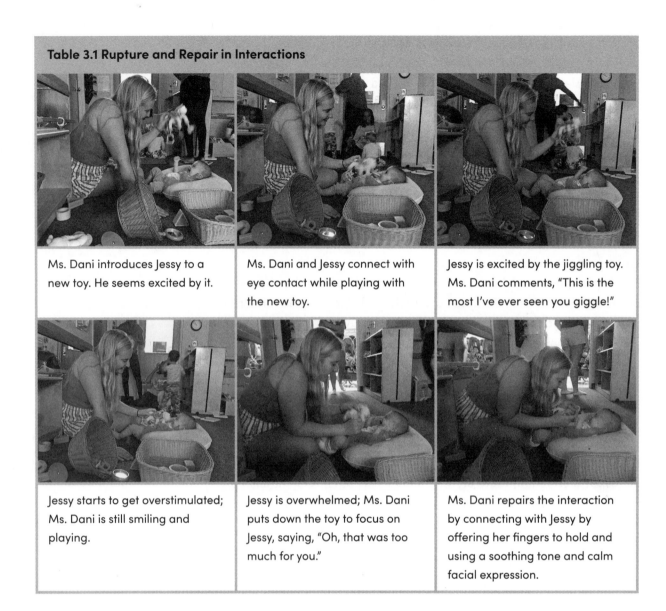

Ms. Dani introduces Jessy to a new toy. He seems excited by it.	Ms. Dani and Jessy connect with eye contact while playing with the new toy.	Jessy is excited by the jiggling toy. Ms. Dani comments, "This is the most I've ever seen you giggle!"
Jessy starts to get overstimulated; Ms. Dani is still smiling and playing.	Jessy is overwhelmed; Ms. Dani puts down the toy to focus on Jessy, saying, "Oh, that was too much for you."	Ms. Dani repairs the interaction by connecting with Jessy by offering her fingers to hold and using a soothing tone and calm facial expression.

Understanding what influences relationships (REL-K2)

Relationships are influenced by factors within each individual in the relationship, as well as external contexts. They are influenced by the here and now and by the past.

Relationships exist in the context of larger relationship systems. Children are members of several relationship systems, such as the early childhood education center and the family. Just as relationships between children and educators are important contexts of development, so too are relationships between coeducators, and between educators and their supervisors. Stress or stability in one part of the relationship system can feed stress or stability in other parts. Educators who feel supported and who trust their colleagues and supervisors are more satisfied with their profession, stay in their positions longer, and form more positive relationships with babies and families. An educator under stress who feels unsupported by the program administrator has less emotional energy to contribute to the educator-child relationship. Disruptions such as staff or administrative changes reflect structural influences on relationships. Program administrators must provide professional supports such as opportunities for professional development and warm, supportive work environments (REL-FC1).

Family systems characterized by stress and tension in parental relationships and ongoing conflict between family members may negatively affect the quality of parent-child interactions. Likewise, major shifts in the family system such as divorce/separation, marriage/union, births, military deployment, moving to a new residence, and incarceration may also impact parent and child behaviors, which in turn can affect their relationships with peers and educators in the classroom.

Systems vary in their ability to take in new information. **Open systems** have flexible boundaries and can take in and adjust to new information. In **closed systems**, the system members may be unable or unwilling to accept new information. They may find it difficult to communicate effectively with those outside the system. For example, it might be easier or more difficult for educators to communicate with some families than others. In chapter 4 on partnering with families, you will learn some strategies for working with families.

Past relationships influence current relationships. Each educator and parent was once a young child who was socialized within their relationships to hold certain beliefs about themselves and others. Prior experiences in relationships often influence our beliefs, practices, and interactions with babies and toddlers. For instance, a caregiver who was punished ("Stop crying or I'll give you something to cry about"), **shamed** ("Quit being a crybaby"), or dismissed ("You're fine. Stop crying") as a child for showing strong emotions, may believe that it is not acceptable to show strong emotions. The adult may have a more difficult time accepting and supporting toddlers' expressions of sadness, anger, or fear. When babies are expressing these strong emotions, adults may become *triggered*, feeling strong emotional reactions that make it hard to respond in a supportive way. For instance, a parent who felt powerless as a child might become angry very quickly if they perceive a child as acting disrespectfully.

Our own relationship histories influence how we perceive and interact with babies. For example, Alissa Huth-Bocks and colleagues (2004) found that pregnant mothers in abusive relationships are more likely to attribute negative intention to their unborn babies (for example, perceiving in-utero kicks as the fetus's deliberate intention to hurt the mother). Dr. Daniel

Siegel (2020) explains that our prior experiences affect our responses to others at neurological and behavioral levels. In the severest contexts, our prior experiences of trauma can result in hypervigilance, continually assessing the environment for threats and perceiving others' behaviors as physically or psychologically threatening. For example, when a child makes an error in following instructions, an educator may perceive the child's behavior as deliberately noncompliant and thus threatening. When this happens, the adult's brain reverts to a fight-or-flight stance in response to the perceived psychological threat. The adult may respond dramatically by completely disconnecting from the child emotionally and physically (fleeing) or becoming enraged at the perceived insult and reacting in anger (fighting).

Adults who have experienced trauma in childhood are at greater risk for mental health concerns such as depression and anxiety, which in turn may contribute to a greater vulnerability to being triggered. All humans have triggers that elicit reactions. This is a key reason why it is very important to become aware of your own triggers and responses. The reflective practice skills you learned in chapter 2 can help you become aware of your triggers.

Understanding the meaning of relationship-based practice (REL-K3)

When programs say they use a "relationship-based" approach, they mean that every decision is made with the quality of relationships in mind—such as how to structure the environment, how to engage in everyday interactions with babies and families, how to create and carry out planned experiences, how to engage with families, and how to work with educators. Relationship-based practices for working with babies and families are consistent with the research on relationships and attachment, and they are part of high-quality practice that supports babies' development and learning.

Infant mental health is a relationship-based approach that supports babies' well-being and development by supporting their relationships with caregivers. The term *infant mental health* refers to the social and emotional health of infants and toddlers in the context of relationships. If a parent is struggling, then their baby is likely struggling too. Experts trained in infant mental health work with parents and educators to gently support adults' awareness of their triggers and build understanding of how these influence their practices. The infant mental health approach has been critical in helping us see that young babies have strong emotions and can struggle or be in distress due to the stress of caregivers. Many states are now offering endorsements in infant mental health–based practices through their state Association for Infant Mental Health organizations. The endorsements are tailored toward individuals working with infants, toddlers, and families in early childhood settings and in-home settings. Visit www.allianceaimh.org for more information on endorsement.

Knowledge of policies and practices that support high-quality, sustained relationships (REL-K4)

Babies can and do form attachment relationships with multiple people, including nonparental caregivers. Attachment relationships in early care and education provide babies with a sense of connection and security that promotes their well-being and emotion regulation and provides a **secure base** for babies' exploration and learning. But it takes prolonged, positive interactions over time for these secure relationships to form. And these relationships cannot form if babies are always cared for by different people, and they will not be secure if caregivers are not warm and consistent. Thus, there is a set of important strategies for promoting secure relationships, including low baby-to-educator ratios and small group size, primary caregiving, and continuity of care. Educators need supportive program policies (REL-FC2, REL-FC3, REL-FC4) to implement these strategies in their classrooms.

Ratio and group size. Having optimal baby-to-adult ratios and small group sizes gives educators the time, space, and energy to build relationships with babies through frequent interactions and reflective practices. Hence, low ratios are linked with higher-quality adult-child interactions. Each state's licensing guidelines provide specific ratios that cannot be legally exceeded, but these legal limits do not always conform to what is recommended by developmental experts based on research. Professional organizations such as the National Association for the Education of Young Children (NAEYC) and Zero to Three (ZTT) recommend one educator to every three infants and toddlers, ages twenty-four months and under, with no more than six in a group. With one educator for every four babies, NAEYC recommends groups of not more than eight infants, twelve months and younger, or twelve toddlers, ages thirteen to twenty-four months. For older toddlers, ages twenty-five to thirty-six months, ratios of one educator to four toddlers with a group size of no more than eight (ZTT) to twelve (NAEYC) toddlers is recommended.

Primary caregiving means that each educator is assigned primary responsibility for connecting with and caring for three to four specific children in the room. Of course, all educators respond to all children, but educators pay special attention to their primary care groups. The primary educator also seeks out and shares information with the parents of those babies. This system allows all of these important relationships to flourish. Primary caregiving gives babies a secure base from which to explore. When babies are focused on their own safety, they have little attention to learn anything else. When they know who is looking out for them, they explore more freely, attend to activities longer, engage more deeply in play, and ultimately gain stronger skills.

Continuity of care means that children stay with the same educators and group of children over time with few big transitions, allowing sustained relationships over time. Research has shown that the longer babies are with their caregivers/educators, the more likely they will have a secure attachment relationship with the educator. Many child care arrangements are set up by child age or by developmental **milestones** (such as crawling, walking, or toilet learning) with transitions to new rooms based on their age or development. However, continuity of care practices keep babies and educators together over longer periods of time. Under the looping model, educators transition with groups of babies as they grow, for two or three years, until the group of babies has "graduated" to older classrooms; then the educators move back down to the infant room to begin relationships with a new group of babies. Another model of continuity creates mixed-age classrooms, where children stay in the same classroom and with the same caregivers during their time in the program. A good model for this is family child care centers, which are mixed age by nature. While these continuity of care models can be logistically hard to manage, they provide the benefit of maintaining relationships over time.

Dispositions

The dispositions that support positive, warm interactions and healthy, secure relationships begin with respecting babies as individuals with their own personalities, needs, and rights (REL-D1). We value all of the relationships that babies experience or witness (REL-D2) and respect babies' contributions to their relationships (REL-D3). Finally, we recognize that comfort with physical contact and affection is developmentally essential for babies (REL-D4).

Respect for the baby as a person (REL-D1)

A critical value embedded in high-quality infant-toddler care and education is respect for the baby as an individual. Magda Gerber, who pioneered the Resources for Infant Educarers (RIE) approach, was one of the first scientist-practitioners to promote the concept of respect for infants and trust in the infant's capacity to develop and learn. Scholar Robin Leavitt (1994) noted that respect for infants means that educators use **developmental power** (shared power in the classroom) rather than **extractive power** (adult control over all aspects of the classroom), **co-constructing** caregiving rituals and routines rather than following adult-determined practices that ignore infants' contributions.

Appreciation for relationships between babies, educators, families, and colleagues (REL-D2)

Educators' varying views influence how they establish relationships with babies and with others. Some practitioners define their role as a teacher providing instruction; some define their role as a caregiver focusing on care and comfort for children; others may see themselves as a babysitter—and their job as just a job, rather than a career—which may mean they are less concerned with establishing strong relationships that last over time. For infant-toddler care and education to be high quality, educators must value and promote healthy relationships not only between themselves and the babies for whom they care, but also between and among children, parents, colleagues, and supervisors.

Respect for babies' contributions and the co-constructed nature of relationships (REL-D3)

Relationships form based on joint interactions between two individuals. Practitioners may see babies as contributors to the relationship to varying degrees. As their knowledge of development grows, educators increasingly recognize and respect infants' behaviors—both **nonverbal cues** and verbal ones—as valuable contributions to interactions and the relationship, and they adjust their interactions to respond to each baby.

Comfort with physical contact and affection (REL-D4)

All humans need physical touch, and babies must have physical touch to survive. Renee Spitz's pioneering work with babies in orphanages more than seventy years ago and Harry Harlow's classic caregiving experiments with rhesus monkeys underscored the importance of tactile comfort and laid the groundwork for us to understand the critical role of touch in healthy emotional development. From the Touch Research Institute in Florida, Tiffany Field's (2019) extensive research on touch in early development identified the ways in which touch is related to emotional development and other developmental domains.

Yet adults vary in how comfortable they are with physical closeness and how much they value positive touch. Sometimes an adult's comfort with physical touch is related to positive or negative experiences in their past. For example, educators who grew up in home environments with little physical affection displayed between family members—or with physically abusive experiences—may feel less comfortable with communicating warmth toward babies through touch. Other educators may feel concerns

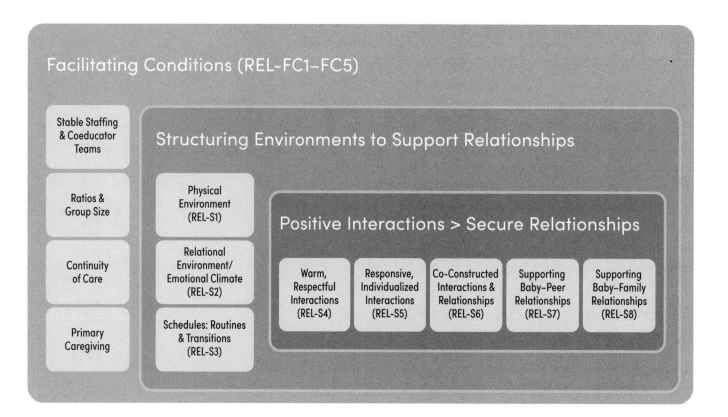

Figure 3.3. Skills and Practices to Build and Support the Network of Relationships among Babies, Educators, and Families

related to touch policies in programs. Adults who are comfortable with touch tend to be attentive to babies' cues for physical affection, holding, rocking, and hugging babies and toddlers in their everyday interactions. On the other hand, adults with less-positive experiences with touch may hold and touch babies only for caregiving activities such as diaper changes. Because affectionate touch is an important component in caregiving, examining personal comfort levels with touch is important.

Comfort with emotional expression (REL-D5)

Babies build relationships by sharing emotions, including joy and excitement as well as sadness, fear, and frustration. As they grow, these emotional experiences become more complex, and their expressions become more intense. Some educators become upset themselves when young children are sad, afraid, or angry, while others believe young children have no reason for these feelings. When we respond in supportive ways, we build trusting relationships in which babies feel accepted and know they can rely on us to comfort them and to help them grow and learn. We must be comfortable letting babies experience their full range of emotions, while sharing some of these emotional experiences with them, to build these secure relationships.

Educators' abilities to build and support relationships are undergirded by the program's facilitating conditions that we described earlier (REL-F1–F5). As summarized in figure 3.3, within this context, educators structure the physical environment (REL-S1), the relational environment (REL-S2), and schedules and routines (REL-S3) to support relationships in the community, and thus babies' development. Within those supportive structures, educators build secure relationships with babies by engaging in warm, respectful interactions (REL-S4) and responsive, individualized interactions (REL-S5) while co-constructing interactions and relationships with babies (REL-S6). Educators also support babies' relationships with peers (REL-S7) and between babies and their families (REL-S8).

Using the physical environment to build and support relationships (REL-S1)

Our respect for relationships and their centrality in babies' lives—as well as our own—should be visible from the moment we step into an early childhood setting. Structural supports for relationships create a calm, safe, welcoming environment for everyone.

STRATEGIES ─────────────────────────────────

Figure 3.4 outlines key strategies for structuring the environment to promote and support healthy relationships.

Figure 3.4. Strategies for Using the Physical Environment to Support Relationships

Support Relationships between Babies and Adults	Promote a Sense of Belonging	Support Adults' Relationships with Each Other
• Provide comfortable spaces for adults to get down on the floor. • Provide rocking chairs and comfortable spaces for adults to be where babies can access them. • Provide spaces in the building for parents to nurse and feed their babies comfortably.	• Display samples and photos of babies' work. • Display photos of babies and educators interacting together. • Display photos of babies with their families. • Provide individual spaces for babies' belongings.	• Provide spaces for coeducators to meet and discuss their work together confidentially. • Provide comfortable spaces for families to talk with educators confidentially. • Provide comfortable spaces for families to interact with one another.

Creating a positive relational environment and emotional climate (REL-S2)

The relationships between the adults who care for children—between coeducators who work as a team, and between educators and families—are the relationship models that children witness. They set the emotional climate that babies experience on a daily basis. The quality and functioning of these relationships have a big influence on how secure children feel and how well they are cared for. We will address the educator-family relationship in chapter 4; here we address the coeducator relationship that sets the relational environment within the classroom.

Some experts have described coteaching as a marriage, and when you think about everything that a pair (or group) of educators must do together to care for a group of six to twelve babies, the analogy makes sense. At the very least, it must be a functional relationship with clear and consistent communication. Ideally it is also a warm and caring partnership so that you can support one another in your work and model this adult relationship for children. However, these crucial relationships are rarely discussed in professional circles.

STRATEGIES ───────────────────────────

Figure 3.5 Strategies to Create and Maintain a Coeducator Partnership

Figure 3.5 describes strategies that create an effective coeducator partnership and set a positive emotional tone in the classroom.

Establish a Partnership	Communicate Weekly	Communicate Daily	Communicate Spontaneously
• Coeducation Model: Determine how you will work together (e.g., What does primary care mean in your classroom?), decide primary care groups, and determine roles and responsibilities. • Professional Philosophy: Talk about beliefs, values, and priorities for your work; identify strengths, joys, and challenges; discuss similarities and differences, and find common ground. • Stress Management: Discuss what stresses you out, how your coeducator will know you're stressed, and what helps you when you're stressed. • Communication System: Create a structure or method for communicating both throughout the day and over the course of the week.	• Babies' well-being and behavior, and any changes needed in daily routines. • Babies' development, including emerging skills and any concerns. • Plan for supporting babies' development. • Anticipated changes in work schedule.	• Check in about each other's well-being; ask for support as needed; offer help as you can. • Communicate about the plan for the day. • Discuss anything out of the ordinary that could affect your work.	• Communicate continually to coordinate monitoring and safety. • Communicate discreetly and respectfully about babies needing extra support to regulate emotions and behavior. • Share your joy in babies' experiences and development. • Signal when you are stressed, overwhelmed, and in need of support.

Educators also model their respect for babies and families as they talk with one another. How you talk with your coeducator about babies can model respect and support or disregard and contempt. Many coeducation teams choose not to talk about babies when the babies are present, but sometimes it is necessary to call attention to a child's actions or needs. In these cases, the tone and word choice are crucial and should model the attitudes you want babies to see and feel. There is a big difference between saying, "It looks like Chamy is about to make a big mess again," and saying, "It looks like Chamy might need your help pouring the water into her cup." Over time, many coeducator teams develop subtle ways to communicate. Likewise, the way you talk to and about babies' families can communicate respect, or not. There is very little reason for coeducators to talk about families in front of children, except to coordinate pickup/drop-off or pass along communication to or from the family. In these cases, tone of voice and word choice can model respect and support.

Using routines and transitions to build and support relationships (REL-S3)

A baby's day is made up of routines and transitions between activities. A stable schedule helps babies feel secure, but caregivers must also remain flexible to babies' individual needs. As much as possible, primary caregivers should work with babies during routines and transitions to build and maintain relationships.

Hellos and goodbyes are crucial transitions for building and reinforcing relationships throughout the classroom community. The way a child enters the classroom in the morning can set the tone for the day; the way they reunite with their family can reflect their feelings about the day and influence their time with family.

STRATEGIES

❋ Greet children and their families by name as they arrive and depart.

❋ Offer children a warm smile and affection upon arrival.

❋ Point out classmates' arrivals to peers ("Carli, did you see that Elle has arrived?"), and point out peers' reactions to others' arrivals ("Elle, Carli smiled when you arrived; she seems excited to see you.")

❋ Develop individualized rituals for how children enter the room—perhaps a particular greeting or something they like to do first. Be flexible, as the child will change these over time.

❋ Work with families to develop individualized rituals for saying goodbyes and hellos (see REL-S8).

www.redleafpress.org/wwb/3-1.pdf

www.redleafpress.org/wwb/3-2.pdf

⁎ Acknowledge children's departures from the class, anticipating when you'll see them again ("Have a good night. I'll see you tomorrow!")

Use care routines throughout the day (such as diapering or helping an infant to sleep) to support babies' relationships with primary caregivers; for example, share affection and talk with babies about what they are experiencing. Use group routines (such as shared meals or putting away toys) to support babies' relationships with each other by modeling conversations and peer-helping behavior.

Be particularly intentional about relationship building during routines in which babies feel most vulnerable, such as sleeping and diapering. It is important to employ the foundational interaction skills in this chapter throughout daily care routines to build and reinforce relationships. In handout 3.1, Relationship-Based Sleep Routines, we describe how the relationship aspects of sleep and naptime support relationships. Also see handout 3.2, Diapering, which describes a diapering routine that reinforces respectful relationships by involving babies in their own care.

Even when policies and practices support continuity of care, changes in relationships are inevitable; for example, a baby or group transitioning to a new class or an educator or a classmate joining or leaving the class. It is important to help babies anticipate and navigate these changes by honoring babies' relationships, giving them warning about upcoming changes, allowing them to have big feelings about the changes (excitement, sadness, even anger), and helping them manage their feelings and adjust to the new circumstances and relationships.

STRATEGIES

⁎ Here are ways to honor babies' relationships and feelings about losing a member of the classroom:

• Have a goodbye party.

• Keep a photo of the past community member where babies can see and point to it to initiate conversations.

• Talk to babies about their feelings and invite babies to express their feelings in creative ways, such as drawing a picture of the person they miss.

⁎ Here are ways to honor babies' own transitions between classrooms:

• Have a celebration of growth around an individual or group transition.

• Have a transition event in which classmates, educators, and families move children's belongings together between rooms.

Table 3.2 Acknowledging and Honoring Important Transitions in Classroom Relationships

Ms. Denise uses a morning gathering in the toddler class to announce that Luke's family is moving away and his last day in the class will be at the end of the week.

Ms. Denise has created a chart to check off each day, counting down to his last day.	She acknowledges that the children and educators will be sad and will miss Luke when he's gone.	Ms. Denise has gotten Luke's favorite snacks to have a goodbye party at snacktime on his last day.

Engaging in warm, respectful interactions (REL-S4)

Warm, respectful interactions are characterized by the following behaviors:

Interact at the baby's level and pace. Position yourself at the baby's level by sitting or kneeling on the floor (rather than standing and bending over). Make eye contact. Adults are often in a hurry, but babies move slowly. Take time to watch and listen to the baby. Be mentally present, as well as physically present, during the interaction, as opposed to thinking of the next thing you need to do.

Show warmth and affection. Practitioners show warmth and affection through a kind tone of voice, an open body posture that invites physical closeness (such as hands resting on your lap with your head up, rather than arms crossed and head down), and offering and accepting affectionate touch. Touch promotes adults' engagement with babies and babies' responsiveness and engagement with adults.

The physiological and neurological changes that occur with touch are really quite astounding. Warm, positive touch, such as a hug, stimulates the release of oxytocin, sometimes called the "love hormone" or "cuddle hormone" because it gives us a sense of affection and well-being. Mothers are flooded with oxytocin when their infants nurse. Touch stimulates additional neurological changes in the brain. Children whose parents are more physically affectionate during play have greater connections in the social areas of their brains than children who experience less touch (Brauer et al. 2016). Comforting a baby with words and touch lowers the baby's

Sasha tries a new climbing experience with Ms. Edson nearby; Ms. Edson is a secure base throughout the day.

heart rate, an indication that it lowers their stress. Tiffany Field has studied touch extensively and has found that touch is related to a broad range of positive health, well-being, and academic outcomes, including better sleep, increased immune system functioning, reduced anxiety, and stronger cognitive and emotional skills. In short, affectionate, supportive touch is an important strategy in promoting relationships, babies' well-being, and long-term development.

Use babies' names frequently in warm and positive ways. Infants are just learning their own names, and toddlers are developing a sense of identity, who they are as individuals. The way we use their names communicates how we see babies and influences how they see themselves. Babies should associate their names with positive feelings, rather than reprimands and directives.

Respond to all invitations to interact. Part of respectful interactions is not ignoring babies' cues to interact. Whenever a baby approaches you or invites you to interact (such as by making eye contact, giving a touch on the arm, or showing you a toy), respond to that cue by acknowledging the baby (this establishes dyadic **joint attention**) and turning your attention to what they want you to see (triadic joint attention).

Share power. Respectful relationships are characterized by shared power, rather than having one person in control of the relationship. We engage *with* babies rather than doing things *to* babies (for example, cleaning up together after a meal or allowing the child to try something first before offering assistance).

STRATEGIES

* Approach the child from the front and narrate what you are doing. For example, when you need to wipe a baby's face after a meal, let the baby see you coming, show her the cloth, and pause and make eye contact as you begin to interact.

* Use **anticipatory talk** (explain what is about to happen). For example, "You have yogurt on your face. I have a damp cloth to wipe the yogurt off. I'm going to wipe your face now."

* Wait for the baby's response, which may be returned eye contact or a **vocalization**.

* Use anticipatory talk when you are leaving ("It looks like Jacob needs help opening the paint. I'm going to get up now and help Jacob. Then I'll come back") or starting a care routine ("We will change your diaper in two minutes. I will go get the table set up, then come back for you").

* Involve babies in their own care. Ask the baby to bring her diaper to the changing table, to turn on the faucet, or to choose whether to have her back rubbed at rest time.

* Narrate and explain what you are doing. "Now I'm going to take off your wet diaper and wipe your bottom so you'll be clean and dry."

* Be flexible in timing whenever possible to respect babies' interests and goals. For example, allow a toddler to finish a block structure by delaying cleanup for her for a few minutes.

* Avoid interruptions and wait for invitations. If a baby is engaged with materials or with other children, watch, wait, and look for an invitation to participate. This might be shown in eye contact, a vocalization, a **gesture**, or a touch (such as touching your arm). If the invitation does not come, avoid interrupting.

Engaging in child-led play (REL-S5).

Engaging with children in play is a primary way to build relationships. When they lead this play, you can learn about babies' interests and skills. You communicate your respect for the baby as an individual and self-driven learner. In child-led play, you will find the most opportunities to intentionally and flexibly support babies' development and learning, which you will learn about in detail in chapter 6. Using all of your skills for warm and respectful interactions (REL-S4), join babies when they are playing.

STRATEGIES ───────────────────────────────

* If the baby is already playing, move to the baby's level, observe their play, figure out what they are doing, and look for openings or invitations to join.

* If you and the baby are starting play together, make sure there are several toys/objects nearby and invite the baby to choose. ("There are many toys. I wonder which one you'd like to play with.") Comment on whatever they choose. ("You chose to play with the cars.")

* Join babies by playing in the same way (both rolling cars side by side) or in a complementary way (rolling cars back and forth to each other).

* Find ways to expand what babies are doing without changing their focus or taking over the play (create a ramp or road for the cars to roll on, or roll the cars up your own body).

* Match babies' pace/speed of play and their general emotional tone (such as calm or exuberant).

* If babies start to lose interest, add something to the play that might engage them or invite them to choose something else. When babies change their focus of play (put down cars, pick up dolls), follow their new interests.

Table 3.3 Respond to Babies' Invitations, Join Their Attention, and Follow Their Lead in Play

Sammy gets Mr. Andrew's attention by walking up to him and making eye contact (dyadic joint attention), then shows him the phone (triadic joint attention), inviting him to play.	Mr. Andrew accepts Sammy's invitation and joins his play. Sammy leads the way by babbling into his phone. Mr. Andrew talks to Sammy as if on the phone.	Sammy directs Mr. Andrew's attention by pointing, and Mr. Andrew follow's Sammy's lead, looking across the room, and talking about what they see.

Engaging in responsive interactions, individualizing to each child (REL-S6)

In chapter 2, Reflective Practice, you learned about the process of observing, reflecting, and responding to infants and toddlers (figure 2.4). Just like adults, babies always have something going on inside—thoughts, feelings, and desires—that are expressed through their behavior. Being sensitive and responsive means looking for and responding to these internal states. Now we are going to take a closer look at how this applies to our ongoing interactions with infants and toddlers.

Observe: What is the baby doing? Watch for babies' cues and apply your skills in objective, focused observation. Think about what the baby is seeing and hearing and what they are doing. Identify the actions, words/vocalizations, and **affect** (the facial expressions and body language) you see. Notice the context. Where is the baby (where in the classroom, where outdoors)? Who else may they be responding to? Use these questions to identify meaningful behavior, expressing an internal state or communicating a need.

Reflect: What might the baby be intending, feeling, or thinking? What might the baby need? Wonder about what the baby is thinking and feeling in the moment, how the baby is experiencing this interaction, and what they might want or need. Bring together your observations of the child and the context with your knowledge of child development and of this child as an individual (temperament, current developmental skills, family/cultural context, recent/current experiences that may influence behavior) to understand what the behavior tells you about the child's interests or needs. Remember that your interpretations are not always right! As you get to know babies well, you can also think about patterns in their behaviors to more accurately interpret what they need. For example, do the behaviors happen at the same time of day, in the same situation, or with the same people?

Use your reflective practice skills in mentalization (RFP-S5) to reflect out loud on the interaction with empathy, compassion, and understanding. "You're working hard with that shape sorter. It looks like you want to get all of the pieces in," or "It looks like you're having difficulty being gentle right now, and you're rubbing your eyes. That makes me wonder if you're feeling sleepy." Reflection in interaction is a foundation for guiding infant-toddler behavior. It's also a great way to build babies' **vocabulary** for actions, emotions, thoughts, and causal associations, which supports development across domains. Reflecting out loud provides examples of reasoning and introduces children to internal states concepts.

Respond: How might you respond to the baby's needs? During sensitive interactions, adults respond to babies' cues in kind, with the same intensity, pace, and similar emotional expressions (affect). Infant psychiatrist Daniel Stern (1984) referred to this matching of affect and energy as **attunement**. Sensitive adults also respond with flexibility (individualizing for different children; changing with a child's changing pace, intensity, needs, and so on). Below are strategies that promote secure relationships.

STRATEGIES

- ❊ Be warm and affectionate. Sometimes educators must be firm, but this is very different from being harsh, cold, or critical. Educators can be firm and warm at the same time.

- ❊ Be timely. **Contingent responses** occur close in time to the baby's behavior. When a baby coos and the educator vocalizes back to the baby within a few seconds, a contingent response has occurred. Contingent responses help the child understand that you are responding to her cues, helping the child link actions and responses. These connections help the baby feel secure in the relationship and understand back-and-forth communication and cause and effect.

❄ Respond with intention rather than simply reacting in the moment. Be intentionally supportive by applying your knowledge of **developmentally appropriate** expectations, developmentally supportive interactions, and the individual baby's unique characteristics, preferences, and needs in the moment to inform how you respond.

Observe Reaction: How did the baby respond to you? After you respond, watch for the baby's reaction. Note what the baby did or said (with face, body, or behavior). Determine whether your response was in tune with the baby's interests and needs, altered their behaviors, or added to their experience. Use your observations to tailor future responses to that baby, continually individualizing your interactions as you build a relationship.

Creating opportunities for the baby to contribute to and co-construct the relationship (REL-S7)

Relationships are co-constructed, meaning that each person contributes to the development and maintenance of the relationship. Through interactions over time, each person develops an understanding of the other's behaviors and role in the relationship. Each responds not only in the moment, but also with the knowledge of their shared history. Creating opportunities for the baby to co-construct means looking for the behaviors, preferences, and cues that are unique to that baby and responding in kind. One baby might like to give high fives, whereas another baby likes to rest her head on your lap. One might show you his belly button while another likes to show you toys brought from home. Your response to these various invitations to interact forms a co-constructed ritual with the baby.

An important place to connect is during drop-off routines. How does each baby prefer to connect with educators upon entering the classroom? Do they prefer a quick hug or a longer cuddle, or do they need a few minutes to sit and watch before reaching out for someone? Imagine a toddler who likes to hug her educator, put her coat away, then walk around the room to see what is available each day. This routine becomes ritual when the teacher supports the toddler by participating. Perhaps the teacher takes a moment to walk around the room with the child, commenting, "I remember you enjoyed painting last week, Char. We have paints out today." Together the teacher and child co-construct this morning ritual that becomes part of their relationship. Other rituals include personalized aspects of routines like naptime (for example, knowing exactly how the child likes to have her back rubbed) and departure (for example, a goodbye unique to an educator-baby dyad).

❊ Pick out one daily routine to start, such as arrival/departure, meal-times, diapering/toileting, or rest/sleep. Practice paying attention to each baby's behaviors and preferences during this routine.

❊ Based on what the baby is telling you through actions and prefer-ences, create a ritual that reflects the baby's expressed needs.

Building a classroom community and supporting babies' relationships with peers (REL-S8)

Though young infants are primarily focused on their relationships with caregivers, by six months old babies pay attention to their peers and enjoy interacting with them. Highly skilled educators intentionally structure their classrooms and practices to promote peer interactions and relation-ships. These peer relationships are important for the quality of babies' daily experiences and their well-being, as well as for supporting babies' growing social skills.

❊ Refer to babies as a group with inclusive words such as *children*, *classmates*, or *friends*. Although babies may not be "friends" as usually defined, making references to "our class" or "friends" builds a sense of community and is associated with toddlers' and young children's prosocial behaviors.

❊ In any game, song, or care routine, make sure each child who wants a turn gets one.

❊ Create small-group experiences for babies (such as painting at a table, building with very large blocks, or exploring at a sensory table), as well as some whole-group experiences (such as songs, stories, dancing outside, or large art projects), but allow children to opt out.

❊ Point out similarities and differences in children's preferences, char-acteristics, clothing, and so on in a neutral tone without any praise or criticism ("You are both wearing stripes today"), but avoid comparing children's behaviors or asking children to be like one another.

❊ Help babies interpret each other's cues, feelings, and intentions ("Colette has her arms over her head. It looks like she is not ready for a morning hug yet").

- Acknowledge helpful intentions and behaviors ("You offered her your family photo; maybe you thought that would comfort her.")

- As toddlers gain skills, invite them to help each other ("Charlie, can you hand Sam a water cup?")

- Engage and scaffold toddlers to negotiate conflict and solve problems with peers ("It looks like you both want to pull the wagon. What could we do?"); be ready to provide ideas and emotional support as needed.

Supporting babies' relationships with their families (REL-S9)

Babies' immediate well-being and long-term development are dependent upon the quality of their relationships with their families; thus it is part of a practitioner's role to support the child-family relationship. Supporting family relationships happens primarily during arrival and departure, and ideally includes daily communication that is responsive to families' needs. In chapter 4, we present competencies for partnering with diverse families and supporting them in their role as their baby's first educator.

STRATEGIES

- Welcome families into the classroom. Create spaces that welcome families by displaying their pictures. Include comfortable furnishings for adults to sit with children. Greet family members by name, and when possible, introduce them to other adults in the room.

- Support emotional school-home connections. Encourage the use of **transitional objects** that have an emotional connection to home, such as a favorite blanket or stuffed animal, or another object that reminds babies of their families. Nonverbal babies should have access to family photos to look at, hold, and initiate conversations about their families. These photos can be laminated or put in plastic pouches.

- Ask about families' preferences for being included. Some cultures and religions do not use photo images of people, and some families may not feel safe having their photos available to others.

In the infant room, family photos are laminated and stuck with Velcro strips where infants can easily find, look at, and hold them.

Reflect Back, Think Ahead

Look back at figure 3.1 at the beginning of chapter 3, which shows the knowledge, disposition, and skill competencies involved in building and supporting relationships. Which of these competencies did you have when you began this chapter? Which competencies did you develop? Which competencies will you intentionally build next? Use the Building and Supporting Relationships chapter of the Professional Learning Guide (PLG [see page 11]) that accompanies this book to support your own professional growth in this domain.

Selected References

Brauer, Jens, Yaqiong Xiao, Tanja Poulain, Angela D. Friederici, and Annett Schirmer. 2016. "Frequency of Maternal Touch Predicts Resting Activity and Connectivity of the Developing Social Brain." *Cerebral Cortex* 26 (8): 3544–52.

Dagan, Or, Arun Asok, Howard Steele, Miriam Steele, and Kristin Bernard. 2018. "Attachment Security Moderates the Link between Adverse Childhood Experiences and Cellular Aging." *Development and Psychopathology* 30 (4): 1211–23.

De Schipper, Elles J., J. Marianne Riksen-Walraven, and Sabine A. E. Geurts. 2006. "Effects of Child-Caregiver Ratio on the Interactions between Caregivers and Children in Child-Care Centers: An Experimental Study." *Child Development* 77 (4): 861–74.

Field, Tiffany. 2019. "Social Touch, CT Touch and Massage Therapy: A Narrative Review." *Developmental Review* 51:123–45.

Gerber, Magda. 2002. *Caring for Infants with Respect*. Los Angeles: Resources for Infant Educarers (RIE).

Harlow, Harry F. 1958. "The Nature of Love." *American Psychologist* 13 (12): 673–85. https://doi.org/10.1037/h0047884.

Huth-Bocks, Alissa C., Alytia Levendosky, G. Anne Bogat, and Sally A. Theran. 2004. "The Impact of Domestic Violence on Mothers' Prenatal Representations of Their Infants." *Infant Mental Health Journal* 25 (2): 79–98.

Jean, Amélie D. L., Dale M. Stack, and Sharon Arnold. 2014. "Investigating Maternal Touch and Infants' Self-Regulatory Behaviours During a Modified Face-to-Face Still-Face with Touch Procedure." *Infant and Child Development* 23 (6): 557–74.

Leavitt, Robin Lynn. 1994. *Power and Emotion in Infant-Toddler Day Care*. Albany: SUNY Press.

Sacks, Vanessa, and David Murphey. 2018. "The Prevalence of Adverse Childhood Experiences, Nationally, by State, and by Race or Ethnicity." *Child Trends*. February 20. www.childtrends.org/publications/prevalence-adverse-childhood-experiences-nationally-state-race-ethnicity.

Siegel, D. J. 2020. *The Developing Mind: How Relationships and the Brain Interact to Shape Who We Are*. 3rd ed. New York: Guilford Publications.

Spitz, Renee A. 1945. "Hospitalism: An Inquiry into the Genesis of Psychiatric Conditions in Early Childhood." *The Psychoanalytic Study of the Child* 1 (1): 53–74.

Stern, Daniel N. 1984. "Affect Attunement." In *Frontiers of Infant Psychiatry*, edited by J. D. Call, E. Galenson, and R. T. Tyson. Vol. 2, 3–14. New York: Basic Books.

Urakawa, Susumu, Kouichi Takamoto, Akihiro Ishikawa, Taketoshi Ono, and Hisao Nishijo. 2015. "Selective Medial Prefrontal Cortex Responses During Live Mutual Gaze Interactions in Human Infants: An fNIRS Study." *Brain Topography* 28 (5): 691–701.

Winnicott, Donald. 1964. "Further Thoughts on Babies as Persons." In *The Child, the Family, and the Outside World*, 85–92. Harmondsworth, UK: Penguin.

CHAPTER 4

Partnering with and Supporting Diverse Families

Working with babies means working with families. Infant-toddler educators play an important role in helping families support their children's development, learning, and well-being by forming **positive, goal-oriented relationships**. Understanding the nature of family systems, as well as what makes families different from one another and different from you, is crucial to forming effective partnerships. It is important to work with each family to understand their living situation, cultures, and values so you can individualize how you work and communicate with them. Figure 4.1 summarizes the dispositions, knowledge, and skills that promote reflective practices with diverse families.

Why is partnering with and supporting diverse families an important competency to have? When families feel welcome, valued, and heard, they work *with* you. Trusting relationships, effective partnerships, and open communication with families make your job easier, yield better care and more optimal development for babies, and encourage families to stay in the care setting for a longer time. Your partnerships with families can also strengthen the baby-family relationship and enrich the child's home learning environment, so you can affect the child's well-being and learning for years after they have left your care.

How is partnering with and supporting families related to other competencies? Throughout this book you will see references to working with families and involving families in your work with babies. Your communication with families is essential to babies' well-being, and your knowledge of the families you work with is the basis for creating culturally relevant materials and experiences for babies. Sharing your observations and reflections can strengthen your partnership and shared goals with families, and these discussions can give you new insights and make your assessments of babies more accurate and useful. Partnering with and supporting families

Knowledge

FAM-K1: Awareness of the importance and characteristics of effective family-educator partnerships

FAM-K2: Knowledge of family relationship systems

FAM-K3: Knowledge of the broad characteristics of culture that shape human experiences and perspectives

FAM-K4: Knowledge of families' circumstances that affect their lives and parenting

FAM-K5: Understanding of one's own cultural traditions and values related to caregiving and education

FAM-K6: Knowledge of local, regional, or state services for families with specific needs

Dispositions

FAM-D1: Respect for the primacy of families' influences on and responsibilities for their babies

FAM-D2: Belief that families are the experts on their own babies

FAM-D3: Appreciation of the strengths each family has to support their baby's development

FAM-D4: Respect for families' individual differences

FAM-D5: Commitment to understanding the role and meaning of cultural traditions in families' lives

FAM-D6: Appreciation of the unique contribution of each family to the community of learners

Skills

FAM-S1: Skills to set up policies and environments that invite family participation and engagement

FAM-S2: Skills to set up effective, regular, bi-directional communication with families

FAM-S3: Skills to create opportunities for families to connect with one another as a community

FAM-S4: Skills to engage in respectful interactions with families of all backgrounds

FAM-S5: Skills to get to know individual families and to learn about babies through their families

FAM-S6: Skills to communicate effectively with families about potentially sensitive topics

FAM-S7: Skills to collaborate with families by synthesizing perspectives and finding common goals

FAM-S8: Skills to utilize families as resources to authentically enrich the learning environment

FAM-S9: Skills to support families' relationships with their babies

FAM-S10: Skills to support families as their babies' educators

FAM-S11: Skills to connect families with other resources or services

Reflective, Relationship-Based Practices

PROMOTED BY Knowledge, Dispositions, Skills, and Facilitating Conditions

Facilitating Conditions

FAM-FC1: Program hours and policies that meet families' needs

FAM-FC2: Consistent staffing and relationship structure

FAM-FC3: Paid time to conduct home visits and parent-educator conferences

FAM-FC4: Physical space for families to meet with educators and each other

FAM-FC5: Resources/materials for a family-educator communication system

FAM-FC6: Educational materials and information on community resources

Figure 4.1. Competencies for Partnering with and Supporting Diverse Families

is particularly necessary in the potentially difficult processes of identifying and supporting babies who need additional social and educational services. Finally, supporting families is essential to mentoring parents—helping them feel confident in their ability to nurture their baby's development.

Facilitating conditions. Program policies and resources set the stage for educators' partnerships with families, beginning with program hours and sick policies (FAM-FC1). Do operating hours allow parents to get to and from work? Do the sick-child policies meet the children's, families', and educators' needs and keep them safe? Being up front about these policies can help to avoid problems down the road. It is common for parents not to question policies, such as sick-child policies, when they first hear them and then disregard the policies when the need arises. Many parents cannot miss work if their child is sick; some might even lose their job. However, this does not mean that the policies, which are there to protect children, families, and staff from illness, can be ignored. Programs can also help families problem solve, such as by helping them identify alternative care if the child is sick.

Program policies that ensure adequate pay, ongoing professional development, and a positive climate promote consistent staffing and thus more consistent educator-family relationships (FAM-FC2). If you are in a larger program, assigning a primary caregiver to a family allows for one person on the team to develop a closer relationship with the family. If you have multiple educators in the classroom, you can also identify provider-family pairs who are a good match.

Paid time to plan and carry out home visits and parent-educator conferences (FAM-FC3) allows educators to get to know babies and families over time through individual conversations. Programs should provide a variety of ways that make it feasible for families to engage with their children's care and learning. Programs need physical space in the building for families to meet with educators, for families to get to know each other (for example, conversations between parents in the program's lending library), and for parents to pump breastmilk or nurse their babies (FAM-FC4). Educators need ways to communicate with families about children on a daily basis. They need systems of communication that are accessible for families and educators, are dependable, allow for privacy, and are easy to use. Some programs use communication apps, while others use text messaging (using a program phone number, not educators' personal phones) (FAM-FC5). Finally, programs should make available a variety of educational materials and information on community resources to meet families' needs or desires for engaging with their child's care and learning (FAM-FC6). See handout 4.1, Family Resources, for examples of resources and materials to provide for families.

www.redleafpress.org/wwb/4-1.pdf

Partnering with and supporting families starts with being aware of the importance of establishing effective partnerships with families and knowing what these should look like (FAM-K1), and understanding family systems and how those may affect your partnerships with families (FAM-K2). Educators should understand how families function and how families differ in their needs, their approaches and communications with educators, and their parenting goals and practices. Educators need to know characteristics of culture that shape parenting (FAM-K3) and circumstances that affect families' lives (FAM-K4). Recognizing that *your* beliefs and approaches to caring for and educating young children are influenced by your culture, values, and traditions is essential to respecting families' perspectives, choices, and traditions (FAM-K5). Finally, you need knowledge of resources and additional services for families in your community, region, and state (FAM-K6), although it is a facilitating condition for programs to compile and provide families with references to these resources (FAM-FC6).

Awareness of the importance and characteristics of effective family-practitioner partnerships (FAM-K1)

The National Center on Parent, Family, and Community Engagement (NCPFCE) describes the optimal parent-practitioner partnership as a positive, goal-oriented relationship. That is, interactions with families are characterized by respect, warmth, and shared goals for supporting the child's development, learning, and well-being. Establishing positive, goal-directed partnerships with families is key to all aspects of your work with their babies. Effective communication ensures that you know how to support the child when their parent is away, and it can help the parent better support their child's development as well. When there is optimal cooperation and communication between home and school, babies do better in the short- and long-term. There will always be differences in expectations between home and school, but if all caregivers communicate about such things as feeding, toileting, and sleeping routines, it can help babies smoothly enter and exit each setting. Family relationships and communication make your job easier and make your effort to support babies more effective. Below we describe several characteristics of positive, goal-oriented relationships.

Communication. An essential component of partnering with and supporting families is effective, regular, bi-directional communication. This way we better understand the child and their world outside of the classroom, which can help us plan our environments and activities to target the child's interests and family culture and better understand the behaviors we see in the classroom. When we share ideas and strategies for supporting the baby, we ultimately build coherent practices and experiences across home and school that synthesize family and professional perspectives and work toward shared goals for the child. Babies fare best when expectations across home and care settings are as consistent as possible.

Trust. Parents must feel confident in entrusting the care of their children to others. When you work with babies, you are often the first nonfamily member to care for the child. You can imagine that families struggle with separation from their baby. Some feel conflicted about having their children in the care of someone they do not know well. While this can be challenging, it also means that relationships between families and their children's first caregivers have the potential to be very close and impactful.

Mutual Respect. The adults who have primary responsibility for the child (we will call them parents, although they may not be the child's biological parents) should feel confident as the ones who know their child best. Most parents see early childhood professionals as the experts about children and child development and can easily be made to feel inadequate. Ensure that parents do not feel undermined or undervalued by appreciating parents' unique role in their child's life, while also honoring your contribution as well. For example, while you may know in general how babies' temperaments and health histories tend to influence their reactions to an environment, parents know their own baby's temperament, health history, behaviors, and habits better than anyone else. When your general knowledge of child development is combined with parents' specific knowledge of their child, everyone can better understand and care for the baby. Children do better when parents and early childhood professionals work together and value each other's roles in their partnership.

Shared Goals. Within a positive, trusting relationship, the educator can talk with the family about their long-term goals for their baby and the family as a whole. Knowing the family's goals can inform your work with the baby, and you can connect the family with other services to help them meet their goals. The skills section of this chapter describes methods for getting to know families' priorities, developing shared goals, and referring families to additional services.

Knowledge of family relationship systems (FAM-K2)

Individuals must be understood in the context of their family relationships. For each child, you should know who lives in the home and who else is important in their life (for example, a sibling living in another household or a grandparent who frequently takes care of the children). What is the role of this child in the family? Do they have older siblings? Is caregiving for the child shared among the extended family or others? Understanding these connections will help you establish a trusting relationship and know how to best communicate with the family.

Family relationship systems differ from one another in three key ways: communication, openness to change, and openness to outsiders. You may find that giving one family member a message ensures that all other members know the information, or you might have to communicate with each family member separately because they will not pass the information along among themselves. Some family systems are very open to change while others prefer to do things the ways they've always been done, perhaps through generations. And families differ in how open they are to outside influence, including whether they seek outside opinions or prefer to make decisions among themselves. Each of these aspects may influence how you establish a partnership with them.

Knowledge of the broad characteristics of culture that shape human experiences and perspectives (FAM-K3)

We are all cultural. You, the babies and families you work with, and other staff members in your program all come from unique cultures, and together you form a new culture within your classroom and your program. Every human is socialized to become a member of their culture, learning the way the culture understands the world, how they operate within it, and what they value. Families are the most immediate cultural context. Outside of that, geography (neighborhood, city, region, country), ethnicity (ancestry and cultural heritage), and race (physical characteristics)—and how you are treated because of these contexts—all influence your values, priorities, and ways of being in the world. This is true for *everyone*, regardless of whether your own cultural heritage is similar to or different from most of the people in your community.

The common understanding of culture often relates to the genealogical background or heritage of an individual. We mean something much broader—the beliefs, values, history, and traditions that influence how we care for children. Many things about a family—including country of origin, historical roots, race, ethnicity, and religion—are associated with their caregiving beliefs and behaviors, but each family develops their own unique cultures as well. We can see these unique family cultures in their caregiving routines, mealtimes and nutrition, naptime and bedtime, and toileting and diapering. Family values and beliefs are also evident in how the family organizes the home learning environment and how they support their babies' development through things like playing, reading, and how they communicate and show love. Families also have different ideas about education and the role of educators. Some might see children as developing without the need for much adult intervention, while others believe that adults must be more active in children's learning. Some might believe that learning should stay within the domain of school and early child education, while home is for family activities; others may see child care as being more about safety and caregiving, while home is a place for training a child in the families' values and practices. Cultural beliefs determine parents' approach to **guidance**, including expectations for babies' behaviors, how much structure is given to scaffold babies' behavior, and what **discipline** strategies are used.

Table 4.1 How Family Culture Is Reflected in Daily Interactions and Routines	
Interaction/Routine	*How Families Differ from One Another*
Sleeping	Whether or not they have a regular bedtime; what the presleep routine looks like (bathing, singing, reading, rubbing their back); whether babies sleep on their own or cosleep with siblings or parents; whether a baby is left to cry themselves to sleep.
Eating	Whether babies eat on demand or on a schedule; whether and when babies feed themselves or are fed by others; how much choice babies have in what and how much they eat; how much and what types of food are provided; whether babies eat by themselves in a high chair or at the family table.
Communication	How much talking, touching, and eye contact there is between family members; the kinds of talk that are directed toward children (directives like "Do this," "Stop," "No", or a diverse range of topics and words); amount of engagement in back-and-forth interactions with children.
Showing Love	How much warmth is shown; how affection is shown (e.g., verbally or physically); how adults respond to babies' requests for affection.
Teaching	How much adults teach babies intentionally versus how much they let the baby explore on their own.

Knowledge of family circumstances that affect their lives and parenting (FAM-K4)

In addition to the family values, routines, and practices described above, other family circumstances and characteristics affect families' lives, their needs and priorities, and the way they care for and educate their babies. But even if you don't know all of the details for each family, thinking about how their circumstances may influence their lives and their parenting can help educators approach families in compassionate ways.

Household composition. Who lives in the house? Who cares for the child? If there is a nonresidential parent, it is important to understand how the parents partner to raise the child. Is there a coparenting schedule? Can the nonresidential parent pick up the child? Transitions between parents' homes can be hard for children, and you can help them prepare for shifts in household composition.

Home language. Which languages do families speak in the home? Which languages does the family want the child to speak? Some non-English-speaking families want the child to speak English in child care/school, while others prefer a dual-language approach. Being up front about what your program can provide and discussing family preference can prevent misunderstandings.

Immigrant status. Is the family newly immigrated? In many cases, early care and education services are the first services that a family receives and can be a tool for acculturation. However, there may be additional barriers to building trust, including language barriers or anxiety about legal status and deportation. They may have experienced trauma as they came to this country. They may be isolated, or they may be treated as an outsider, subjected to racism or xenophobia, which can influence the levels of trust they can have in their new community. If they have not connected with a community of people, you can help be that connector.

Military. Does the family experience deployments? Long separations can be especially hard for babies who do not have a sense that their parent continues to exist and will return. In addition to feeling a loss they may not fully understand, young children also sense the other family members' stress. It may be confusing for young children to be in contact with their deployed parent using technology, but it may also provide a sense of connection the child would not otherwise have. Reunions, while highly anticipated, can also lead to disruptions in routines. Families may come to rely on you as a source of consistency as they go through separations and reunions.

Mandated separations from parents. Is the child in foster care, or is one of the parents incarcerated? In some cases, parent-child separations are mandated by the court system. It is important for you to know what the plans are for long-term placement, adoption, or reunification. Does the noncustodial parent have visitation rights? Children who have an incarcerated parent may visit their parent, or they may have no contact. It may be helpful in these situations for you to know about visits, which can disrupt a child's routines or affect their behavior in the classroom.

Neighborhood. It is critical for you to know your own and your families' communities so you can identify learning opportunities and other resources and services available locally.

Social support. Is the family embedded in a system of support, such as their extended family, church, or community? The family can turn to these systems if a child is sick and cannot attend school, as well as for parenting support and social interactions. If a family does not have this kind of network, they may be more reliant on you. You can also help connect them with other families in the program.

Family risk factors. What kinds of demographic risk factors does the family experience? Some demographic risk factors can cause stress for families and challenge their abilities to provide a stable and supportive environment for their child, despite their best intentions. Some examples include poverty, low social support, frequent moves, fewer caregiving adults, underemployment, teen parenting, or low levels of education. Research has found that the greater number of risk factors a family has, the harder it can be to maintain a stable household and positive parent-child relationships. However, not all families who experience demographic risk factors respond to them in the same way. Families can be very resilient, so you cannot make assumptions based on demographic factors. But knowing this information can help you understand the behaviors you see and may give you some clues for how to help, if necessary. Part of the risks families face because of their demographic characteristics is due to the ways others treat them, rather than a direct effect of the characteristics themselves. Families may also face unique stressors due to discrimination they experience based on their demographic characteristics. For example, LGBTQ parents have not traditionally had the same rights as heterosexual parents. When a heterosexual married couple has a baby, both parents are identified as legal parents. However, such presumption is not always the case in same-sex married couples who have a baby or adopt a baby. Families who do not speak English often face discrimination and challenges in communication. Families with black or brown skin are faced with systemic racism that impacts physical and mental health. For example, Black women are at vastly greater risk for premature birth than their white counterparts. This is due in part to the chronic stress of the racism they are subjected to, and in part to the racism they encounter in the medical system during pregnancy; this includes less access to consistent, high-quality prenatal care, and medical professionals who don't take the symptoms of Black women as seriously as they do those of white women. Another example very important to early childhood education comes from Walter Gilliam and colleagues (2016) who found that Black boys are more likely to be viewed as **aggressive** by their early childhood educators and even face expulsion as a result. Further, early child educators may justify this choice is by blaming families for children's behaviors, rather than realizing their own biases (Martin, Bosk, and Bailey 2018).

Parent stress. Life events like a change in work, a move, or a marriage, whether negative or positive, affect family well-being and routines and can cause the parent to have less time to focus on parenting. Parents also face stress from their past adverse childhood experiences. Adverse childhood events (ACEs), such as early exposure to trauma, violence, or loss, have been found to predict health and well-being outcomes in adulthood (e.g., Felitti and Anda 2010), as well as a person's parenting behaviors. Some family members you work with may have experienced early life adversity, and some of the children you are working with may be currently experiencing adversity. You can be a resource to families experiencing current stress or affected by past stress and can also be a link to mental health services. Program administrators should retain current information on community supports (FAM-FC6).

Understanding your own cultural traditions and values related to caregiving and education (FAM-K5)

Becoming aware of your own culture and how it has influenced your beliefs, values, and behaviors is a first step in understanding how it influences your work with babies and families. At times you will react strongly to a belief or practice of a family you work with because of your own belief system. If you understand your own reactions, it can help you to step back and respond to the family. Review the broad characteristics of culture (FAM-K3) and the circumstances that affect families' lives (FAM-K4); reflect on these aspects of your own experience to become more aware of your own culture and how it has influenced who you are as an individual and as a practitioner of early care and education. It may be helpful to discuss your feelings with peers or a supervisor.

Knowledge of local, regional, or state services for families with specific needs (FAM-K6)

It is important that you know about local, regional, or state services for your families, such as basic necessities like food and shelter in times of crisis, local parenting education programs, community mental health services, services for children with disabilities, and local libraries. Program administrators should provide up-to-date information to educators (FAM-FC6). As the person whom a family entrusts with their baby, you are in a unique, trusted position to help the family link to services. In doing so, you are not only helping the family but also ensuring the baby's long-term well-being.

Dispositions

Many practitioners go into the early childhood field to work with children, not realizing they will also be working closely with adults. But working with babies means forming positive relationships with families too: respecting the unique roles that parents play in their children's lives, understanding their influence on their children's development and their ultimate responsibility for their children's well-being (FAM-D1), and knowing that families are the experts on their own babies (FAM-D2). Successful practitioners also value the strengths each family has to support their baby's development (FAM-D3), the differences between families that make them unique (FAM-D4), the meaning that culture and traditions hold for families (FAM-D5), and the contributions each family can make to the care setting (FAM-D6).

Respect for the primacy of families' influences on and responsibilities for their babies (FAM-D1)

Parents are the first and longest-term educators, and they are the ultimate decision-makers for their babies. While you may spend many hours with the children in your care, their parents are with them their whole lives, when they go to sleep at night, and when they are sick. The family is the child's primary environment. This means that important decisions like changes in feeding, dropping a nap, or starting toilet training should not be made without the family's input and consent.

Belief that families are the experts on their own babies (FAM-D2)

While you know more about child development than most families will, and you know babies in the context of the classroom or program, each parent/family is the expert on their baby. They have known the baby the longest and have seen the baby in many different contexts. It is important to reinforce parents' confidence as the experts on their children. This may pose a challenge if you see the baby very differently from what the parent describes. In this case, you can discuss how the baby's behavior may be different in different settings. You can invite parents into the classroom to see the behaviors you see, but be careful not to undermine parents by suggesting they could be incorrect about what their child is like at home.

Appreciation of the strengths each family has to support their baby's development (FAM-D3)

The home environment is a baby's primary learning context. Each family has unique strengths and resources to support their baby, but families vary in how conscious they are of these strengths and how intentionally they use them. When educators identify and value the resources that each family brings, they can help families become more confident in their strengths. Taking this strength-based perspective helps build strong educator-family partnerships.

Respect for families' individual differences (FAM-D4)

You will work with families in many different circumstances. It is important to convey respect for families' individual differences and adhere to professional ethics and values regarding diversity. When you recognize yourself as cultural—recognizing how your own characteristics, circumstances, and experiences have shaped who you are—it is easier to see the ways you are similar to the families with whom you work and to value the ways you are different.

Commitment to understanding the role and meaning of cultural traditions in families' lives (FAM-D5)

Families' cultural traditions and values support a baby's development and learning. Children who are aware of their own cultural heritage and have positive attitudes about it enjoy better mental health and better relationships with peers, and do better in school than children who don't. Thus, our commitment to understanding families' lives and cultural traditions, rather than making assumptions or judging, will help us aid families in supporting their children.

Appreciation of the unique contribution of each family to the community of learners (FAM-D6)

Families each have diverse strengths, skills, knowledge, and talents that can contribute to richer learning in your program—for babies, educators, and other families. When you identify and value families' unique contributions, you can invite them to share with the community of learners. Families' cultural traditions can add meaning and richness to your program. When babies grow up in more diverse communities, particularly when they see that their parents and caregivers have positive relationships with those who are different from them, they grow to have more accepting attitudes toward others.

Skills

When building partnerships with families, we first engage families by creating welcoming physical environments (FAM-S1), communication systems (FAM-S2), and opportunities to connect with other families (FAM-S3). Next we partner with families, interacting respectfully with all families (FAM-S4), getting to know families (asking and listening; FAM-S5), and sharing information about sensitive topics (FAM-S6). Then we collaborate

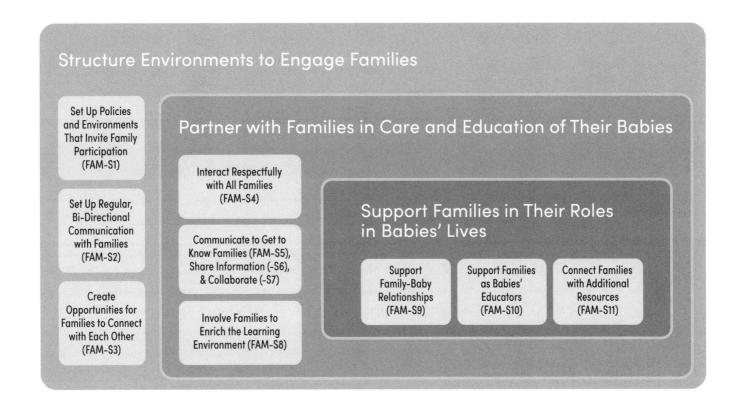

Figure 4.2. Skills and Practices to Build and Maintain Partnerships with Diverse Families

with families by synthesizing educators' and families' perspectives to develop common goals for babies (FAM-S7) and using families as resources to enrich the learning of all babies in the learning community (FAM-S8). Finally, we support the family-baby relationship (FAM-S9), support families as their babies' educators (FAM-S10), and connect families with additional resources they may need (FAM-S11).

Setting up policies and environments that invite family participation and engagement (FAM-S1)

The first step to ensuring that families feel welcome is for directors or administrators to set up policies and environments that invite family participation. As we noted, policies should meet families' needs (FAM-FC1) *as much as possible*. Educators should be knowledgeable about program policies to provide consistent information to families and avoid misunderstandings. Having a relationship-based model that includes continuity of care and primary caregiving (explained in chapter 3) builds both the child-educator relationship and the family-practitioner relationship. Programs that support such practices are promoting consistent staffing and relationship structure (FAM-FC2).

Family engagement. Several practices at the classroom level can invite families to be vital members of the community.

✳ Have open-door policies for classrooms, with families welcome to visit anytime.

✳ Invite families to engage in activities in class or share favorite recipes, family traditions, and family experiences.

✳ Send home weekly newsletters about classroom experiences.

✳ Ensure that parents are aware of program policies and include them in decision-making groups, such as a parent policy council, parent-educator association, or the board of directors.

Welcoming physical environment. The physical environment of the program should welcome all families with comfortable spaces to sit and interact. The environment can recognize each family with a photo and honor their cultures and languages: having signs and handouts in all of the languages of the families served by the program, noting all holidays celebrated, and reflecting diverse children and families in the posters, photos, books, and other materials used as decoration or educational materials.

A cozy reading corner in this toddler classroom intentionally welcomes families by placing family photos prominently for all to see.

Setting up effective, regular, bi-directional communication with families (FAM-S2)

Effective educator-family relationships are characterized by frequent two-way communication about babies' experiences, needs, well-being, and development.

Family-educator meetings. Home visits allow for educators to understand more about the family, their caregiving practices, and their priorities for their babies' well-being and education. This can be a time to understand families' priorities and share your own. Home visits are helpful as the care relationship begins, then should follow at least annually or with any transition between classrooms. Family-educator conferences, held two to four times per year, allow in-depth conversations about babies' experiences, behavior, well-being, and development. You will learn more about the skills for these conversations in FAM-S4–S7.

Newsletters. Newsletters can reflect back on what children learned the previous week and communicate educators' plans for the coming week. Families learn a lot when newsletters share child development information that is geared to the babies' ages, explain the curriculum, invite families to contribute at home and at school, and communicate other important information and reminders about the program. When parents know what their babies are doing each day, they can reinforce this learning at home. Consider the following structure for a newsletter article:

1 We've noticed that the children are really fascinated by . . . (their own bodies, taking care of baby dolls, the colorful leaves on the playground, objects that roll).

2 To support these interests, we are . . . (using words to label body parts; adding diapers, bottles, blankets, and clothes to the house play area; gathering leaves to use in making art; adding ramps for children to roll toys down and learn about gravity).

3 How does your child show this interest at home? What do you do at home to support his or her learning about this? Please share your ideas!

Daily bi-directional communication. Babies cannot speak for themselves, so educators and families must be in daily contact with one another. Parents can let educators know whether the baby is teething, sleeping poorly, or eating off schedule. At the end of the day, the parent needs to know any news that might affect their evening schedule. Daily routines of drop-off and pickup provide frequent, though often brief, opportunities to share information in both directions and build the educator-family relationship. Even short interactions can bolster a parent's trust in you, as well as their confidence as a parent. During these times, educators can demonstrate their understanding of the important and unique role that the parent has in the baby's life, as well as the importance of a responsive connection between the baby's home and the group care setting. Programs can structure staffing so that a knowledgeable educator (who will spend/has spent

Families of toddlers in Ms. Graham's class get a weekly newsletter about what their children are doing and learning. The newsletter includes important notes about events and other ways families are invited to engage in the program.

much of the day with the babies) is available and has time to talk with families (FAM-FC2).

Sending updates via texts and taking photos or videos of babies playing, learning, or meeting new milestones can alleviate parents' worries, reinforce trust in the educator, and strengthen the baby-family relationship. Whether you use technology, send daily notes home on paper, or both, you need the program resources, materials, and policies to support daily communication (FAM-FC5).

When families are very busy or stressed, engaging deeply with practitioners can be hard for them. It can also be challenging when families are new to the community and don't yet feel connected to the other families or the educators.

STRATEGIES

※ Communicate your open-door policy explicitly, making sure families know they are always welcome. Share the general schedule so they know when babies will be sleeping.

※ Invite family members to find a day to visit the classroom for a longer stretch of time.

※ Try to use the communication method that is easiest for each family, such as a phone call, text, email, note sent home, or quick conversation at drop-off or pickup.

Ms. Rachel sits near the door to greet families as they enter the room; she takes the opportunity to talk with Sefina's mom about an upcoming transition.

Creating opportunities for families to connect with one another as a community (FAM-S3)

Events that invite all of the program's families to come together can communicate important information, build educator-family relationships, and connect families as a community. These events should strive to be accessible and welcoming to all families served by the program, regardless of home language and culture, household composition and work schedules.

STRATEGIES ────────────────────────────────

❊ Use annual family orientation events to communicate key program information and intentionally connect families with one another. Provide name tags and make opportunities for families to talk in classroom groups if possible.

❊ Be inclusive of all cultures and religions when planning seasonal social events and holiday celebrations. Consider whether the learning experiences you plan for children celebrate only the **majority culture's** histories (for example, holidays such as the Fourth of July or traditions such as Santa Claus). Also, guard against **cultural appropriation**. This occurs when the majority culture disrespectfully uses an image or characteristic of a nonmajority group without permission and without a deep understanding of the other group's culture and history. Common examples of cultural appropriation in mainstream society include sports teams named after Indigenous peoples or the use of costumes characterizing minoritized or nonmajority groups. Don't plan events on days when families may have religious observances.

❊ Make sure all families can contribute in some way to fundraising events, regardless of their income. Invite families to donate items or volunteer in other ways.

❊ Help families get to know one another at events like picnics, field trips, or a tea-with-educators event. Intentionally make personal introductions if you think two families have things in common with one another or might become friends.

Families of young children are typically very busy and often stressed and exhausted. Planned events should offer opportunities for families to connect with their baby's educators and with each other in meaningful and fun ways to encourage them to engage. Ideally, all events should be open to children or provide care. Including a meal is a good idea, particularly if events are at typical mealtime hours. These practices are all made possible by program-level factors, including physical space (FAM-FC4) and paid time for educator-family meetings (FAM-FC3).

Engaging in respectful interactions with families of all backgrounds (FAM-S4)

Having structures in place for communication (FAM-S1–S3) lays a foundation, but educators really build these partnerships as they communicate with families individually. Though you may have some contact outside of the classroom, most interactions with families will be during drop-off and pickup. When you interact with babies' families, you model respectful interactions and warm relationships for all the babies in your classroom. You communicate to the baby that you care about their parents, which builds the baby's trust in the educator.

Nonverbal. Nonverbal behavior communicates a lot even before we open our mouths. The skills for engaging in respectful interactions with families are parallel to those you use with babies (see chapter 3). This includes being at their level physically—both standing or both sitting. An open body posture communicates that you are open to the relationship and interaction. Your facial expression and verbal tone should be warm and accepting. This can be hard sometimes, and you may need to consciously monitor your reactions to what families communicate. When you feel threatened or triggered, use your reflection skills to pause, become aware of your reactions, consider the other person's perspective and needs, then respond thoughtfully. Observe their reactions as you interact, try to understand what they are experiencing, and modify your approach as needed.

Verbal. Both what we say and how we say it matter. Here are four characteristics of respectful, professional speech:

❋ **Kind:** First and foremost, our communication should be kind, especially concerning difficult topics. Avoid speaking about other babies or families, or do so only in positive ways. For example, say, "One baby went home sick today, so watch your baby for symptoms," rather than "Lula came to school sick today, so your baby will probably get it soon."

❋ **Inclusive:** Watch your own use of inclusive terms like *we* and *us*, as compared to exclusive terms like *them* and *they*. For example, the phrase "*our families* who are recent immigrants" communicates something different than "*the immigrants* in the program"; likewise, "*Our* families who work two jobs struggle to find time" is more inclusive than "*Those* families don't make time."

- ❋ **Person-first:** Part of our professional ethics of **inclusion** of children with additional support needs involves always putting the child first, before the description of their needs or condition (for example, "baby with Down syndrome" rather than "special needs baby"); this avoids communicating that we see babies as a label, diagnosis, or problem. We should apply the same with families who need extra support to meet expenses rather than "poor families" or "lower-class families."

- ❋ **Strength-based:** Use strength-based language when talking about babies' behavior and development. Consider these two ways of communicating the same information: "Charlie is enthusiastic about socializing with his classmates, and his enthusiasm is not always matched by his peers," versus "Charlie wants to play with other children, but he's so pushy they don't want to play with him."

Getting to know individual families and learning about babies through their families (FAM-S5)

While parents often look to educators as the *experts* in child development, educators often see parents as the *experts* in their own children. When families join a program, educators ask about the family's priorities and goals, as well as the child's needs, strengths, characteristics, and interests. Over time, educators partner with parents and can serve as sources of child development information (see figure 4.3). But the first part of building a partnership with families is to ask questions and listen. Asking questions sensitively and listening thoughtfully will help you learn about families' priorities for their child and their values, strengths, and needs.

Many programs practice home visiting so educators can get to know the family before their child starts attending the program. Although a home visit can be a logistical challenge and feel intimidating at first, generally the visits help make a smooth transition into the group care setting. Watching how the parent and baby interact at home offers a lot of information about their relationship and about the baby. For example, whether they stay in close contact or are more distant, how the baby likes to be held or comforted, whether they establish eye contact, what languages are spoken, and so on.

Each child and family is embedded in their own cultures and belief systems, which affect perceptions, behaviors, and interactions. Each of us is also embedded in our own cultural background. Even when there is a racial or ethnic match between practitioners and families, differences in cultures may still exist, and it is important not to assume that you know what a family's belief system includes. When in doubt, it is best just to ask. Ask **open-ended questions** to elicit information about families' beliefs, practices,

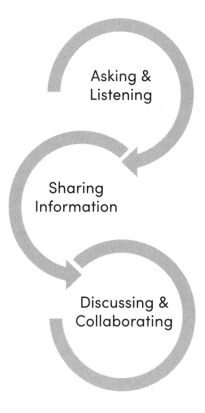

Figure 4.3. Communication Processes for Building Partnerships with Families

www.redleafpress.org/wwb/4-2.pdf

and goals for their children as well as broader family goals, such as, "In order for me to best work with your child, it is helpful for me to know how you feel about _____." Handout 4.2, Getting to Know You, has examples of questions you might ask as you get to know the family.

Skills to communicate effectively with families about potentially sensitive topics (FAM-S6)

Having open communication and a warm relationship is helpful as stressful issues emerge in the classroom or at home. At times you may have concerns about a family, such as their level of stress or lack of basic resources or perhaps about their child's development. Families are more likely to hear your concerns and react constructively if you have established ongoing communication and have built a partnership together.

We addressed sensitive and respectful communication earlier; it is also important to be accurate and clear about program policies, your own philosophy, and babies' behaviors or experiences. Your approach to this will communicate a lot to families. When you have a clear understanding of your program's policies and the reasons for them, you can avoid using explanations such as "These are the rules because that's how we do things here," or even "It's required by licensing." Instead, you can explain, "This is what we need to do to provide a safe and stimulating environment for children. Please let me know if you have any questions so I can explain why we have taken this approach. We want to meet your and your baby's needs, so please tell us if you have concerns about our policies." When you believe a child may require additional assessment or **early intervention**, communication must be accurate, clear, jargon-free, sensitive, and respectful to describe how children are doing based on your observation and assessment results.

There will be times when your classroom policies and practices will not fit with families' beliefs, goals, and practices. For instance, you may allow children to dress up in any costumes they desire, while a particular family may not want their child to wear a gender-discordant costume (like a boy wearing a pink tutu). In these cases, it is important to be respectful while adhering to your program policies and beliefs. You may not change a parent's belief, but it is important that you find a way for them to feel comfortable with their child being in your setting. Cultural mismatches often arise over issues of sleeping, eating, and sick-child policies.

Collaborating with families by synthesizing perspectives and finding common goals (FAM-S7)

Once you have established respectful interactions, asked questions and listened deeply, and provided information and explained program approaches in clear ways, you are prepared to engage in discussions that synthesize a family's belief systems with your own professional knowledge of child development and best practices and identify shared goals for their baby. As you listen to families' answers to your questions, identify the priorities and goals you hear. For example, if a family says, "I want her to learn her ABCs and numbers," they are probably telling you about their goal for their child be ready for preschool and kindergarten. If they tell you, "I just want him to be happy and have fun," they are telling you that their priority is their baby's sense of well-being and emotional development. Find common ground between the family's priorities and goals and your own, and describe how you help babies meet those goals. Having common ground lets you use activities or strategies that children know from home, and it often opens families to extending classroom activities at home. This consistency between home and school greatly enriches children's learning.

Overall, families and educators want the same things for babies—that they feel loved and happy, and that they develop to their full potential. It is more common that educators and families differ in their approach to these goals or disagree on the timing of outcomes rather than the goals themselves. However, you will need to synthesize a family's belief systems with your professional knowledge about child development and best practice. This requires not only the communication skills described above but also flexible thinking. For instance, consider a family who plans to potty train their four-month-old using a traditional method of holding the child over a sink and making a "shh" noise. From your experience, you know that babies this age do not have control over their bodies. However, this does not mean the family's practice is *wrong*, just based in their cultural practices. You will need to think creatively with the family to accommodate their cultural practice with your policies. When you do identify a potential source of conflict, consider whether the differing approaches at home and school might be complementary (that is, they each provide something good), or whether they really counteract each other. When you are open to learning from families and adjusting your practices, over time you gain knowledge and expertise in family culture. Handout 4.3, Family Discussions, contains ideas for questions to ask, information to share, and discussions to have to build a family-practitioner partnership that supports babies' development.

www.redleafpress.org/wwb/4-3.pdf

Utilizing families as resources to authentically enrich the learning environment (FAM-S8)

Reflect family culture in the classroom. Knowing that diversity is always at the family level, it is clear that just having a book about a culture or pictures of diverse families on the walls is not enough to be culturally responsive. Children should see visual representations of their families and people who look like them, but practices need to go deeper. You can adapt feeding or naptime interactions to better mirror the baby's experiences at home. When babies are old enough to discuss, you can have conversations about how mealtimes, bedtimes, and holidays are all different in different households. Bringing in familiar items, phrases, or actions from the children's home cultures helps the whole class to begin to understand that all families are different.

Invite families to share their home life in the classroom. Utilize **collaborations** with families to authentically enrich your learning environment for all babies. Invite families to share their own interests, hobbies, or talents. Know that many families will not know what is appropriate to share with babies, and they may need some ideas on what and how to share. Some ideas include singing a favorite song, sharing a recipe, reading a special book, or bringing in an object for babies to explore.

Supporting families' relationships with their babies (FAM-S9)

The parent/family-baby relationship is a main influence on development not only in infancy but throughout a child's development. Thus, bolstering this relationship can support a baby long after they leave your care.

STRATEGIES ───

* Comment about families' importance to their baby.

* Help them notice how their baby responds to them ("She got such a big smile on her face when she saw you through the window").

* Tell them what toddlers say about them ("Jill told me you made cookies together this weekend; then she pretended to bake cookies in our kitchen area." "He was really missing you at naptime today, so he drew a picture of you this afternoon").

In most programs, an educator's most consistent opportunity to support the family-baby relationship is during daily goodbyes and hellos (drop-offs and pickups). This can be a vulnerable time, and therefore it is a prime opportunity to support families' relationships with their babies.

Work with families to create drop-off rituals. Babies—and parents—often feel strongly about being separated. Experiencing daily separations when babies are in a care setting can challenge parents' and babies' attachment relationship. These separations are harder for some than others, depending on their relationship, the age and temperament of the baby, and the stress and uncertainty of the parent. When a baby does not settle into a classroom easily, parents may feel distressed or worry about their baby's well-being.

Some families will need your support during separations. Talk with parents about how you can help the baby feel comfortable entering the classroom together. Parents will vary in how much they want you involved in the process and how open they are to talking about it. Come up with a predictable routine for the baby, including when the parent will leave and how the baby will be comforted, ideally with the same educator each day. For example, the parent gives their baby a hug and kiss and leaves, then the caregiver takes the baby to the window to watch for the parent to wave goodbye. Or the parent and baby read the same story together every morning, then the caregiver reads the story with the baby after the parent leaves. It is *not* good for the baby for the parent to sneak away when the baby isn't looking. This might be easier for some parents because they don't have to see their baby upset, but it is much harder for the baby, who learns that their parent is unpredictable and might leave at any time without warning. After the parent has left and the baby has calmed, sending a text or a photo can be a great comfort to parents, reducing their stress and enabling them to turn their attention to their work.

Support family relationships through reunions. Reunions between babies and families are shaped by family culture. They can be joyful and affectionate ("I'm so happy to see you! I missed you!"), they can be practical and down-to-business ("Find your shoes while I get your lunch bag; let's go"), and they can be distressing. When babies don't want to leave the classroom or show distress when their parent arrives, it can be stressful, upsetting, and even embarrassing for parents. Parents may need help understanding their baby's behavior. If a baby is angry or distant when a parent returns, they may be saying, "I was sad and angry while you were away, and I need some time to adjust to your being back," or "Even though I missed you so much, I was settled into my routine and I'm not ready to go yet." Crying could also mean, "I was scared all day, but I distracted myself; now that you are here, I can show how upset I've been." Consider the messages you send parents in your reaction and comments. For instance, when a child cries at pickup, you could hug them and say, "You like being here so much you don't want to go." But the message the parent may hear is "Your child likes it here better than at home," or "I can comfort your child better than you can." An approach that supports babies' relationship with their families is to acknowledge the situation and normalize it by explaining the baby's behavior—for example, "The end of the day can be hard for everyone when we're all tired. Let's think together about how to make it easier on everyone," or "Your child held it together all day, and now that you are here, she is telling us how hard it is to move between home and school." This way you can use reunions to reinforce the family-child relationship and their long-term development.

Supporting families as their babies' educators (FAM-S10)

Parents vary in how much they see themselves as educators for their children and in their confidence in this role. Practitioners can actively help build families' skills in observing their child, their knowledge of child development, and their confidence in supporting their babies' learning.

Invite families to observe their child at play. Ask what skills they notice in their child, and point out what you notice, specifically linking the skills to the behaviors you observe. ("She is using the pair of tongs to move the blocks one by one. She has really been working on her hand coordination and using tools more. What kinds of tools does she like to use at home?")

Create a family-child activity. Set up a table with small and large chairs for a family-child activity. Sensory experiences work well for families of infants or toddlers, and a make-and-take activity can work well for families of toddlers. Explain the skills babies will practice during the activities.

Use home visits to help families enrich the home learning environment. The biggest and longest-lasting positive effects of early child care and education occur when educators support families to help them create a rich home learning environment. **Home visiting programs** provide child development and family support services in the families' homes. While logistics make it hard for group care educators to visit families' homes, occasional home visits yield great rewards. As described above, an initial home visit gives you insight into the family culture and what you can do to ease the transition for families and babies. Occasional home visits can help families understand how their home, daily routines, and interactions support babies' development. Doing home visits allows time to intentionally support each parent's learning about their roles as their baby's educators. Parents can be supported to observe their babies' behavior then plan routines and experiences to promote new skills. In home visits, educators can help families understand what they are already doing that supports their goals for their baby, then collaborate on additional ways to support development in their everyday routines and interactions. While this is most easily done in the home setting, not every family is in a position to invite you into their home. It is possible to engage in the same interactions and discussions in other settings when necessary.

Connecting families with other resources or services (FAM-S11)

When we asked infant-toddler educators how much they know about their families, most educators said they didn't know and generally didn't ask about family income and resources, culture and religion, discipline and guidance strategies, or daily caregiving routines at home. But most families we surveyed said they feel comfortable telling their baby's educators about almost all aspects of family life. Further, when we asked families who could help with their biggest parenting challenges—such as understanding their babies' behavior and development, figuring out effective discipline strategies, and developing good routines at home—they said they wanted advice from their baby's caregiver.

Over time, you will learn about families' strengths, resources, goals, and needs. If you develop the skills to have potentially challenging conversations in clear, supportive, and nonthreatening ways, your unique trusted role can help you link families to other services. These sometimes difficult and personal conversations are easier when there is a history of respectful interactions and a feeling of collaboration in supporting their child's development. Sometimes a resource-based assessment tool such as the Family Map (www.thefamilymap.org) can help gather information about family strengths and needs. The Family Map is a series of questions that provides you with information on a broad array of family resources and needs. It can be used to generate family goals, and you can also use it over time to track changes as you work with families.

Remember that it can be hard for families to share sensitive information. It may take time for them to open up to you. Listen with the benefit of the doubt, without blaming the parent. Be thoughtful in making assumptions about others' histories and experiences (such as adverse early life experiences, maltreatment, substance use, and so on). We cannot really understand what it means to be in someone else's skin. Even if we know some of their history, we don't know what the experience was like for them. You may hear things that are concerning or that you feel you cannot handle on your own. This is when you can call in additional supports and services. Knowing about the services available in your community is important so you can be a resource for families (FAM-K6).

Reflect Back, Think Ahead

Look back at the figure at the beginning of this chapter showing the knowledge, dispositions, and skills involved in partnering with and supporting diverse families. Which of these competencies did you have when you began this chapter? Which competencies did you develop? Which competencies will you intentionally work on building next? Use the Partnering with and Supporting Diverse Families chapter of the Professional Learning Guide (PLG [see page 11]) that accompanies this book to support your own professional growth in this domain.

Selected References

Felitti, Vince. J., and Robert F. Anda. 2010. "The Relationship of Adverse Childhood Experiences to Adult Medical Disease, Psychiatric Disorders, and Sexual Behavior: Implications for Healthcare." In *The Impact of Early Life Trauma on Health and Disease: The Hidden Epidemic*, edited by Ruth A. Lanius, Eric Vermetten, and Clare Pain, 77–87.

Gilliam, Walter S., Angela N. Maupin, Chin R. Reyes, Maria Accavitti, and Frederick Shic. 2016b. *Do Early Educators' Implicit Biases Regarding Sex and Race Relate to Behavior Expectations and Recommendations of Preschool Expulsions and Suspensions?* New Haven, CT: Yale Child Study Center. September 28. https://medicine.yale.edu/childstudy/zigler/publications/Preschool%20 Implicit%20Bias%20Policy%20Brief_final_9_26_276766_5379_v1.pdf.

Martin, Karin A., Emily Bosk, and Denise Bailey. 2018. "Teachers' Perceptions of Childcare and Preschool Expulsion." *Children & Society* 32 (2): 87–97.

National Academies of Sciences, Engineering, and Medicine. 2016. *Parenting Matters: Supporting Parents of Children Ages 0–8*. Washington, DC: National Academies Press.

National Center on Parent, Family, and Community Engagement. "Building Partnerships: Guide to Developing Relationships with Families." https:// eclkc.ohs.acf.hhs.gov/family-engagement/building-partnerships-guide -developing-relationships-families/building-partnerships-guide-developing -relationships-families

Roggman, Lori A., Lisa K. Boyce, and Mark S. Innocenti. 2008. *Developmental Parenting: A Guide for Early Childhood Practitioners*. Baltimore: Brookes.

CHAPTER 5

Guiding Infant and Toddler Behavior

— with Jean Ispa

Guidance is helping infants and toddlers meet behavioral expectations appropriate to their developmental skills in a way that supports their short-term well-being and long-term development. We do this by structuring an environment that supports desired behaviors, interacting in ways that model and support positive behavior, and scaffolding children's **behavior regulation**. Over time, guidance supports babies' development of independence (self-driven behavior toward goals), **autonomy** (confidence in voicing and pursuing their own opinions and interests), and self-regulation (self-constraint to stop, wait, or modify their actions). This definition of guidance as support for development includes classroom management, but it is distinctly different from punishment. With developmentally supportive guidance, caregivers set babies up for success by maximizing their joyful learning and ability to do things for themselves, while providing the support they need to meet behavior expectations. We have summarized the competencies for guiding infant and toddler behavior in figure 5.1.

Why are competencies in guidance important? Effective guidance of infants' and toddlers' behavior is essential for infant-toddler well-being, building and sustaining positive educator-child relationships and peer relationships, and supporting babies' long-term development of autonomous and regulated behavior. Effective guidance creates a calm and predictable environment where infants and toddlers know they are safe and know what to expect from adults, and older toddlers know what is expected of them. Promoting babies' behavioral competencies helps them gain other skills, such as self-care and care for community, emotional expression and regulation, prosocial behavior with peers, and much more.

How is guidance related to other competencies? Guiding babies' behavior in ways that support well-being and development springs from

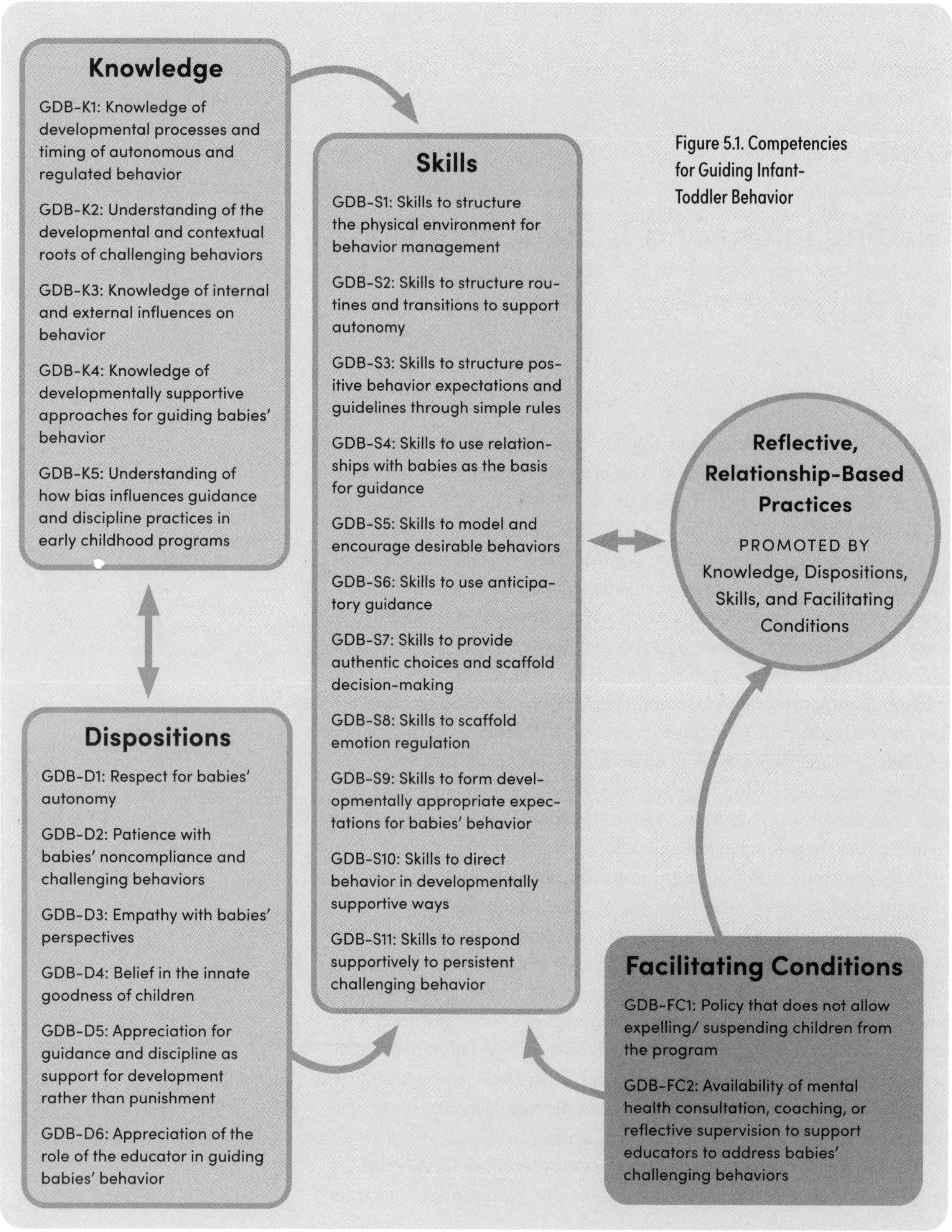

Knowledge

GDB-K1: Knowledge of developmental processes and timing of autonomous and regulated behavior

GDB-K2: Understanding of the developmental and contextual roots of challenging behaviors

GDB-K3: Knowledge of internal and external influences on behavior

GDB-K4: Knowledge of developmentally supportive approaches for guiding babies' behavior

GDB-K5: Understanding of how bias influences guidance and discipline practices in early childhood programs

Skills

GDB-S1: Skills to structure the physical environment for behavior management

GDB-S2: Skills to structure routines and transitions to support autonomy

GDB-S3: Skills to structure positive behavior expectations and guidelines through simple rules

GDB-S4: Skills to use relationships with babies as the basis for guidance

GDB-S5: Skills to model and encourage desirable behaviors

GDB-S6: Skills to use anticipatory guidance

GDB-S7: Skills to provide authentic choices and scaffold decision-making

GDB-S8: Skills to scaffold emotion regulation

GDB-S9: Skills to form developmentally appropriate expectations for babies' behavior

GDB-S10: Skills to direct behavior in developmentally supportive ways

GDB-S11: Skills to respond supportively to persistent challenging behavior

Dispositions

GDB-D1: Respect for babies' autonomy

GDB-D2: Patience with babies' noncompliance and challenging behaviors

GDB-D3: Empathy with babies' perspectives

GDB-D4: Belief in the innate goodness of children

GDB-D5: Appreciation for guidance and discipline as support for development rather than punishment

GDB-D6: Appreciation of the role of the educator in guiding babies' behavior

Reflective, Relationship-Based Practices

PROMOTED BY Knowledge, Dispositions, Skills, and Facilitating Conditions

Facilitating Conditions

GDB-FC1: Policy that does not allow expelling/ suspending children from the program

GDB-FC2: Availability of mental health consultation, coaching, or reflective supervision to support educators to address babies' challenging behaviors

Figure 5.1. Competencies for Guiding Infant-Toddler Behavior

your reflective practice and the relationships you've built with babies. Guidance is crucial for keeping babies safe and supporting their development and learning (chapter 6).

Facilitating conditions. At the program level, guidance must be supported by relationship-based program practices (REL-FC1–FC4) and structures for communicating with families (FAM-FC5), as well as paid time for educators to carefully consider the behaviors they see and develop thoughtful responses (RFP-FC2). Deepening this competency to ensure that guidance is relationship-based and equitable across all children requires both thoughtful program policies and supportive supervision practices. Many programs have implemented no-expulsion/suspension policies (GDB-FC1). But these policies are just a first step, and educators need support to address behaviors in a way that is equitable and supportive of all children, including access to infant/early childhood mental health consultation, coaching, and/or reflective supervision (GDB-FC2).

Knowledge

The foundation of effective guidance includes knowledge of the development of babies' autonomy and regulation skills (GDB-K1), knowledge of the developmental reasons for behaviors often labeled "challenging" (GDB-K2), and knowledge of influences on behavior from within the baby (how they feel) and outside the baby (things in the home and school context) (GDB-K3). Knowledge of developmental skill sequences and milestones (see appendix A QR code on page 126) helps us understand what we can and cannot expect of babies. You also need to know about developmentally supportive strategies for guiding behavior (GDB-K4) and be aware of how educators' strategies may be influenced by biases (GDB-K5).

Knowledge of developmental processes and timing of autonomous and regulated behavior (GDB-K1)

Particularly when we want to guide a child's behavior, we must understand the development of autonomy, **self-control**, and behavior regulation, or babies' skills for initiating, controlling, and regulating their own behavior (figure 5.2). You can learn more about the development of emotion and behavior regulation in appendix A.

Self-Direction. Babies spend their first two years learning what their bodies can do. In the first six months, infants find their hands and feet and learn to move their legs and arms intentionally. Between six months and one year of age, they use their voices to get adult attention and use their arms and hands to reach objects and explore them with purpose. As babies

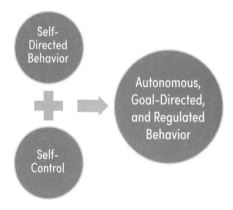

Figure 5.2. Development of Regulated Behavior

learn to walk early in their second year, they learn to direct their bodies to reach goals. Throughout the second year of life, toddlers take more and more initiative and find joy in learning what they can do for themselves. This **goal-directed behavior**, which grows throughout infancy and toddlerhood, is related to later **mastery motivation**, creativity, and love of learning.

Self-Control. At the same time toddlers are learning to direct their actions toward goals, they must learn constraint. This is part of learning to control their own bodies, but it is often in response to someone else. This means that toddlers are learning to be both the action initiator ("Look what I can do!") and the action constrainer (having to wait or stop doing what they want to do). This is physically, cognitively, and emotionally challenging. First, children must have the physical control to stop their moving bodies. Life for a toddler is as if you just learned how to use roller skates but haven't learned how to use the brakes yet! Second, children must have the cognitive skills (called **executive function**) to stop an action and then carry out a different action based on adult guidance or a community rule. Third, children must have the emotional skills to manage disappointment or frustration about stopping what they wanted to do or doing something they don't want to do. That's a lot to ask of a young child!

Behavior regulation. In their third year of life, toddlers begin to recognize the social norms and rules for behavior that their families and communities follow. But they often need adult guidance to follow these rules and meet expectations. When we are verbally guiding children's behavior, we must think about whether they have the **receptive language skills** to understand our directions ("Use walking feet in the classroom," or "Put the cup on the table so it doesn't spill") and the executive function to stop their current behavior and follow our directions. We cannot expect toddlers to follow our community rules on their own until they have the verbal skills to understand the rules and the cognitive skills to internalize and remember them. The challenge in learning to be both the action initiator and the action regulator is most obvious when we see toddlers try and fail to change their actions based on a rule or guidance from an adult:

> Harper was sixteen months old and loved lotion. Her mom, Kristen, had told her many times not to open the lotion bottle. Kristen would shake her head and say, "No, Harper, don't touch the lotion. That is just for Mom to use." One morning, Kristen left the lotion out, and she looked over to see Harper with the bottle open and pointed down toward the carpet. Harper looked up at Kristen, shook her head, then looked back at the lotion. Still looking at the lotion bottle, she shook her head again, then stopped and squeezed the bottle of lotion into the carpet, much to her mom's frustration.

Harper is struggling between being the goal-directed action initiator and the rule-directed action regulator. We see her struggle as she looks to her mother for guidance, shakes her own head, indicating that she understands that she is not supposed to have the lotion bottle, but fails to regulate her behavior in line with her mom's rule. Harper needed more support from her mom in order to follow the rule. Many adults misinterpret toddlers' struggles at this stage, even seeing defiance ("She *looked right at me* and shook her head! So I *know* she understood the rule, but she did it *anyway!*"), rather than valiant but failed attempts to follow the rules. Understanding the development of autonomy and self-regulation and the conflicts between the two are keys to understanding toddlers' struggles and what we think of as challenging behaviors.

Understanding of the developmental and contextual roots of challenging behaviors (GDB-K2)

Some of babies' autonomy behaviors are challenging for adults, and thus we call them challenging behaviors. The baby is not intentionally challenging us. Rather, we are challenged by behaviors that are a natural part of early development. Babies' behaviors can sometimes be hard to handle, particularly aggression or resistance to being guided. But these behaviors help babies develop autonomy and sense of self, and they ultimately lead to behavioral regulation. Lacking socially acceptable ways to communicate, babies often express their unmet needs with challenging behaviors. For example, toddlers' physical need for movement may manifest as squirming when they are expected to be still. An emotional need for connection may lead to clinginess. In addition to the developmental explanations below, learn more about developmental processes in chapter 6 and milestones in appendix A (see page 126).

Mouthing and biting. Infants explore other people with their mouths, just like they explore objects. They have more control over their mouth and sensation in their tongues than other parts of their body, so they explore textures as well as flavors orally. Biting can also bring some relief to teething pain. Finally, toddlers bite when they feel threatened or closed in and don't have another way to communicate their feelings and needs. When verbal toddlers are still biting, they may need support for regulating behavior.

Rough touch. Infants love to explore other babies and familiar adults with their hands as well as mouths, and often do so in rough ways. They are learning about others' bodies, others' reactions, and the effects of their actions on others. However, they don't yet understand that others feel pain and can't interpret the words or facial expressions that result from their rough touches.

Instrumental aggression. In toddlerhood, aggressive behavior (pushing, hitting, biting) is usually instrumental, or functional. That is, it's not intended to be mean but rather as a means to an end, such as moving someone out of the way or getting a toy. It's common in **preverbal** babies, those who have delays in language, and verbal toddlers who are upset and can't find their words.

Vigorous physical activity. Toddlers need to run, climb, jump, throw, kick, and bang to exercise their muscles, learn the effects they can have on the world and others, and ultimately learn to control their bodies.

No! Saying no is a developmental milestone that indicates a child's growing sense of self, defining themselves as separate individuals. They are learning that they can want something different than their caregivers and are learning how to make decisions. You have to know that you can say "no" before "yes" really means anything. Toddlers are still learning they can say no, and they love to practice this new skill! Many times you'll find that toddlers say yes almost immediately after saying no.

Mine! Toddlers define their identities according to what belongs to them or who belongs with them, and also by what they like. Eventually "My truck" becomes "I like trucks," and "My mommy" becomes "This is my family." Saying "mine" is often the first sign of a growing sense of identity. But toddlers don't have an adult sense of possession; they see everything that they want or like as theirs.

Vigorous emotional expression, aka tantrums. Babies can be easily overwhelmed by their emotions. Verbal expression is difficult, and they have not yet learned strategies to solve the problems that led to their big feelings. Overwhelmed emotions can result in physical acting out, such as screaming, lying on the floor, kicking, or hitting. This indicates that the child has an unmet need.

Knowledge of internal and external influences on behavior (GDB-K3)

There are seven main influences on babies' short-term behavior and long-term development. The first three affect babies in similar ways and are responsible for changing behavior from one day (or minute) to the next: internal states and needs, immediate context (what's going on in the physical and social environment), and developmental skills. The last four underlie differences between babies in their behavior and development over time: temperament, security of close relationships, family culture, and stress and trauma. All of these are important as you try to understand an individual baby's behavior, particularly when you identify a difference or change that concerns you. Use your knowledge of these seven influences to better understand babies' challenging behaviors. (See handout 5.1, Behavior Detective.)

1. Physiology first! To interpret babies' behavior, we first consider their physical states and needs. We call this the Physiology First principle. Only after ruling out physiology do we consider the other six influences. Is she hungry, tired, cold, or in pain? Could he be teething or sick? Has she had enough activity and exercise today? Are her senses overwhelmed

www.redleafpress.org/wwb/5-1.pdf

by too much noise, light, or people? Another physiological influence is the baby's gestational age (whether they were born prematurely) and their birth weight, which influence their general health, brain development, and the regulation of biological rhythms, emotions, and behaviors.

2. Immediate and recent context. Babies' behavior is highly contextual. Qualities of the baby's immediate context—at home or school—that affect behavior and development are safety, security, and stimulation. Educators should look first to the immediate context in the group care setting to explain babies' behavior before considering how the child's home context might be affecting behavior in the classroom.

In safe environments, routines are predictable and children are free to explore without danger. Babies can become overwhelmed by social or sensory input, including lighting, sound, and the number of people in a room. In an environment with chaos and constant change, babies have difficulty concentrating and can easily become dysregulated, particularly if they are not sleeping enough.

Children feel secure when they feel connected, respected, and valued, and when their caregiver is a secure base for exploration. Babies are affected by the absence or loss of a familiar caregiver in out-of-home care; this is why consistent staffing and continuity in the caregiver-child relationship is so important. Secure relationships at home can be disrupted by family changes, be it happy changes like a new sibling or sad changes like a divorce. Close and consistent relationships with educators can be a buffer for babies experiencing change at home and can also reduce anxiety, withdrawal, and aggressive behavior.

Stimulating environments offer developmentally appropriate learning opportunities that invite and excite children while also offering breaks. When children are not engaged in play and learning and not challenged by their environment, they seek challenges for themselves. This can result in challenging behavior! When a child's behavior challenges you, ask whether they are engaged by the environment. Calm, consistent contexts that are both safe and stimulating support regulated behavior, active exploration, and, ultimately, development and learning.

3. Development across domains. When we notice behavior change or see a behavior that concerns us, we ask whether the baby is developing new skills. For example, infants get more frustrated during challenging tasks once they have the cognitive skills to plan and carry out goals (goal-directed behavior). A toddler will become more possessive of toys once they develop a sense of identity connected to their belongings. When babies are developing a new skill (like crawling or walking, or scooping and dumping), they spend a lot of time practicing it, which can be exhausting. Babies may become tired and dysregulated, cry or fuss more, or be clumsier (falling over, running into things, or dropping things more than usual). Toddlers may make more messes, as when a child dumps cereal on to a table because they are exploring in/out relationships. This can seem like a **regression** in regulatory skills, but it is usually just a temporary disruption in regulatory behavior. When you see children practicing a behavior over and over, including in ways that are unsafe (climbing shelves) or that create extra messes (dropping food on the floor, dumping things out of containers), consider what skill they are practicing, then offer them safer or cleaner alternatives to meet the same goal.

4. Temperament. Temperament influences how babies behave and learn. It includes a set of nine biologically based traits that a baby is born with that influence the way they react to and engage with the world, such as how quickly and strongly they react to changes and new people, places, and objects; the amount of time they need when making a transition between activities; and their overall mood. The nine temperament traits include the following:

* *activity level*—how wiggly a baby is

* *regularity*—in eating, sleeping, bowel movements, and so on

* *adaptability*—how quickly and easily they adjust to changes in routine

* *approach/withdrawal*—in reacting to new people, food, toys, situations

* *physical sensitivity*—awareness of noises, differences in temperature, texture, taste

* *intensity of reaction*—positive and negative emotional reactions

* *distractibility*—how easily the child is distracted

* *positive or negative mood*—whether they are in a good or bad mood most of the time

* *persistence*—how long a child continues an activity, including a difficult one

While there are also social and cultural influences on temperament, we understand it to be a stable part of who babies are as individuals, and thus we respect these differences and work with them as we respond to behavior and support development. To learn more about temperament, we recommend completing a temperament chart for yourself and your class. Examples of such tools include the IT3 Infant Interactive Tool, available from Head Start's Early Childhood Learning and Knowledge Center.

5. Close relationships. Babies' behavior, moods, and willingness to explore are all highly influenced by their relationships with caregivers, as well as by the relationships between their caregivers. When relationships are consistent and caring, a baby feels secure and loved and can freely explore their environment, sure that their caregiver will be there whenever they need anything. When a baby does not know whom they can trust, they will feel anxious and scared, often becoming dysregulated (more crying and fussing, clumsier physical behavior) or not feeling free to explore and learn. Babies also pick up on the emotional tone of relationships between others—between their parent and educator, or between coeducators—which influences their sense of security.

As we described in chapter 3 (Building and Supporting Relationships), a baby's special relationship with his parents (attachment) influences his general sense of security in the world, and thus his attachment-related behavior in the classroom, even when his parents aren't there. Babies can establish a trusting and secure relationship with consistent and caring educators, even if their relationships with parents are less consistent. When babies constantly monitor their caregivers' location in the classroom instead of playing and exploring, this is an indication that they don't trust that the caregivers will be there for them. (This is why we always let children know when we're going to leave, rather than sneaking away, even if our goodbye makes them sad.) If you see a baby who does not explore, who tends to stay in one spot, or who constantly watches the adults in the room, consider whether he has a secure relationship or special bond with at least one educator.

6. Culture. Family culture and the culture of the group care environment both influence baby behavior. For example, psychologist Heidi Keller and anthropologist James McKenna have written extensively about the ways in which cultural values and norms inform caregiving and infant behavior. Culture shapes the physical and social environments, as well as the customs of caring for and educating children. For example, some cultures practice cosleeping, which means a baby entering group care will not be used to sleeping by herself and may have a difficult time adjusting to the classroom sleep practices. In some cultures, babies are encouraged to feed themselves. In others, caregivers spoon-feed them, which encourages interdependence among family members. Communication styles may also differ. For example, in some cultures it is not respectful for a child to make eye contact with an adult. If you find that a child avoids eye contact with you, consider whether this reflects the family's culture. Some cultures view pointing as rude, while others encourage it as a communication tool. For some cultures, it is disrespectful to touch a child on the head; for others it is a sign of affection. If a child recoils from being touched, consider whether this touch means something different in their home culture.

7. Stress and trauma. Chronic stress and intense trauma have immediate and long-lasting effects on babies' behavior. Common sources of chronic stress for babies are unpredictable and chaotic environments at home or at school or neglect of their physical and emotional needs. Emotionally chaotic

www.redleafpress.org/wwb/5-2.pdf

environments tend to have high levels of anger, fear, or sadness. Unpredictable people and routines are most common in families who abuse drugs or alcohol. Traumas include living through natural disasters, witnessing violence against family or community members, experiencing physical, sexual, or emotional abuse, or having a family member die or leave for another reason. Babies can experience the same emotions that adults do during prolonged stress or during or after a trauma, including fear, anxiety, sadness, grief, anger, and being overwhelmed. But babies don't have coping tools or ways of making sense of what is happening. Preverbal babies cannot tell us about the stresses and traumas they experience, but their behavior can give us clues about what they are feeling. Read handout 5.2, Respond to Trauma, to identify behavioral indicators of stress and trauma and what they tell us about underlying emotional needs.

Knowledge of developmentally supportive approaches for guiding babies' behavior (GDB-K4)

Developmentally appropriate and supportive guidance uses and encourages children's skills. All guidance should support children's well-being, reinforcing the connection between children and their educators and peers. Developmentally appropriate guidance is based on expectations that children are capable of meeting, given their current developmental skills, temperament, emotional states, and contexts. In the skills and practices section of this chapter, we describe guidance techniques that are developmentally appropriate and supportive for infants and toddlers.

Common techniques that take a punishment approach are less effective and *not* developmentally supportive. Punishment includes any penalty inflicted on children for their behavior. Research shows that imposing a penalty on children—in *any* form—to stop a behavior damages the adult-child relationship, discourages trust, and inhibits development. Punishment often models the very behaviors we want to stop and thus works against positive behavior development. Toddlers learn and do what they see and what they experience, not what they are told to do. Thus, if we want to socialize babies to have positive interactions, we need to model them. Below are five common punishments and their negative effects on babies.

Dismissing children's feelings or needs includes saying, for example, "Big girls don't cry," or "That's nothing to cry about." Children feel misunderstood and often become sadder or angrier, escalating the behavior in an attempt to be understood.

Shaming includes teasing or belittling children for their feelings or behavior, such as calling them "fraidy-cat" or "chicken" when they are scared or nervous, or laughing or looking in disgust at their expressions of sadness, fear, or anger.

Intimidation includes fear-inducing behaviors such as slamming a door, hitting an object near the child, yelling, giving children dirty or very stern looks, looming over them, or otherwise using physical size or threat of force to intimidate.

Physical punishment, including **spanking**, shaking, yanking an arm, pushing, shoving, or other rough handling induces fear and stress, erodes trust, damages the adult-child relationship, and teaches children that physical force can solve social conflicts. Use of physical punishment is more common in some cultures than others. It is more harmful to some children than others, depending on the child's temperament and family culture. However, decades of research have shown that spanking and other physical punishment is harmful to children's development in *every* culture. There are much more effective ways to guide babies' behavior and socialize the skills and behaviors we want them to have.

Separating infants or toddlers from caregivers or the classroom community can damage babies' sense of connection and threaten their sense of security. **Exclusion** includes time-outs or not letting children join desired activities. **Love-withdrawal** involves acting in a cold, aloof way toward the child, either intentionally or as an unintentional reaction when the caregiver is angry or annoyed. Expulsion or suspension is an extreme form of separation as punishment. Expulsion and suspension are not options for high-quality child care and education programs. This is a strong rejection of the child and the family and severely damages the child's relationship to education, setting them up for a poor educational trajectory. Sadly, there are racial disparities in expulsions in child care that speak to our societal biases on ongoing systemic oppression of Black and brown children and families.

Understanding of how bias influences guidance and discipline practices in early childhood programs (GDB-K5)

Research by Walter Gilliam (2005), a national expert on early childhood expulsion, reports that young children are expelled from child care and preschool at substantially higher rates than high school students. It bears repeating: *Expulsion and suspension are not options for high-quality child care and education programs.* These experiences are harmful to babies' well-being and deprive working families of resources they need to support their families economically. What is worse, these expulsions happen disproportionately more to children who are Black and/or Hispanic/Latino. Research by Gilliam and colleagues (2016b) has shown that early childhood educators watch children of color more carefully, expecting them to misbehave. Other research shows that early childhood educators are more likely to interpret the behavior of children of color as challenging, aggressive, or less socially skilled, even when it is completely age appropriate. Thus, educators are harsher or stricter with certain groups of children than others. Importantly, when educators attribute babies' challenging behaviors to things happening at home that are out of the educators' influence (such as chaos or trauma), they are more likely to initiate expulsion. Thus, educators should look to what is happening in the classroom context first and do what they can to support the child in that context, regardless of what they see as the root cause of the behavior. Biased educator reactions harm children's well-being and development and are difficult for parents as well. Educators need support to manage their classrooms and effectively guide babies' behavior (see GDB-FC1 and GDB-FC2, above), as well as an understanding of children's development and behavior.

Human beings are biased because our brains are designed to make quick decisions based on incomplete information. This is a fact of human life. But we can disrupt the negative influences our biases have on young children and their families by (1) becoming aware of our biases through conscious reflection, (2) questioning our own beliefs about and behaviors toward children, and (3) attempting to counteract our biases in conscious ways. Learn more in this chapter's Selected References, as well as the Resources and Further Readings online.

Dispositions

The dispositions critical for effective guidance include our beliefs about and approach to children (GDB-D1–D4) and beliefs about guidance (GDB-D5, GDB-D6), and they follow on the dispositions for building relationships with babies. It becomes easier to form attitudes that support guidance when we choose to view babies' behavior through a developmental lens rather than as a threat to our authority.

Respect for babies' autonomy (GDB-D1)

Respecting babies' autonomy means respecting who they are as people, with their own personalities, needs, desires, interests, and goals. From birth, babies are active, self-driven learners, each with their own ways of experiencing and interacting with the world.

Patience with babies' noncompliance and challenging behaviors (GDB-D2)

Babies have not yet internalized the rules of their families, schools, or communities. This socialization process takes years. They cannot predict what is unsafe or empathize with others' feelings. They have a different sense of right and wrong than adults do, and it is primarily about getting what they want. Thus, they do things that place themselves in danger and hurt others. Patience with these behaviors helps us use them as learning opportunities.

Empathy with babies' perspectives (GDB-D3)

To respond in supportive ways, we must try to understand the world from babies' perspectives, including their goals and intentions, emotional reactions, and their limited understanding of themselves, others, and rules. When we can see the world through the baby's eyes, we can provide guidance that is truly sensitive and supports their development.

Belief in the innate goodness of children (GDB-D4)

Beliefs that babies are selfish, manipulative, and bad cause us to look for and see "bad behavior" where there is none and react accordingly. Then babies feel misunderstood and act out to try to get their message across, which causes us to see more "bad behavior." Instead, we respond supportively when we understand that babies are innately motivated to connect with and please others and when we know that their behavior is a result of their developmental limitations.

Appreciation for guidance as support for development rather than punishment (GDB-D5)

When we think guidance must include punishment, we end up training children to comply only when they fear being caught. When we approach guidance as support for development, we socialize children to understand community rules, empathize with others, and regulate their own behavior to meet shared goals.

Appreciation of the role of the educator in guiding babies' behavior (GDB-D6)

Some educators feel that it is a parent's job to guide their child's behavior, and that classroom behavior is a reflection of what is expected or accepted at home. While babies' home lives influence their behavior, babies also adapt to each social context and learn to follow rules and norms in each setting. Thus, educators have a strong influence on babies' behavior in the classroom and their development of autonomous and regulated behavior.

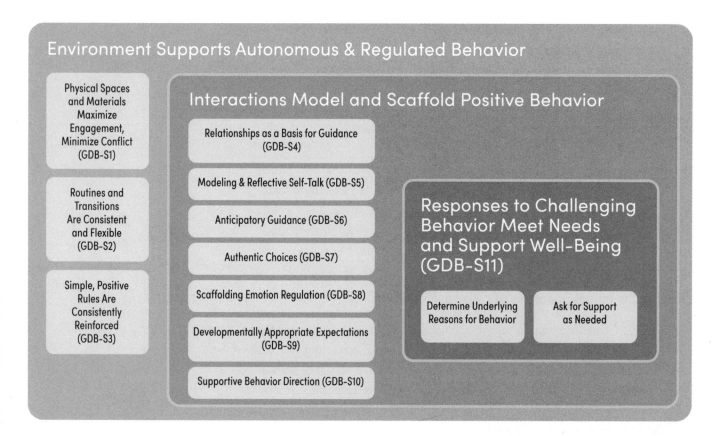

Environment Supports Autonomous & Regulated Behavior

Physical Spaces and Materials Maximize Engagement, Minimize Conflict (GDB-S1)

Routines and Transitions Are Consistent and Flexible (GDB-S2)

Simple, Positive Rules Are Consistently Reinforced (GDB-S3)

Interactions Model and Scaffold Positive Behavior

Relationships as a Basis for Guidance (GDB-S4)

Modeling & Reflective Self-Talk (GDB-S5)

Anticipatory Guidance (GDB-S6)

Authentic Choices (GDB-S7)

Scaffolding Emotion Regulation (GDB-S8)

Developmentally Appropriate Expectations (GDB-S9)

Supportive Behavior Direction (GDB-S10)

Responses to Challenging Behavior Meet Needs and Support Well-Being (GDB-S11)

Determine Underlying Reasons for Behavior

Ask for Support as Needed

Figure 5.3. Skills and Practices for Guiding Behavior to Support Well-Being and Development on a Daily Basis

Skills

The skills and practices for effective guidance are like those for building relationships and supporting development. They start with structuring the environment for success (GDB-S1–S3), then use everyday interactions within ongoing, positive relationships to model and reinforce the behaviors and skills we want children to develop (GDB-S4–S9). Then finally, when needed, practitioners direct or redirect children's behavior to keep them safe and support their development (GDB-S10, GDB-S11).

Structuring the physical environment for behavior management (GDB-S1)

We set up physical environments to provide natural limits on behavior, as well as to maximize babies' engagement in meaningful play. Limits and boundaries provide predictability, safety, and security. In chapter 6, you'll learn more about balancing safety, security, and stimulation in the environment. Here we focus on setting up "yes environments," structuring space to allow for monitoring and maximizing child engagement.

Turn "no environments" into "yes environments." When the child-accessible spaces and materials are in good repair and don't present any dangers, we can say yes to the things children want to do. In yes environments, everything is safe and developmentally appropriate. Adults can see all children at once, so we can easily monitor them and spot any risks as they occur. Adult furniture is against the wall and facing into the room. Low shelving or other furniture defines spaces while allowing us to see over it. We make sure there are few "blind spots" where children are out of view. Even when we are engaging in babies' play, we can sit against the wall so we can scan the room without disrupting our interactions.

When children are engaged, they rarely misbehave. We set up environments to maximize babies' sustained engagement in self-driven exploration and play and to reduce competition for resources. Babies should have access to multiple kinds of engaging materials, and there should be enough materials to go around. This minimizes aimless wandering, conflicts, and challenging behaviors.

Table 5.1 Structuring the Physical Environment for Behavior Management

Yes environment

- Space structured for global view.
- Adult materials out of reach.
- Runways minimized using barriers or speed bumps.
- Intentional design to accommodate different moods.
- Protected space for nonmobile infants.

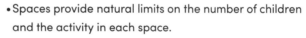

Natural and flexible boundaries

- Spaces provide natural limits on the number of children and the activity in each space.
- Spaces have natural boundaries to protect children's concentration and creations.
- Furniture is movable to allow children to manipulate their environments.
- Flexibility supports children to carry out their plans.

Engaging materials

- Range of stimulating materials is always accessible to children.
- Enough materials to go around minimizes conflict.
- Moderate amount of materials prevents babies from being overwhelmed.
- Materials are well-organized to minimize clutter and confusion.
- Materials can be moved to accommodate children's plans.

Here are babies' cues that the environment is under- or overstimulating:

❋ **Unfocused** wandering, not sustaining attention on anything

❋ **Reverting** to "younger" ways of interacting with toys, such as dumping, throwing, or kicking toys in a way that is not purposeful

❋ **Aggressive** behaviors with other children, like pushing

❋ Other **attention-seeking** behavior

❋ **Withdrawing** into a corner of the room or other quieter space

Structuring routines and transitions to support autonomy (GDB-S2)

Consistent, predictable routines help children feel safe, secure, and competent in participating. At the same time, being flexible in timing and carrying out routines supports babies' autonomy, active participation, and developing skills in caring for themselves and their community. Use transitions to intentionally support emotion and behavior regulation.

STRATEGIES

Post a visual schedule with pictures of daily routines. Draw children's attention to it as you go through the day. For toddlers, the daily schedule may be relatively consistent in sequence, with a lot of flexibility in timing as needed. For example, it takes a lot longer to get outside when the group must put on winter gear than it does when all they need are jackets. For young babies, a group schedule does not make sense since their sleep and mealtimes are individual and rapidly changing. Instead, the daily schedule is more of a list of experiences that happen sometime each day.

Use forecasting between routines, telling children ahead of time what to expect next and when to expect it. This allows children to prepare emotionally for the upcoming change and actively participate in the transition.

Give children authentic choices as much as possible to empower them in transitions and routines, and respect the choices they make. Read section GDB-S7 for more information about providing authentic choices and supporting children's decision-making.

Support relationships throughout routines by connecting with the child at each step. Handout 3.2 (see page 52), Diapering, describes using relationship-based guidance practices throughout a hygienic diapering routine to support children's autonomy and regulation.

Structuring positive behavior expectations and guidelines through simple rules (GDB-S3)

Young children need consistent limits to provide predictability, safety, and security. But setting limits is different from exerting adult control. Limits provide boundaries within which babies can safely explore as they choose. This promotes babies' own sense of autonomy and mastery of their environment. On the other hand, exerting control through unnecessarily rigid rules (such as rules about moving a toy around the classroom or dictating where or how to sit during group experiences) inhibits creativity, autonomy, and mastery motivation. Such control is particularly damaging if it is unpredictable or if it singles out or excludes some children.

Expect that toddlers will frequently test limits. They learn limits by testing them. Give gentle, consistent reminders about limits. Effective guidance is flexible when possible, enforces firm boundaries when needed, and is always kind.

The schedule in Ms. Denise's class is a series of photos stuck to a Velcro strip that can be rearranged each day.

Two friends find familiar events on the day's schedule.

Short and simple rules. Develop a short list of positively worded, simple rules. All rules should be relevant to children's daily experiences and within their behavioral control. Post the rules visually in key places in the classroom and refer to them when reminding children about them. For example,

1 Use gentle touches.

2 Eat the food on your own tray.

3 Hold the railing on the stairs.

Reinforce rules with positive directives. Babies respond better to positively worded directions than to negative ones like "don't." Their understanding of language is still developing along with their ability to apply our words to their behavior. Phrase directions as actions *to do* ("Walk slowly") rather than as what *not to do* ("Don't run"). Logical reversals are also difficult, so instead of saying, "You're going too fast," say, "Walk slower." Link your directives to reasons and classroom rules so children begin to understand the consistent limits in their community. Each negative directive below has been reworded to one that toddlers can understand and learn from:

❄ Get off the shelves. ➔ Put your feet on the floor. You could fall and hurt yourself.

❄ No pulling hair! ➔ Use a gentle touch. We use gentle touches so we don't hurt our classmates.

❄ Don't eat food off other children's plates. ➔ Remember our classroom rule: Only eat the food on your own plate. If you would like more, I will get more for you.

❄ No running in the hall. ➔ Remember, we walk in the hallway to stay safe. We can run when we get outside.

Using relationships with babies as the basis for guidance (GDB-S4)

Guidance occurs in the context of educator-child relationships and should reinforce the child's trust in the educator. Children crave connection and are motivated by it. They want to please their caregivers and be part of their community. Thus, guidance is most meaningful to children, and most likely to result in learning, when it occurs as part of warm, supportive, daily interactions over time, and when it reinforces, rather than undermines, connections to caregivers or peers. Relationship-based practices, such as primary caregiving and continuity of care, support strong connections between each child and their primary educator so educators understand each child's needs, strengths, and limitations.

Guidance with affection and connection leads to **committed compliance**, when toddlers have internalized the rules and the principles behind them. Once they have internalized rules, they will follow them even when no adult is guiding them. On the other hand, punishment that makes the child feel ashamed or isolated results in **conditional compliance**, when toddlers follow a rule only when they think they could be caught and punished.

STRATEGIES ————————————————————————

The Three *T*s of relationship-based guidance reinforce relationships:

Touch. We reinforce children's trust through our physical actions. We move to be next to the child rather than yelling across a room; we get down to their level to eliminate a threatening stance; we make eye contact to get their attention and communicate respect; and we use affectionate touch, like a gentle hand on their shoulder or arm, to reinforce our connection and help them stay calm.

Togetherness talk reinforces the child's connection to the caregiver or the community. It often expresses guidance in terms of a common goal or community principle: "*Let's* clean up the blocks *together*. Which color blocks should *we* clean up first?" or "Remember, *we* use only gentle touches with *our* classmates." Children are more likely to go along with what we ask when we are working together, rather than when they feel forced to comply.

Time-in, not time-out. During **time-in**, children receive connection and comfort from a trusted caregiver after an upsetting situation or misbehavior. It supports the baby to move from a negative emotional state (angry tantrum) to a calm, connected state. Once the child is calm and connected, they are more open to talking about what happened. Time-in is an alternative to **time-out**, which isolates the child, is less calming, and can induce shame.

Modeling and encouraging desirable behaviors (GDB-S5)

Children learn behaviors and attitudes by watching us more than by obeying us. Thus, we use daily positive interactions to draw children's attention to appropriate and prosocial behavior (ours and theirs) in an authentic, respectful way.

STRATEGIES ————————————————————————

Model and narrate your own positive behavior. Show babies what you want from them so they see and experience it. Narrate as you model desirable behaviors so babies begin to understand your reasoning. If you want them to use quiet indoor voices, use your quiet indoor voice ("I'm going to lower my voice now that we're inside because other children might be resting and I don't want to disturb them"). If you want them to treat their peers gently, then use only gentle touches ("Use gentle touches with your friends, like pats or hugs, just like I touch you"). If you want them to use deep breathing when they are upset, let them see you do it too ("I'm feeling overwhelmed right now, so I'm going to breathe in really slowly, then let it all out").

Comment on children's positive behavior. Children naturally want to please and connect to caregivers and peers. Commenting on children's desirable behavior connects with them and reinforces that behavior ("Charlie, you handed Charlotte her cup. That was so helpful," or "Simon, I notice you tried two new vegetables. You're exploring new tastes"). However, avoid acknowledging children in a shaming or manipulative way. Don't compare children implicitly by talking *about* one child's actions to others ("I really like how Salem is putting his dishes in the sink") or shaming children by acknowledging some but not others ("David, Ann, and Jamal are being so helpful today!"). Instead, speak directly to the child you wish to acknowledge. Avoid manipulating children into doing things they don't want to do ("It makes me really happy when you finish all your lunch"). When children feel shamed and disconnected from us, or they only feel accepted when they please us, their self-worth is damaged. Ultimately these strategies backfire by triggering the behaviors we want to discourage.

Acknowledge and encourage instead of praise. Praising children for personal qualities ("You are so smart") or using exaggerated praise ("Your painting is *sooo* beautiful!") can backfire by lowering motivation and self-worth when children face challenges. This counterintuitive reaction happens because the children become overly concerned with others' opinions. When they don't succeed, they worry that a setback means they are unworthy. As a result, they may avoid challenges. Such praise teaches children to look for external rewards rather than doing things because they are intrinsically valuable. Praise given frequently can become meaningless to children. Instead of praise, we acknowledge children's efforts, processes, or strategies: "You're trying so hard," "You put all the blocks into the basket," or "You figured out that if you put the big blocks on the bottom, your building won't fall." **Encouragement** lets children know why you appreciate what they did ("When you put your leftovers in the trash, you help keep our classroom clean," or "Thank you for bringing Lily her socks. That was very helpful"). Acknowledging effort is a general tool that can be used almost anytime to encourage a positive behavior. Handout 5.3, Encourage Positive Behavior, has examples of rewriting praise to acknowledgment.

www.redleafpress.org/wwb/5-3.pdf

Using anticipatory guidance (GDB-S6)

Anticipatory guidance happens when the educator tells the baby about upcoming changes and events. It communicates respect for children's self-directed activities and can involve children in transitions and prevent challenges.

STRATEGIES

* **Foretell:** Letting children know what you are going to do before you do something to them shows respect for their personhood ("I'm going to set you down now because I need to go help Sarah").

* **Forecast:** Telling children what to expect next and when to expect it helps them anticipate and prepare for change ("I'm going to change your diaper after we read this book").

* **Foresee and Forestall:** Anticipating what might happen lets you prevent conflicts. For example, when you see that a toddler is about to take another's toy, preemptively suggest a positive peer interaction ("Hanif, it looks like Zaya is interested in what you're building. Can you give her some blocks so she can build next to you?").

Ms. Akiba foretells an upcoming diaper change for baby Azura, showing her the purple gloves she always wears for diapering.

Ms. Denise foresees that Carla and Emi may bump each other as they both try to climb into the box, so she places a hand between them to provide physical guidance and forestall a conflict over space.

Providing authentic choices and scaffolding decision-making (GDB-S7)

Providing young children with authentic choices shares power in a way that keeps them safe and healthy while building their skills in decision-making. When children get to make choices often, they are more willing to go along with adults' decisions when needed. Notice how giving an authentic choice is much more engaging than a simple directive: "Sarah, we need to clean up the blocks. Do you want to clean up the blue ones, the green ones, or the pink ones?" rather than "You need to clean up those blocks now, Sarah." Below, we describe characteristics of authentic choices and provide strategies for offering authentic choices and scaffolding children's decision-making.

Developmentally appropriate. First, options must be safe and within babies' capabilities. Second, the child must understand their choices. Avoid offering choices about increments of time because babies don't understand the difference between two and three minutes. Instead, offer a choice about sequence, such as "Do you want to put on your shoes first and then jacket, or your jacket first, then shoes?" Third, the decision process itself must be simple enough for the baby to do. We use simple choices with infants, then expand them with toddlers. We ask an infant, "Would you like peas or corn?" but ask a verbal toddler, "What would you like for snack today?"

Equivalent in value. To be authentic, rather than coercive, choices must be equivalent in value. Adults often pretend to offer children choices when they are really threats: "If you're not going to put on your shoes, then I guess you'll have to stay here. It's your choice." In reality, the child won't be left; this is an empty threat disguised as a choice. Contrast this choice—"Polly, it's time for your diaper change. Do you want to hop, crawl, or walk to the diaper table?"—with this disguised threat: "It's time for your diaper change. Are you going to come with me, or do I need to come get you?"

No wrong answer. Offering authentic choices means there is no wrong answer. We offer two or more options we really can say yes to. This is key in turning "no environments" into "yes environments." Adults often ask questions to which the only good answer is yes, such as, "Do you want to hang up your jacket?" or "Can you pick up your toys now?" Babies will not understand these questions as directives, and their answer may well be no. We confuse children when we give directions in the form of questions, particularly children whose families give more direct commands. We might even misinterpret children's responses as defiance or disobedience when we did not make our expectations clear to them.

* **Get the child's attention** and reduce distractions when offering a choice so the child can think about it. Walk over, get down to the child's level, make eye contact, then offer the choice.

* **Use nonverbal cues** with infants and younger toddlers to clarify and reinforce your verbal message. For example, if you are offering a baby a choice between two toys or two foods, hold out both options at equal distance to them. Encourage them to reach for what they want.

* **Wait for a response.** Repeat the question or try asking in a different way if the child doesn't respond.

* **Scaffold decision-making.** If you don't get a clear answer, help by narrating what you are doing. "I can't tell what you want to eat, so I'm going to give you applesauce and see if you like it."

* **Let children change their minds.** Children change their minds— sometimes immediately or several times—because they are practicing their decision-making skills. Let them change their minds within practical limits.

* **Follow through with limits.** A child may make a choice, then fail to follow through. For example, a toddler may choose to hop to the diaper table but run the other way. Caregivers must stick to necessary hygiene and safety limits, stating firmly but kindly, "You can come back over to the diaper table, or I will come carry you."

Scaffolding emotion regulation (GDB-S8)

When babies are distressed, they can do little to regulate their behavior. We must first help them regulate their emotions, providing comfort and support as needed.

Use mind-minded reflections to acknowledge babies' experiences. Use *your* words when babies can't. Infants can't use words yet, and even toddlers lose their words when they are upset. We look to nonverbal clues to tell us about their experiences, and we provide words for them using informed guesses (mind-minded reflections).

Observe, reflect on, and describe the ABCs of babies' experiences: *Affect* refers to babies' facial expressions and other indicators of emotions ("Your eyebrows are down"). *Behavior* refers to what children do and say ("You're kicking that shelf"). *Context* refers to what has happened ("That car keeps falling on the floor every time you try to put it on the shelf"). Connect these ABCs to their possible internal states—what they may intend, want, feel, and think ("You seem really frustrated"). This builds babies' vocabulary for internal states, which eventually helps them communicate their feelings and needs and better understand themselves and others. You don't need to connect all three ABCs out loud every time, but it helps to reflect on each yourself before offering babies support.

Offer coping strategies and solutions. After you've acknowledged their experience, work with the baby to address the emotion (emotion-focused coping; "Calming our bodies helps when we're frustrated. Let's get the breathing ball") or a solution to the problem (problem-focused coping; "Can I help you put the car where it won't roll off?"). See table 5.2 for emotion coregulation strategies, and handout 2.2 (see page 29), Mindfulness for Babies, for additional ideas.

Table 5.2 Emotional Experience, Underlying Needs, and Strategies to Scaffold Emotion Regulation		
What I Feel	*What I Need*	*What You Can Do*
Frustration	I need to feel capable of accomplishing my goal.	Acknowledge my feelings. Help me find a solution to the problem so I can reach my goal.
Anger	I need to feel understood and validated.	Tell me it's okay to feel this way; help me find safe ways to express my feelings. If possible, help me find a solution to the problem.
Overwhelmed	I need to feel contained.	Help me find spaces that calm me, and spend one-on-one time with me.
Sadness and grief	I need to feel connected and loved.	Comfort me, invite me to interact. Help me find ways to soothe myself, but let me feel sad for as long as I need to.
Fear and anxiety	I need to feel safe.	Let me know you will protect me. Make my environment, routines, and adult behavior calm and predictable.

Forming developmentally appropriate expectations for babies' behavior (GDB-S9)

Before we can effectively direct babies' behaviors, we must understand what we can and cannot expect of them. What we can reasonably expect of an individual baby depends upon their developmental skills, temperament, and current context. There are three steps to forming developmentally appropriate expectations for individual children in specific contexts.

Step 1: Developmental Task Analysis. Consider the emotional, sensorimotor (physical), cognitive, communication/language, and social skills a baby needs to behave the way you wish. Form developmentally appropriate expectations by comparing these skills to what individual babies can and cannot currently do. Appendix A (see page 126) provides more specific information on the general timing and sequence of developmental skills in each domain. But more important than the average timing is whether the child has the ability right now. Handout 5.4, Developmental Task Analysis, provides practice in conducting developmental task analyses.

Step 2: Take the Baby's Perspective. When considering the baby's perspective, draw on your belief that the baby is a unique person with their own thoughts, feelings, and goals. Figure 5.4 provides questions to ask yourself about what would make it harder or easier for a baby to comply, even if they do have the developmental skills to do the behavior.

Step 3: Consider the Context. Consider the home and classroom influences on behavior described in section GDB-K3 above, or use the list of questions in handout 5.1, Behavior Detective. Then consider how you could alter the classroom context to best support each baby.

Once you understand generally what a child can do, you will understand the kinds of directions you can reasonably expect them to follow. But always be prepared to support babies gently and kindly if they cannot follow your directions themselves.

www.redleafpress.org/wwb/5-4.pdf

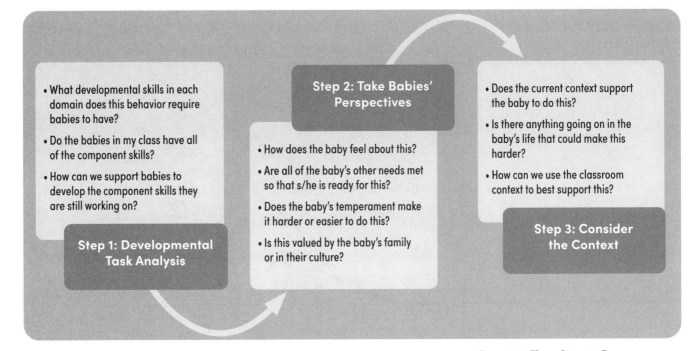

Figure 5.4. Three Steps to Form Developmentally Appropriate Expectations for Each Baby's Behavior

Directing behavior in developmentally supportive ways (GDB-S10)

Before you direct or redirect the child's behavior, you should be physically close, get their attention and establish connection, then deliver your message (see figure 5.5).

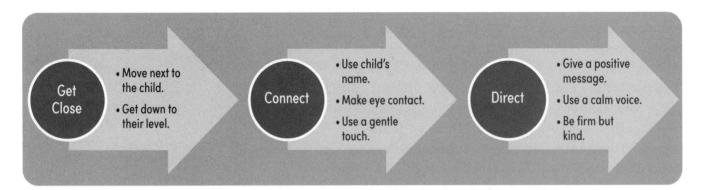

Figure 5.5. Three Steps to Directing Behavior in Developmentally Supportive Ways

We use five general types of messages to guide babies' behavior, and we combine them differently in various situations. Each message has a specific purpose for supporting children's behavior and well-being in the moment as well as their development in the long term. In every situation, we use simple words, positive statements, and short sentences so that babies are more likely to understand and be able to follow our directions. Handout 5.5, Direct Behavior, describes how each type of message supports development

Ms. Samantha gets at the toddlers' level to help Luke and Elli figure out who will pull the wagon.

and shows how the messages can be combined in different situations to support behavior and development.

※ **Reflection.** Describe the child's actions or experiences in words, mirroring some of their emotion in your face and voice. Briefly connect actions to affect, behavior, or context. Focus on behavior if you need to redirect it ("Ruby, you hit Sam. Maybe you were upset because he took your bear," said while mirroring the child's facial expression).

※ **Reason.** Briefly explain reasons or state rules, especially if you are directing the child to change behavior ("Ouch! Hitting hurts!" while showing a hurt facial expression).

※ **Redirection.** State what you want the child to do in positive terms, offering a choice if possible ("You can shake your head to tell Sam, 'No!' or put your hand out to say, 'Stop! Don't take my bear'"). Babies are not expected to share or take turns, so if there is a conflict over materials, offer a replicate ("We can get another bear from the cozy corner").

※ **Authentic choice.** In nonurgent situations, offer authentic choices ("Do you want to ask Sam for the bear back or play with something else?").

※ **Scaffold and follow through.** Follow through to make sure that the child successfully carries out your direction or their choice. Scaffold the child's behavior to help complete the task if needed, explaining how you'll help them ("If you want the bear back, I will help you ask Sam for it").

www.redleafpress.org/wwb/5-5.pdf

Responding supportively to persistent challenging behavior (GDB-S11)

Sometimes, despite all of our efforts to provide a safe, secure, nurturing environment with clear expectations and scaffolds for behavior regulation, babies still have persistent challenging behaviors. Concerning behaviors can include displaying targeted aggression toward a specific peer, biting others regularly after teething and oral exploration have subsided, hurting themselves intentionally, playing violent themes while pretending, having sudden changes in eating or sleeping patterns, screaming or crying for no clear reason, and not initiating, frequently avoiding, or withdrawing from interactions with peers and adults. All of these indicate that something is troubling the child. We must work with the family to understand the behavior so we can help. Sometimes it is also up to us to seek help from infant and child mental health professionals.

Become a behavior detective. Observe babies regularly to detect patterns or triggers for behaviors such as aggression, tantrums, or withdrawal. Take systematic notes when you see concerning behaviors. Describe each worrisome behavior clearly, objectively, and in detail, as well as what happened right before and after the behavior (you'll learn more about the Antecedent, Behavior, Consequence observation method in chapter 7 on assessment). Write down the date, time of day or routine, who else was around, what had happened just before the behavior, and as many details as you can about the behavior itself and the child's emotional expressions. After you have gathered several observations, look for patterns in the context around the behavior. Use the table in handout 5.1, Behavior Detective, to reflect on these contributing factors.

Observe all children. According to research from Gilliam and colleagues (2016), early childhood educators tend to watch Black or Hispanic boys more closely than white children, expecting to see problem behaviors when they are just being typical toddlers. Educators tend to perceive more challenging behavior and impose harsher punishments for boys and girls who are from minoritized racial/ethnic groups, including time-outs, expulsions, and suspensions. We must be vigilant about our own biases and put systems in place that help us treat children equitably. If you are concerned about the behavior of a child from a minoritized group or from a culture different from your own, invite a colleague to observe with you. Observe multiple children systematically to avoid singling out the child and seeing problems where there may be none.

Observe all behaviors. Challenging behaviors come in two basic forms: active or aggressive **externalizing behaviors** and unengaged and withdrawing **internalizing behaviors**. Internalizing behaviors are often subtler but potentially just as problematic as externalizing behaviors. We must observe all behaviors systematically, even if the behavior itself does not draw our attention.

Recognize stress and trauma. According to data from 2016 reported by Johns Hopkins Bloomberg School of Public Health (Bethell et al. 2017), more than one-third (35 percent) of children under age five in the United States have experienced at least one significant traumatic event, and 12.1 percent have experienced two or more traumatic events. While there are no more recent national data on childhood trauma from the federal government, these numbers are likely increasing with the advance of COVID-19, the detainment of young immigrant children and their families, and the widespread police brutality toward Black and brown communities and protestors. When a baby feels trauma or stress because they are unsafe or lack security, they show persistent challenging behaviors. Babies are also affected by their family's trauma and stress when things happen to the important people in their lives. Helping babies feel safe, connected, contained, and validated can help them tolerate stress and prevent some of the long-term damage to babies' brains, health, and development. Handout 5.2, Respond to Trauma, details symptoms of chronic stress or trauma in babies.

Ask for help with infant mental health. Guiding behavior is one of the most challenging aspects of working with babies. Many infant-toddler educators find it overwhelming at times or feel they lack the skills or resources to support all children. They need access to mental health consultation, coaching, or reflective supervision (GDB-FC2). Handout 5.6, Help with Challenging Behavior, lists signs that it's time to seek help and explains what you can expect from infant mental health specialists.

Involve families to help you respond supportively to challenging behaviors. Handout 5.7, Involving Families, includes strategies for having sensitive and productive discussions with families about behavior.

www.redleafpress.org/wwb/5-6.pdf

Reflect Back, Think Ahead

Look back at the figure at the beginning of this chapter that shows the knowledge, disposition, and skill competencies involved in guiding infant and toddler behavior. Which of these competencies did you have when you began this chapter? Which competencies did you develop? Which competencies will you intentionally work on building next? Use the Guiding Infant and Toddler Behavior chapter of the Professional Learning Guide (PLG [see page 11]) that accompanies this book to support your professional growth in this domain.

www.redleafpress.org/wwb/5-7.pdf

Selected References

Ball, Helen L., Cecilia Tomori, and James J. McKenna. 2019. "Toward an Integrated Anthropology of Infant Sleep." *American Anthropologist* 121 (3): 595–612.

Bethell, C.D., M.B. Davis, N. Gombojav, S. Stumbo, K. Powers. 2017. "Issue Brief: Adverse Childhood Experiences among US Children, Child and Adolescent Health Measurement Initiative," Johns Hopkins Bloomberg School of Public Health, October 2017: htpp://www.cahmi.org/projects/adverse-childhood-experiences-aces.

Child and Adolescent Health Measurement Initiative. 2013. *Overview of Adverse Child and Family Experiences among US Children*. Data Resource Center for Child & Adolescent Health. www.childhealthdata.org/docs/drc/final-ace-nd-children-(2).pdf.

Dweck, Carol S. 2007. "The Perils and Promises of Praise." *Educational Leadership* 65 (2): 34–39.

Gilliam, Walter S. 2005. *Prekindergarteners Left Behind: Expulsion Rates in State Prekindergarten Systems*. New York: Foundation for Child Development.

Gilliam, Walter S., Angela N. Maupin, and Chin R. Reyes. 2016a. "Early Childhood Mental Health Consultation: Results of a Statewide Random-Controlled Evaluation." *Journal of the American Academy of Child & Adolescent Psychiatry* 55 (9): 754–61.

Gilliam, Walter S., Angela N. Maupin, Chin R. Reyes, Maria Accavitti, and Frederick Shic. 2016b. *Do Early Educators' Implicit Biases Regarding Sex and Race Relate to Behavior Expectations and Recommendations of Preschool Expulsions and Suspensions?* New Haven, CT: Yale Child Study Center. September 28. https://medicine.yale.edu/childstudy/zigler/publications/Preschool%20 Implicit%20Bias%20Policy%20Brief_final_9_26_276766_5379_v1.pdf.

Grey, Kathleen. 1995. "Not in Praise of Praise." *Exchange Magazine*, 7.

Heller, Sherryl Scott, Allison Boothe, Angela Keyes, Geoffrey Nagle, Margo Sidell, and Janet Rice. 2011. "Implementation of a Mental Health Consultation Model and Its Impact on Early Childhood Teachers' Efficacy and Competence." *Infant Mental Health Journal* 32 (2): 143–64.

Howes, Carollee, Alison Wishard Guerra, Alison Fuligni, Eleanor Zucker, Linda Lee, Nora B. Obregon, and Asha Spivak. 2011. "Classroom Dimensions Predict Early Peer Interaction When Children Are Diverse in Ethnicity, Race, and Home Language." *Early Childhood Research Quarterly* 26 (4): 399–408.

Keller, Heidi. 2020. "Children's Socioemotional Development across Cultures." *Annual Review of Developmental Psychology* 2:27–46.

Kochanska, Grazyna, and Nazan Aksan. 1995. "Mother-Child Mutually Positive Affect, the Quality of Child Compliance to Requests and Prohibitions, and Maternal Control as Correlates of Early Internalization." *Child Development* 66 (1): 236–54.

NAEYC (National Association for the Education of Young Children). 2009. "Developmentally Appropriate Practice in Early Childhood Programs Serving Children from Birth through Age 8." www.naeyc.org/sites/default/files /globally-shared/downloads/PDFs/resources/position-statements/PSDAP.pdf.

Opendak, Maya, Elizabeth Gould, and Regina Sullivan. 2017. "Early Life Adversity during the Infant Sensitive Period for Attachment: Programming of Behavioral Neurobiology of Threat Processing and Social Behavior." *Developmental Cognitive Neuroscience* 25:145–59.

CHAPTER 6

Supporting Development and Learning

—with Maria Fusaro and Kalli Decker

Early educators strive to support development and learning in intentional and individualized ways. How do we do this? What is curriculum for babies? We define *curriculum* as the intentional support of babies' development and learning through the following:

* the ways we structure the environment (physical, social, and daily routines)

* the daily interactions between babies and their educators (within care routines, play, transitions, and behavior guidance)

* planned but flexible learning opportunities individualized to each child through observation and reflection

Curriculum relies on the physical and social environments for structuring safe, stimulating learning opportunities. This chapter does not provide a curriculum but rather an approach to creating curricula to intentionally support babies' development and learning across domains (see figure 6.1 for a summary of the competencies that support development and learning).

Why is supporting children's development and learning important? Humans develop and learn more in the first three years of life than they will at any other time. During this period of rapid growth, babies are most influenced by their experiences. It makes this time the most vulnerable but also our best opportunity to support lifelong well-being. Caregivers and educators of young children are literally brain builders. Infants and toddlers may not be able to tell you what they are learning, but the skills, habits, and knowledge—of themselves, others, and the world around them—that

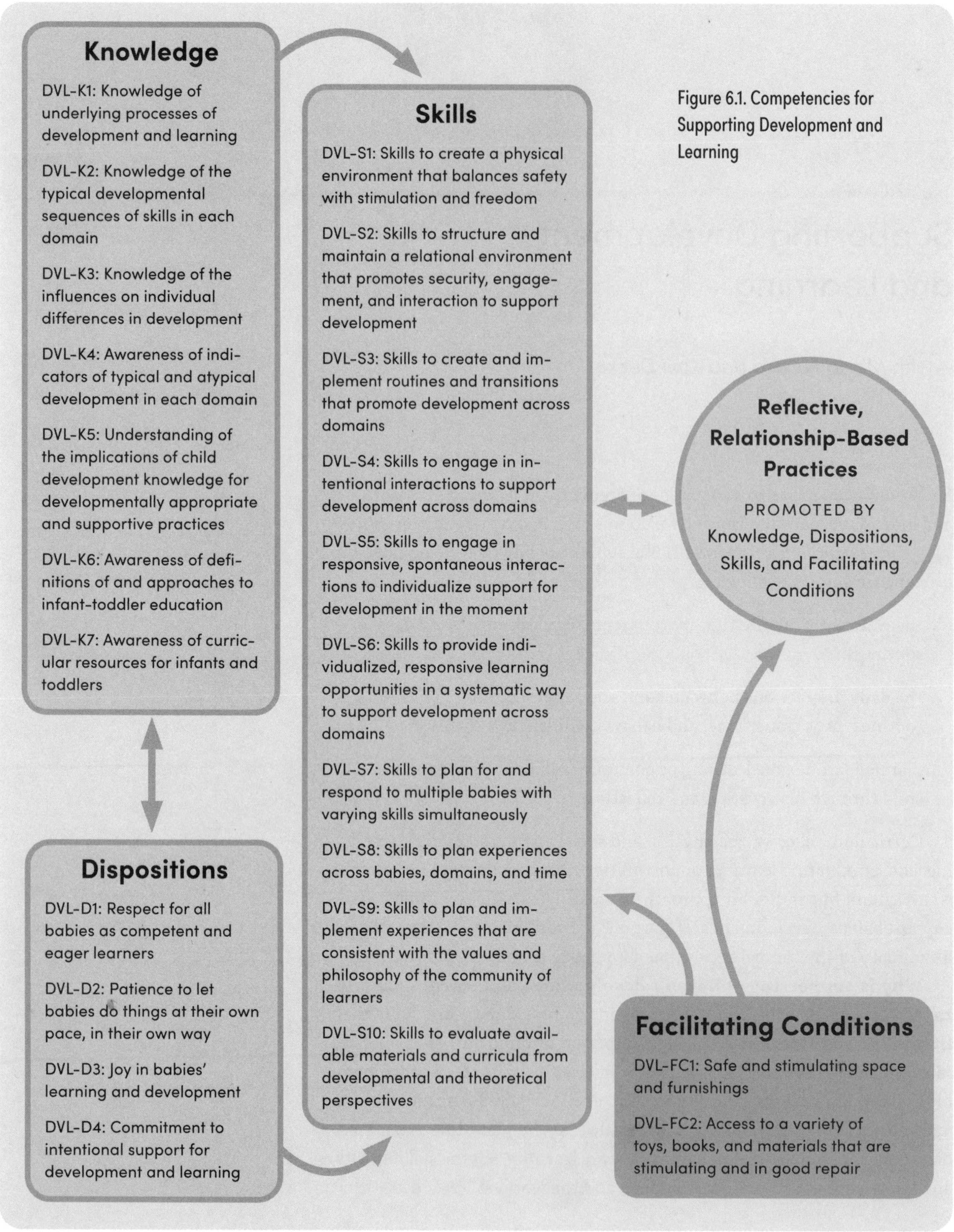

Knowledge

DVL-K1: Knowledge of underlying processes of development and learning

DVL-K2: Knowledge of the typical developmental sequences of skills in each domain

DVL-K3: Knowledge of the influences on individual differences in development

DVL-K4: Awareness of indicators of typical and atypical development in each domain

DVL-K5: Understanding of the implications of child development knowledge for developmentally appropriate and supportive practices

DVL-K6: Awareness of definitions of and approaches to infant-toddler education

DVL-K7: Awareness of curricular resources for infants and toddlers

Dispositions

DVL-D1: Respect for all babies as competent and eager learners

DVL-D2: Patience to let babies do things at their own pace, in their own way

DVL-D3: Joy in babies' learning and development

DVL-D4: Commitment to intentional support for development and learning

Skills

DVL-S1: Skills to create a physical environment that balances safety with stimulation and freedom

DVL-S2: Skills to structure and maintain a relational environment that promotes security, engagement, and interaction to support development

DVL-S3: Skills to create and implement routines and transitions that promote development across domains

DVL-S4: Skills to engage in intentional interactions to support development across domains

DVL-S5: Skills to engage in responsive, spontaneous interactions to individualize support for development in the moment

DVL-S6: Skills to provide individualized, responsive learning opportunities in a systematic way to support development across domains

DVL-S7: Skills to plan for and respond to multiple babies with varying skills simultaneously

DVL-S8: Skills to plan experiences across babies, domains, and time

DVL-S9: Skills to plan and implement experiences that are consistent with the values and philosophy of the community of learners

DVL-S10: Skills to evaluate available materials and curricula from developmental and theoretical perspectives

Reflective, Relationship-Based Practices

PROMOTED BY Knowledge, Dispositions, Skills, and Facilitating Conditions

Figure 6.1. Competencies for Supporting Development and Learning

Facilitating Conditions

DVL-FC1: Safe and stimulating space and furnishings

DVL-FC2: Access to a variety of toys, books, and materials that are stimulating and in good repair

develop in the first three years are the foundation for a lifetime. Because of the vulnerability and promise of these first three years, we cannot think of work with babies as babysitting. Keeping babies safe, fed, dry, and happy allows them to learn, but it is not enough. Conversely, setting up a miniature kindergarten with teacher-driven activities is even further from our goal. Babies need stimulation and support to learn and master their bodies and their environments.

How are competencies to support development and learning related to other competencies? The skills and practices to support development and learning build on the skills of reflective practice, building relationships, partnering with families, and guiding behavior from prior chapters. In later chapters, you will enhance your ability to support development and learning with competencies in assessment, inclusion, and professionalism.

Facilitating conditions. In addition to paid time for observation, reflection, and planning (RFP-FC2), educators must have support from their programs to structure their environment to support babies' development across domains. They must have the space, time, and resources to create safe and stimulating environments that meet licensing codes, with furnishings that are safe, comfortable, and in good repair (DVL-FC1). It requires a variety of toys, books, and materials that are developmentally appropriate, stimulating, and in good repair (DVL-FC2) that can be switched out at least monthly. There should be enough toys and materials that interested children can use them simultaneously and in increasingly complex ways, for example, building bigger and bigger block structures or using a greater variety of kitchen tools in the dramatic play area.

Knowledge

To effectively support babies' development and learning, you need research-based knowledge of each domain of development, its influences, and practices that support it (DVL-K1–K5), awareness of your own and others' approaches to working with young children (DVL-K6), and awareness of professional resources for supporting development and learning (DVL-K7).

Knowledge of underlying processes of development and learning (DVL-K1)

The following principles of learning summarize what we know from the science of child development and are relevant across all developmental domains. We use the terms *development* and *learning* to mean two different things, though babies are doing both at once. Development includes the growth of skills and knowledge that develop naturally for humans, such as crawling, walking, talking, and experiencing and expressing emotions. These tend to be driven by **maturation**, that is, biologically timed growth. As long as the infant has the basic social and physical inputs expected in any human environment, these skills will eventually develop. They tend to be consistent across cultures and home contexts, though they may look different or show differences in timing. Learning, on the other hand, is the acquisition of knowledge or skills that one must be taught, such as brushing teeth, reading, or saying please and thank you. Learned knowledge and skills tend to be more culturally specific. However, just because learned knowledge and skills are taught doesn't mean infants always have to be explicitly instructed or forced to practice them. These skills are woven into our daily lives, and babies learn them as they participate with us.

Six basic principles of development and learning apply across domains of development:

1. Babies are born developing and learning. Development and learning begin before birth and are more rapid in the first three years than at any other time. Babies' brains are born to take in information from their environments and figure out what it means.

Babies learn before birth. Newborns recognize and prefer their parents' voices; later, babies prefer foods their mothers ate during pregnancy.

Babies have computer brains. Babies detect patterns and sequences, learning from the statistical probabilities of common sights and sounds. For example, given how fast adults speak, how do babies know when one word ends and another begins? How do they know that the sounds in *happyday* are broken into the words *happy day* rather than *hap pyday*? By listening to lots of language, their brains detect how often these sounds occur together so they can figure out what the separate words are and how they pair with different objects or concepts.

Babies have social brains. How do babies know what information is meaningful? They learn from us! Infants come into the world wired for social connection, ready to interact with and learn from others. Babies and their caregivers' brains synchronize during face-to-face interactions, which helps them establish joint attention (when a caregiver and child pay attention to the same thing). This then sets the stage to learn lots of other things.

2. Babies develop in the same order but at different paces. Humans develop in predictable ways on somewhat predictable timelines. The pace varies for each baby, within certain windows, but the sequence is usually the same. Sequences of skills are more useful to know than age-based milestones because they help you anticipate and support next steps in development. However, knowing age-based milestones helps us detect when development is *significantly* delayed.

Babies develop in a predictable sequence. We are genetically programmed to develop in a particular predetermined sequence, building foundational skills that set us up for more advanced skills. This is true across domains of development. For example, a baby rolls over, then the muscular strength from rolling over helps her sit upright, first with support, then on her own. In the emotional domain, a baby must experience and express an emotion before she can recognize it in others. In language a toddler must have a couple dozen words in his vocabulary before he makes short sentences.

Babies develop with their own individual timing. Babies' skills develop in the same order, and they have biologically timed **sensitive periods**, but this timing varies somewhat. Some individual differences are somewhat predictable because they are based on things like babies' sex (female, male), temperament, or environmental exposure. For example, on average, girls develop faster than boys across a variety of domains (language, emotion, cognitive, social). Babies with more easygoing temperaments will develop self-regulation and attention skills earlier, while more social babies will develop earlier communication skills. Normal development is based on broad age windows rather than specific months of age. We watch those windows to determine whether a baby's development is typical or delayed (see DVL-K4). It is also crucial that we get to know each baby individually to understand their developmental timing.

3. Babies develop in multiple domains that influence each other. What we think of as separate domains—language, cognitive, social—don't actually develop separately. Babies' skills in one domain influence others and are often influenced by the same things.

Skills in one domain can drive development in another. For example, a baby's motor skills (crawling, walking, grasping an object, stacking) can drive their cognitive skills (exploring, testing causal relationships, problem solving). As babies use motor skills, they learn about their bodies and the world around them. Once a baby learns eye-hand coordination to reach out and grasp objects, they begin to explore them. They learn about objects' properties (the rattle is bumpy, and it makes a noise) and physical principles such as cause and effect (when I move the rattle, that's what makes the noise).

Delays in one domain can delay another. A toddler's expressive language skills help them develop social skills as they communicate with peers. **Late-talking toddlers** have difficulty initiating and maintaining social interactions with their peers and thus miss opportunities to improve social skills.

Emotions motivate or disrupt learning across domains. Emotions are crucial to learning across domains. Emotions of joy, pride, and a sense of mastery motivate children to learn; fear and anxiety get in the way of learning.

4. Babies are motivated to actively explore, learn, and master. Babies come into the world with reflexes, instincts, and drives, including the drive to explore and master their social and physical environments. Their behaviors naturally elicit reactions from their own bodies, environments, and other people, all of which they learn from.

Babies are explorers! Natural curiosity leads babies to explore their environments and the materials and people in them. First they visually explore things within their sight; then explore things within reach of their mouths, hands, and feet; then finally use their growing locomotion skills to explore spaces. Babies also explore their own bodies to learn what they can do.

Babies are scientists! Babies test, experiment, categorize, and problem solve. For example, after hearing the sound a spoon makes when it hits a bowl, they will hit it against a cup, a table, a plate, and maybe their own hand or head to find out other sounds a spoon makes. They also experiment through trial and error, such as trying out different solutions with simple puzzles like shape sorters. Eventually they come to anticipate when something will or won't fit. These scientific skills help babies gain conceptual knowledge of the world as well as functional knowledge of how to do things.

Babies are construction workers! Infants and toddlers construct their understanding of the world as they interact with it. They build their understanding of objects as they handle them, combine them by banging or stacking, and even throw or kick them. As they gain new knowledge, their perspectives change. For example, once a baby can crawl, they notice edges and boundaries and become wary of heights.

Babies are masters of their worlds! Infants and toddlers have natural motivation to master challenges, called mastery motivation. They tackle challenges (crawling up a ramp, putting a lid on a bottle, hopping on two feet) and practice, practice, practice. Babies can get frustrated when they try for a long time without success, but they need opportunities to keep practicing to build their skills.

5. Babies learn in social contexts. The human brain is a social organ, shaped by its interactions and connections with others. Even as newborns, babies pay more attention to human faces and face-like images than to anything else. These connections with others—individual interactions that turn into relationships—form the context for babies' learning.

Babies learn in interactions with others. In the sensorimotor domain, babies develop their brain-body maps through touch. Babies get to know their own bodies as they feel the sensation of being touched by caregivers and map the nerve pathway from their brains to that part of their body. In the language domain, babies learn to communicate through exchanges with others using facial expressions, hands, and voices long before they have words. By making eye contact with caregivers and sharing attention on interesting objects and events, babies learn that words are not just random sounds.

Babies learn by watching others. Babies watch others closely. Babies are born with the neurological reactions to imitate other people's actions and learn from them—if you stick your tongue out at a newborn, they will copy what you do. By twelve months old, babies use **social referencing**: looking to their caregivers' facial expressions to learn how to react to a new situation, toy, or person. By around eighteen months old, toddlers understand the difference between an intentional and accidental action (such as pouring water from a cup to a bowl versus accidentally pouring the water on the floor next to the bowl) and will imitate the intentional actions. Although babies are natural explorers, toddlers can be limited by what they see others do. If an adult demonstrates how to use a new object and indicates there is only one way it works ("This is what it does"), a toddler will not explore it to find other things it might do. But if the adult says something more open, like "I wonder what happens if we do this," then the toddler will continue exploring new ways to use the object.

Babies learn in homes, communities, and cultures. Babies apply their skills in interpreting facial expressions, identifying intentional actions, and detecting meaningful behavior to learn about social norms and rituals in their family, community, and culture. They learn through everyday routines what is important in their family, school, and culture, such as washing hands, sharing food, and giving a hug good night. They also learn from weekly, monthly, or annual events related to religious customs, cultural rituals, and family traditions. By watching and participating in these interactions, and eventually talking about them, babies learn what is acceptable and expected and understand what these customs mean to their communities. Eventually these traditions are internalized until babies become culturally socialized community members.

6. Babies learn from all of their experiences—but some experiences are better than others.

Because babies come into the world with so many mechanisms for learning, they learn from all of their experiences. But babies don't all have the same experiences, and thus not all babies develop and learn the skills that will help most in their future.

Timing matters. When a baby is going through rapid growth in a specific developmental domain, this creates a sensitive period in which their learning and development is highly influenced by their experiences. For example, the first year of life is a sensitive period for learning language, when the amount of language babies hear influences how quickly they learn it. Optimal development relies on certain experiences that are expected for most humans during a particular period of time; the skills that rely on these inputs are called **experience expectant**. There are also **critical periods** in which a baby *must* have certain types of input to develop in a healthy or typical way. An example is the attachment bond babies form with a primary caregiver in the first year of life. Babies must bond with a consistent caregiver, or without intervention they may develop **reactive attachment disorder**, which is the inability to bond with others in normal loving relationships.

Risk and lifelong opportunities for resilience. Because babies are so vulnerable in the first three years of life and because these years are so important to later development, there is a tendency to think that a baby who has experienced many risks will have lifelong deficits. While early experiences have lifelong impacts and it can be hard to overcome adverse childhood experiences (ACEs), particularly during critical periods, there are opportunities for recovery and resilience throughout a lifetime. Research on **risk and resilience** has revealed a whole collection of factors that support development throughout a child's life, including relationships with parents, educators, mentors, and other important adults. Opportunities to support a child's development always exist, from infancy through adolescence and beyond.

Knowledge of the typical developmental sequences of skills in each domain (DVL-K2)

Development occurs in the same basic sequence within each domain, with new skills based on prior skills and each domain influencing others. You need to watch each baby and recognize their skills so you can understand what is likely to come next for them. Appendix A contains tables of the development of skills from birth to three years old in seven domains: health and safety, behavior regulation, emotion, sensorimotor, cognitive, language, and social. Reference these tables as you observe individual babies to get to know their current skills. We also recommend reviewing the *Head Start Early Learning Outcomes Framework* for infants and toddlers and watching videos from the Centers for Disease Control and Prevention (CDC) developmental milestones video library.

Knowledge of the influences on individual differences in development (DVL-K3)

The timing of babies' development varies and is influenced by factors inside and outside of each child. As you learned in chapter 5 (GDB-K3), there are seven major influences on babies' behavior, and these also influence their development. Knowing each baby's unique personality, context, and culture will help you support their learning in the most developmentally appropriate ways. Handout 6.1, Developmental Detective, includes questions to guide your understanding of individual babies' development.

www.redleafpress.org/wwb/appendix-a.pdf

www.redleafpress.org/wwb/6-1.pdf

1. Physiology first! Babies born prematurely or at a low birth weight are at risk for a number of health and neurological conditions that can affect short- and long-term development, as can the mothers' stress, exposure to toxins, and nutrition during pregnancy. After birth, babies will not explore, play, and learn when they are tired, hungry, uncomfortable, or in pain. If their physical needs are not met quickly on a regular basis, babies become anxious and learn they cannot trust their caregivers. This distrust can become its own source of stress, which further compromises learning. Finally, sleep is crucial to help babies process new information and form long-term memories.

2. Immediate and recent context. The immediate social and physical environment influences babies' abilities to practice new skills, to concentrate on play, and, ultimately, to develop and learn. Babies' contexts at home and school support development best when they are safe (predictable, free of danger), secure (connected to caregivers and classroom community), and stimulating (offer appealing materials and opportunities for exploration and elaborate play). Changes at home or school can disrupt routines or affect the physical or social environments. Even good changes can cause children to feel less safe and secure, thus disrupting their learning and development.

3. Development across domains. Development happens in multiple domains that influence each other. Thus, to understand individual differences in a baby's skills in one domain, you must look at what is happening in the other domains. For example, newly mobile infants become more cautious in exploring once they begin to use social referencing, looking to a caregiver's facial expressions to learn how to react.

4. Temperament. Babies react to new people, situations, and objects based on their biologically based temperament. Supporting babies' development requires us to know their temperaments so we can predict their reactions to new things, understand when they might be overwhelmed, and develop individual strategies to support them. Learn more about temperament with the Infant Toddler Temperament Tool Supporting Goodness of Fit (www.ecmhc.org/temperament).

5. Secure relationships. Babies' sense of security in the world is based on the security of their relationships with caregivers (parents, educators). Babies' brains need secure relationships so they can learn. The brain's hippocampus is responsible for storing long-term memories (that is, learning). It sits right next to the amygdala, which monitors the environment to make sure we are safe. If the amygdala doesn't feel safe, it disrupts learning to focus only on things relevant to safety. That means babies need to feel safe and secure in order to learn. A calm and predictable environment makes babies feel safe, and relationships with caregivers they trust make them feel secure. In chapter 3 on building relationships, you learned about the qualities of caregiver-child interactions that help babies feel secure (REL-K1 and REL-S4–S6). Having a secure base with educators enables children to play more creatively in the classroom, increasing cognitive skills and improving relationships with peers.

6. Culture and language. Infant-toddler behavior, development, and learning are influenced by culture and language. Culture shapes the physical and social environments, the common customs of caring for and educating children, and the beliefs, expectations, and values of parents and other caregivers. If you notice differences between one baby and another in their developmental skills, consider how the children's home cultures may be influencing them.

7. Stress and trauma. Babies' developing brains feel the effects of chronic stress (chaotic and unpredictable environments that make them feel unsafe, regularly going hungry) or acute trauma (being physically hit, witnessing violence against their parents, being in an accident or natural disaster). Chronic stress or intense trauma can cause **toxic stress**. The neurochemicals released due to toxic stress erode the foundations of the brain and cause long-term consequences to health and well-being. However, if a baby has a secure relationship with a caregiver who helps them feel safe in the midst of the stress, what could have been toxic stress may become **tolerable stress**, avoiding long-term damage.

Awareness of indicators of typical and atypical development in each domain (DVL-K4)

Although each baby has their own personality, and developmental timing varies, certain signs indicate that a baby needs our help to stay healthy or safe. Likewise, certain behaviors or delays in skills can predict a child's diagnosis with a specific **disability**. When we recognize these signs, we can help families obtain additional supports. However, we must consider whether these differences are **false alarms** caused by inappropriate expectations or other influences on the child's behavior and development, such as those described in DVL-K3 above. Thus, to optimally support development and fulfill professional obligations to children and families, you must be aware of atypical behaviors and development (**red flags**) in each domain, as well as false alarms from other influences. You must also understand your professional responsibilities to respond to them. For example, in the health and safety domain, these include signs of illness and your responsibilities for illness prevention, as well as signs of maltreatment and your obligations as a **mandated reporter** (see PRO-K6 in chapter 10). In the emotion domain, this includes behavioral indicators of infant mental health challenges and your role in referring families to mental health resources. Red flags and false alarms in each domain are described in appendix B.

www.redleafpress.org/wwb/appendix-b.pdf

Chapter 7, Assessing Behavior, Development, and Environments, describes ways to screen for delays and disabilities (ABD-K8), and chapter 8 on inclusion describes the process of determining whether a baby is eligible for special services (INC-K1), as well as the knowledge, dispositions, and skills for working with infants and toddlers with additional support needs and their families.

Understanding how child development underpins developmentally appropriate and supportive practices (DVL-K5)

Chapter 5, Guiding Infant and Toddler Behavior, described how to apply knowledge of child development to understand what you can and cannot expect of a child in a particular situation (GDB-S9). Here we apply child development knowledge to understand what to expect of ourselves—the principles and practices we follow to support babies based on the science of learning and development. Developmentally appropriate practices are based on developmentally appropriate expectations of babies' behavior. They support babies' immediate well-being and their long-term development. They draw on developmental and learning principles (DVL-K1) and take into account influences on development (DVL-K3). Figure 6.2 illustrates how we apply the principles of development to understand best practices.

Figure 6.2. Developmentally Supportive Practices

Babies . . .		So we . . .
. . . are born developing and learning		. . . view babies' behavior as meaningful . . . intentionally support learning from birth . . . support the development that is already happening
. . . develop in the same order, but at different paces		. . . respect differences by individualizing supports for learning . . . look to current skills, rather than age, to individualize support . . . adapt materials and experiences so all babies can participate
. . . develop in multiple domains that influence each other		. . . form behavior expectations that reflect skills across domains . . . support learning in integrated ways . . . remain flexible when babies change the goal of an experience
. . . are motivated to actively explore and learn		. . . follow their lead . . . encourage and support them to make choices . . . provide opportunities to practice emerging skills . . . offer them challenges
. . . learn in social contexts		. . . engage them in interactions and conversation . . . model behavior and attitudes we want them to learn . . . include them in meaningful social rituals . . . honor family and cultural contexts
. . . learn from all of their experiences, but some experiences are better than others		. . . provide safe environments, secure relationships, and stimulating learning experiences to support development across domains . . . learn about each domain of development so that we know how best to support it

Awareness of definitions of and approaches to infant-toddler education (DVL-K6)

Perspectives vary on what infant-toddler education actually *is*, not to mention what adults' roles should be in supporting development and learning. Educators must be aware of their own definition of infant-toddler education or curriculum but also know that definitions and approaches vary among educators and across programs. Here we describe what infant-toddler education is *not*, consider approaches for defining what it is or could be, and lay out the definition and approach we take in this book based on the science of child development.

What infant-toddler curriculum is *not*. The word *curriculum* might bring to mind specific materials, planned activities, or **learning objectives**. That definition is too narrow when we work with infants and toddlers. Some programs require a specific curriculum, and using a curriculum that includes a predetermined series of activities is often considered a marker of high quality. However, a developmentally appropriate and supportive curriculum for infants and toddlers must always be individualized and responsive. Though a structured curriculum can support educators to implement high-quality experiences for babies, it can also be challenging to use a predetermined set of activities in a high-quality way. Infant-toddler education is *not* any of the following:

* miniature kindergarten

* babysitting—basic care, without intentional support for learning

* cute curriculum—a collection of arbitrary crafts and activities that are chosen and directed by adults (such as those available on blogs and websites like Pinterest)

Adult-directed activities and crafts are only meaningful if they are individualized to support development. They need a learning objective and must be implemented so as to be responsive to each baby's interests, skills, and needs.

Approaches to supporting learning and development. There are a few well-articulated philosophical models for early childhood education, including Reggio Emilia, Resources for Infant Educarers (RIE), and Montessori. They offer different perspectives on the role of adults in infant-toddler development and education. For instance, the Reggio Emilia approach emphasizes classroom community and child-driven content, and the adult is viewed as a co-learner and collaborator, as well as instructor. They plan lessons and activities based on children's interests and document children's development through these experiences. Magda Gerber, who developed the RIE philosophy, offers more of a hands-off perspective. She advocates that infants and toddlers should pursue their own interests within a resource-rich environment and supportive relationships. In this approach, adults do not plan specific learning experiences for infants and rarely join infants' activities physically, instead reflecting out loud on what infants are doing. The Montessori method stresses self-driven and hands-on learning. The adult intentionally provides a specific environment and set of materials, facilitates experiences, and nurtures development. You will find an approach that works for you and the children you work with. Consider your own philosophy and beliefs about development and adults' roles so you can support babies' learning in consistent and systematic ways and also explain your approach to families and other practitioners.

Infant-toddler curriculum as the result of intentional and flexible processes. Infant-toddler education is intentional, flexible, and individualized. Curriculum is the result of a process of providing environments; interacting, observing, planning, and implementing developmental experiences; then reflecting and modifying what we do (see figure 6.3). Supportive relationships are at the center of the process, surrounded by the context of environments, intentional interactions, and planned experiences. The curriculum process surrounds the core experiences: intentionally planning experiences (based on observing and reflecting on the baby's abilities and interests), implementing the plan, and then evaluating based

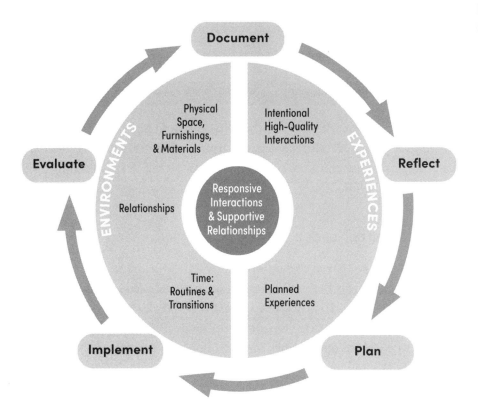

Figure 6.3. Structure of Curriculum for Infants and Toddlers

on your observation of your own and the baby's experience. Then this observation starts the cycle again. Longer-term planning around physical space, social-emotional climate, and routines are critical in supporting the day-to-day curriculum work.

When you absorb the concept of this approach, it may feel intuitive for one-on-one or small-group activities. However, you usually care for a larger group of young children. It takes time and experience to learn how to balance the needs of an individual child with the needs of the whole group. With practice, you can learn how to individualize an experience for different children at the same time. Learning how to balance your time, attention, and energy in ways that are manageable for you and responsive to the children in your care is not easy. We are not always successful in achieving the optimal balance, and it is always a work in progress. Advance planning, reflection, and intentionality do help!

Awareness of curricular resources for infants and toddlers (DVL-K7)

There are no curricula for infants and toddlers that have been proven by science to support development, but there are some systematic curricula available that are based on what we know about how young children develop and learn. These can be good resources for creating learning experiences for infants and toddlers when used in conjunction with the process approach described above. Handout 6.2, Curriculum Resources, offers resources for creating specific learning opportunities for infants and toddlers, defining developmental learning objectives, and identifying rich materials.

www.redleafpress.org/wwb/6-2.pdf

Dispositions

The attitudes, values, and approaches that promote practitioners' abilities to support babies' development and learning are centered in the respect, patience, joy, and intentional support of children's self-driven learning processes (DVL-D1–D4).

Respect for all babies as competent and eager learners (DVL-D1)

When we believe that all babies are motivated to learn and seek out the learning experiences they need, we can confidently follow their lead, supporting their choices in play and learning. Without this belief, we are more likely to direct babies' activities or force them to do things they are not interested in, which undermines the playfulness of learning.

Patience to let babies do things at their own pace, in their own way (DVL-D2)

Working with young infants requires us to slow our adult pace, moving slowly and speaking softly. This requires an inner calm that is hard for some adults. With toddlers, we exercise self-control to allow them to take a long time to do things for themselves (such as put on mittens or clear a plate). A patient disposition helps us remain calm and in control of ourselves.

Joy in babies' learning and development (DVL-D3)

Babies take joy in doing and learning. They want to share this joy with us, expanding the experience and motivating themselves to learn more. Our joy in babies' learning helps us connect with families as we share our experiences with their children.

Commitment to intentional support for development and learning (DVL-D4)

Supporting babies' development—whether through environment, interactions, or planned experiences—takes constant intentionality. Babies change quickly and do unexpected things. This means we often need to change our plans, but it also gives us new opportunities to support their development. Thus, we must remain both flexible and intentional in this work.

Skills

Planning curricula, or experiences that support development and learning, is more complex at this age than any other. This is not rocket science—it's *much* harder! It is challenging enough to plan supportive, stimulating experiences for one rapidly changing baby—but then you are simultaneously planning across domains and for multiple children who are all very different. This requires an incredibly complex set of skills, and the ability to apply those skills with **flexible intentionality**. The expert educator has goals for babies' development and systems for supporting them but can adjust instantly to meet the babies' immediate needs or shifting interests. Nonverbal or nonmobile babies are even more challenging because educators must accurately read their cues to structure their environment, interactions, and experiences. Educators must practice and develop these skills over time while remaining patient with themselves.

The skills to support development and learning are built upon the skills for observation and reflection (RFP), building relationships (REL),

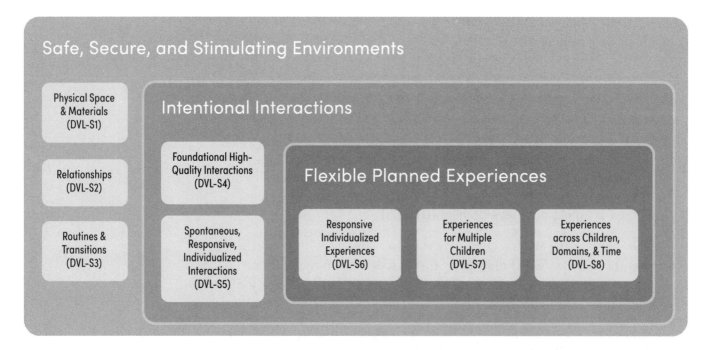

Figure 6.4. Skills for Supporting Babies' Development and Learning on a Daily Basis

partnering with families (FAM), and guiding behavior (GDB). Figure 6.4 shows how the skills to support babies' development every day are related; these also reflect the concepts of infant-toddler curriculum (figure 6.3). Supporting development begins by structuring the learning environment (DVL-S1–S3), then interacting in intentional and flexible ways (DVL-S4–S5), and finally planning and implementing rich learning experiences (DVL-S6–S8). Skill set DVL-S6 is about creating responsive planned learning experiences for individual children; DVL-S7 extends this process to multiple children; and DVL-S8 expands this across domains over time. Skills DVL-S9 and DVL-S10 increase the quality of these experiences by creating and evaluating them from developmental or theoretical perspectives.

Creating a physical environment that balances safety with stimulation and freedom (DVL-S1)

Across the physical space, relationship, and time dimensions, there are common principles that promote babies' safety, security, and stimulation:

❊ We keep harmful things out of babies' way, rather than expecting them to avoid potential harm. We recheck the environment regularly and monitor babies' activities.

❊ We support babies' sense of safety with organization, consistency, and predictability, avoiding overstimulation and chaos.

❊ Babies' security is based on their sense of connection and belonging. This includes connection to their educators, connection between their family and educators, and connection to the environment, which is familiar and represents them and their family.

✳ Babies are stimulated by novelty, variety, and challenge while actively choosing their own interests.

In the guidance chapter, you learned about structuring "yes environments" where adults can see all children at once and physical spaces and materials are safe, so there is little reason to say no. You need basic support from your program to create safe and stimulating environments that meet licensing codes (DVL-FC1). Here we describe an environment that balances safety, security, and stimulation so children stay engaged in self-driven exploration and play. Chapter 10 (Becoming an Infant-Toddler Professional) discusses environmental safety and health related to child care licensing.

The physical environment affects the way babies and caregivers interact, the way babies move their bodies and use materials, and the way babies feel. Babies need comfortable spaces to rest and relax and space to move freely with vigor. Our mood, energy, and activity levels—for both children and adults—are affected by lighting, color, and sounds. Some of us are more affected than others, as influenced by our temperament, security in relationships, and exposure to stress and trauma.

As much as possible, arrange your space to balance safety, security, and stimulation. To maintain stimulation, change some materials weekly. Make materials that are most interesting to babies available (almost) all the time, such as water, household items, toys that roll, things to build with, and any other materials or toys that individual babies are persistently interested in. This requires that you have access to a variety of toys, books, and other materials that are developmentally appropriate and in good repair (DVL-FC2). See handout 6.3, Balanced Environment, for considerations you should make when setting up physical space, including the layout of the room, furnishings (such as furniture, pillows, mats), lighting, sound, decor, materials, and posted information. The Resources and Further Readings for this chapter will direct you to online articles (with videos and podcasts) on assessing and designing spaces for infants and toddlers.

www.redleafpress.org/wwb/6-3.pdf

Structuring and maintaining a relational environment that promotes security, engagement, and interaction (DVL-S2)

The relational environment also sets the stage for the emotional climate. It is crucial to a baby's sense of safety and security, as well as their willingness to engage and explore. Babies only feel safe when they feel connected to trusted adults and when those adults are connected to one another (this includes a connection between parents and educators as well as among educators). Structuring and maintaining the relational environment starts with the skills discussed in chapter 3. These consistent, close relationships are supported by the physical space of the classroom and by the communication systems that allow regular contact with families. This relationship structure supports development and learning in several ways.

Mr. Drew and Hanif share a book in the cozy corner.

Secure base. Primary caregiving supports development and learning by providing babies with a secure base. With this security, babies explore freely, attend to their own activities longer, engage more deeply in play, and ultimately gain stronger skills.

Engaged educators. Low baby-to-educator ratios (no more than three infants or three to six toddlers per caregiver) allow educators to better share joy in their learning and provide stimulation and challenges as babies explore, discover, practice skills, and learn.

Systematic planning and monitoring. Primary caregiving and low ratios allow educators to systematically observe babies' development, allowing them to plan enriching, individualized experiences. Educators also need paid reflection and planning time. This is usually out of educators' control, but it is a support you need to best use your skills.

Creating and implementing routines and transitions that promote development across domains (DVL-S3)

A day in the life of every baby in our care will include certain experiences they can count on, supporting their sense of safety through predictability. Daily routines including arrival and departure, play, caregiving (eating, sleeping, diapering, dressing), and transitions between activities are all part of the curriculum. While keeping babies healthy and safe is the primary purpose of most caregiving routines, these are not just something we do to or for children. Rather, they are crucial opportunities for babies to learn life skills. Each routine has opportunities to build the caregiver-baby relationship, promote babies' autonomy, and enable babies to learn and practice skills. In chapter 5, Guiding Infant and Toddler Behavior, you learned about structuring a daily schedule with consistency and flexibility, using routines and transitions to support autonomy, mastery, and regulation. Handout 6.4, Meals Support Development, provides examples of how meal routines support learning across domains. Consider how other caregiving routines and the accompanying transitions can also be used to support development.

www.redleafpress.org/wwb/6-4.pdf

Interacting intentionally to support development across domains (DVL-S4)

After setting up a stimulating and safe environment where we can be available and responsive to babies, what do adults *do* that supports and stimulates development? We use opportunities within everyday interactions—in child-led play or caregiving routines—to support development in intentional and flexible ways. We use all of our adult skills (emotion, social, motor, language, and cognitive), our whole selves, to respond to and support babies' whole selves (see table 6.1). With our emotions, we share babies' joy in discovery, enjoy their pride of accomplishment, and reflect their frustration or disappointment when things don't go their way. We reflect, share, and expand their emotional connections to their learning. We use social modeling to show babies, in unspoken ways, how we want them to behave and to treat one another, us, and our shared space and belongings. With our motor skills, we demonstrate actions or physically assist babies in carrying out their goals, while leaving room for their own discoveries of how things work. We use language to reflect and guide babies' behavior and provide the words for babies' experiences to build their understanding of concepts as well as vocabulary. This includes everything from parallel talk to explanations and reasoning. We use our cognition to scaffold babies' learning, analyzing a task and babies' skills to understand what they can and cannot do independently. We offer hints or just enough support to help children get to the next level of challenges, sometimes making things easier, sometimes harder.

Table 6.1 Educators Use Skills in Each Domain to Support Babies' Development across Domains

Domain	Learning Principles	What We Do
Emotion	Emotion and emotional connections motivate learning.	**Share** joy in babies' discovery and learning, encourage their curiosity and persistence, and reflect frustrations.
Social	Babies are sociocultural learners who make meaning of social rituals.	**Model** the attitudes and behaviors we want babies to develop.
Motor	Babies learn by imitating others and understand when actions are intentional.	**Demonstrate** how to do some things and encourage babies to discover others.
Language	Babies construct mental representations of the world through language.	**Talk** by labeling, describing, explaining, reasoning, analyzing, wondering.
Cognitive	Babies actively construct learning and learn best when challenges build on current skills.	**Scaffold** by analyzing a task and baby's skills, determining what they can and cannot do alone, and offering incremental help and challenges.

Ms. Liu shares babies' joy in exploring and learning as she supports their learning by talking about what babies see and hear, demonstrates turning book pages, and scaffolds their interactions with materials and each other through physical support.

Scaffolding requires flexibility and creativity to figure out how to do our least to support babies most. That is, we use **incremental support** to provide the smallest amount of help possible to support the baby to the next step; then we increase our help as needed if our smallest help wasn't enough. Another approach starts by providing maximum support, then provides less and less as babies take over. Scaffolding calls for moving across a range from most to least support in response to what a baby needs. Strategies go from most to least intervention to maximize babies' active role in learning. More intensive scaffolding is provided as practitioners model and narrate explorations with materials, such as modeling how to problem solve a puzzle. The practitioner gradually shifts from initiating explorations and inviting participation to following the baby's lead, providing encouragement, and extending the child's explorations. Practitioners do not exert control over a baby's explorations; rather, they continually observe the baby's needs and interests to carefully scaffold learning and development.

STRATEGIES

* Model and Narrate—Adult completes action while child watches (adult models/demonstrates and narrates): "I'm going to put this puzzle piece on the board. I'll twist the piece to help it fit."

* Child Assists Adult—Adult invites child to help (asks child to put hand on object or on adult's hand to do it together): "Put your hand on this puzzle piece. Let's twist it together to fit it in."

* Adult-Led Collaboration—Adult and child operate collaboratively, with the adult leading (adult puts hand over child's hand, pushing pieces in together; adult physically guides child's movement while narrating): "I'll help you push this puzzle piece into place. Let's twist it just a little more to the left."

* Child-Led Collaboration—Adult and child operate collaboratively, with the child leading (child hands adult puzzle pieces and indicates where they should go, while adult fits them in; adult may ask questions): "Where should I put this piece?" "Which one should we do next?"

* Adult Assists Child—Adult offers explicit verbal guidance while child performs actions with occasional physical assistance: "I think this piece goes right here." "You can tap it down to fit it in."

* Strategy and Encouragement—Adult offers guidance on strategies (suggests how to make something easier, with little specific direction, possibly modeling strategies with empty-handed gesture; offers encouragement to keep going): "Hmm, I wonder where you can put that piece." "It looks like it doesn't fit; where could you try it next?" "What else could you try?"

* Challenge and Extend—Adult challenges the child to solve the problem, puzzle, or task in a new way or to extend the activity: "Can you put all the red ones on the bottom?" "Can you stack a tower of eight blocks?" "How high can we stack it?"

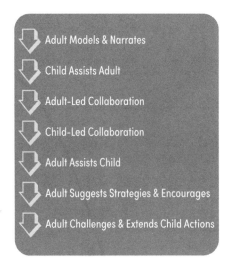

Figure 6.5. Seven Strategies for Scaffolding Learning, from Supporting Least-Developed to Most-Developed Skills

Responding spontaneously to individualize support for development in the moment (DVL-S5)

We combine our skills for using interactions to support development (described above) with our skills for observing and responding to babies' cues, needs, and interests (described in chapter 3) to intentionally individualize supports for each child. The same steps of Observe, Reflect, Respond, and Observe Reaction are applied to supporting babies' development and learning.

Observe: Watch carefully to determine what the child is doing and experiencing.

* Watch: Watch and learn what babies are doing and experiencing in the moment. What is the baby seeing or hearing (perception)? What

Ms. K'Sandra provides incremental support—increasing physical and cognitive support in small increments—to assist Trini as she completes the multistep task of putting a mask on her bunny.

are they doing (behavior)? How do they feel? Are they interested, engaged, and concentrating? Are they content, excited, or frustrated?

☀ Identify: Apply your knowledge of development to identify the baby's skills and learning processes. Are they exploring an object with their eyes, hands, or mouth? Are they practicing a sensorimotor skill, such as using vision to guide their hand to an object?

Reflect: Analyze how to support development and learning.

☀ Interpret: What does the baby need to support learning in this moment? Do they need to feel connected or share the joy of discovery? Encouragement to stick with a challenge? Scaffolding to get to the next step? Words to help them understand what they're doing? Or just the opportunity to persist without interruptions?

☀ Learn: As you reflect on your observations over time, you learn about babies' individual interests and styles of exploration. You will see how they pursue their goals and how easily they get distracted or frustrated.

Respond: Act with sensitivity and warmth.

☀ Decide: First, determine whether you will do anything at all. Sometimes the best response is just to watch. Adults often rush to help young children, denying them the opportunity to solve problems and learn from challenges. Sometimes the most supportive response is simply to watch, making sure children are safe and do not become too overwhelmed or discouraged. Sometimes providing reflective language is all that needs to be done.

☀ Choose your moment: Look for invitations or cues that tell you the baby is ready for input. Overall, try not to disrupt babies' thought processes or flow of activity.

☀ Implement: Whether your response is sharing emotion, talking, modeling, demonstrating, or scaffolding, each response should be warm, friendly, and affectionate to reinforce your relationship.

Observe Reaction: Watch for the baby's response.

☀ Observe: Apply your observation skills. How did they respond to what you did or said? Did it expand the baby's experience, keep their attention on the task, or distract them from it? Did they enjoy sharing their learning with you, or were they overwhelmed by your response?

※ Reflect and learn: As you reflect on interactions over time, you will learn more about each baby's cues and invitations and how you can support their own self-directed learning.

Handout 6.5, Interact to Support Development, describes a story in which a toddler was practicing and learning new skills and the teacher responded. Review the story and consider how you might choose to respond to intentionally support development.

www.redleafpress.org/wwb/6-5.pdf

Planning and implementing individualized systematic supports for development across domains (DVL-S6)

Planned experiences are learning opportunities that we plan ahead of time with flexible intentionality to support development in a purposeful way. They can be unstructured, in that we provide some materials but let babies explore while we respond to their actions. Or they can be more structured, so the experience has a particular flow of events that we guide, such as story sharing, cooking from a recipe, or playing a game of freeze when the lights go out. Having an off-the-shelf curriculum (Creative Curriculum, High-Scope, or Great First Eight: Infant & Toddler) can help you generate ideas for learning opportunities, but it is not necessary—you can generate your own ideas.

We create individualized supports that are responsive to babies' interests, needs, and current skill levels by following the cyclical process of Document, Reflect, Plan, Implement, and Evaluate (DR.PIE; see figure 6.6). In reality, each of the five steps in this cycle requires its own skills, but we present them here as one overarching skill set because together they result in high-quality learning experiences. Engaging in this process of curriculum planning will take time when you are not responsible for caring for children. Some settings allow for planning time and others do not. If your setting does not currently provide you planning time, you might discuss with your supervisor the reasons why it would improve your work with children.

Document. Document babies' current and emerging developmental skills. This starts with writing down your observations, likely writing anecdotal records about what babies do and say throughout the day. Documentation can also involve videos or a series of pictures. Sometimes a picture really is worth a thousand words! However, technology in the classroom can detract from your face-to-face interactions with babies, and so should be used sparingly. Following a systematic approach helps make sure you document behaviors across domains and observe all babies. We will address additional skills and practices for this in chapter 7 on assessing behavior and development.

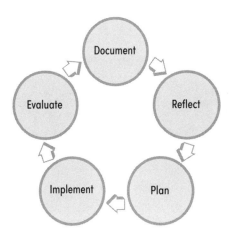

Figure 6.6. DR. PIE: The Cycle of Curriculum Planning

Reflect. Review the collection of anecdotes one baby at a time, looking for developmental skills. You may use the developmental skills in appendix A (see page 126) of this book, or other available sources, to help identify the skills you observe. A skill is mastered when babies can use it flexibly across situations. Emerging skills are new and can only be used in certain situations or with support. Also identify challenges, areas in which the baby can use additional support. Using a systematic assessment tool that is connected to a curriculum can help you identify emerging and **mastered skills**.

Plan. Plan environments, routines, and experiences to respond to babies' interests, needs, and emerging developmental skills. Use your reflections on babies' mastered and emerging skills to set objectives for the development and learning you want to support next. Setting appropriate objectives is a complex skill in itself. While a developmental goal is a "destination," an objective is an observable step toward that goal. For example, for the developmental goal of walking independently, objectives include (a) pulling her body up to a standing position, (b) walking sideways while holding onto furniture, (c) walking forward while holding on to an adult's hands, (d) walking a few steps independently, (e) standing up from the floor without support after she falls, and (f) walking across the room without holding on to anything. Setting appropriate objectives for children's development and learning requires that we know the typical progression of skills as well as the child's current skills. After identifying the developmental objective, create a plan to support this objective by doing one or more of the following: modify the environment (add materials, shift furnishings, or alter routines), engage in intentional interactions, or create a specific learning opportunity. Planning to support development relies on your knowledge of developmental processes (DVL-K1), influences on development (DVL-K3), and the implications of these principles for supporting development (DVL-K5). Once you have chosen one or more ways to support the child's emerging skills, write down your plan for the developmental experience as a guide for what to do. Save the plans you write. Even though we offer individualized experiences, you can expect that the same experience will be useful for other babies in the future. Figure 6.7 is an example of a written plan for supporting one baby's visuospatial skills based on a prior observation that can be saved to be used with other children.

Implement. Flexibly implement intentional environments, routines, and experiences, modifying as needed to follow babies' needs and interests in the moment. You might think that after you've done the work of documenting, reflecting, and planning, implementing the experiences should be the easy part. But implementing these plans flexibly is the key to making sure experiences are responsive to babies and ultimately support

Educator: __Ms. C_____   Date: ____10/8/20_____

Domain(s): <u>Cognitive: visuospatial, problem solving</u>

Developmental Objective(s): <u>Understanding relationship of container-to-</u>
<u>contained: Using containers; predicting what containers will hold based on</u>
<u>size of objects</u>

Environment & Materials: <u>Containers of various sizes and sets of objects</u>
<u>of various sizes and shapes to go into the container; place in baskets or</u>
<u>buckets on low shelves where children can access them</u>

Interactions: <u>When children are holding objects or using containers, use</u>
<u>language to point out container-to-contained relationships, such as "Jordan,</u>
<u>you are holding a lot of pieces in your hand. What could help you hold those</u>
<u>pieces?" "You are using a container to help you hold all the pieces at once."</u>
<u>"A container helps us hold many things at once. How many pieces can fit</u>
<u>into your container?"</u>

Planned Experience: <u>Use three containers of various sizes, blocks with</u>
<u>different shapes, cotton balls. Invite children to see how many pieces they</u>
<u>can hold in their hands, counting with them to support developing number</u>
<u>sequence. Then invite them to find how many pieces can fit in each of the</u>
<u>three containers. Use words like *container, fit, full, more, less, some, all.*</u>

Figure 6.7. Sample Written Plan for Supporting Development

their development. And flexible intentionality is challenging! Babies are actively motivated to explore and learn, and their interests in the moment don't always match what we have planned. Here you must use your skills in responsive interactions to be flexible (DVL-S5) while also being intentional about supporting development.

What helps with this flexibility is remembering other principles of development and learning: *babies can learn from all of their experiences*, and *babies develop in multiple domains that influence one another*. Recognize the development happening right in front of you in each experience. Read how an art experience intended to support babies' self-expression and fine-motor skills turned into a sensory experience that supported a baby's sensory and language skills.

Ms. Jessica planned an art experience for her class (ages eighteen to twenty-six months). The objectives were (a) self-expression through art (painting), and (b) exploring tools (paintbrushes, toy cars) to make marks. She set out the paper, paint, and tools and invited babies to the table, saying, "We have paint with paintbrushes and cars today. Would you like to paint?" Asha toddled over and sat down. Ms. Jessica helped her get her smock on, then sat across from her. Asha picked up a car and put it in the paint and made a mark on the paper. She stuck her hands in the paint, used a finger to swirl the paint in her palm, and then held out her hands. Ms. Jessica commented, "You have blue paint on your hands," then stuck her own fingers in the paint and rubbed them together, saying, "It feels cold and slippery between my fingers." Asha used her fingers to make dots on the paper, saying, "Bu, bu." "You're using the blue paint, Asha, making dots on the paper." Asha wrinkled her nose and shook her hands. Ms. Jessica said, "It looks like you're all done. Let's go wash the paint off your hands." In the bathroom, Asha turned on the faucet and put her hands under the water. Ms. Jessica helped her get soap, commenting, "The bubbles are soft and foamy. Look, mine are turning blue from the paint!" "Blue!" said Asha as the blue paint ran off her own hands into the sink. When Ms. Jessica realized that Asha was interested in using her hands and exploring the sensations (color, texture), she followed the child's lead and supported her sensory and language development.

Asha explores fingerpainting and hand washing; Ms. Jessica follows her lead to intentionally support development.

Evaluate. Evaluate your intentional supports for development and learning by observing and reflecting on babies' experiences and learning processes. Then modify as needed. Once again, we rely on observation and reflection skills. Whether you have gathered documentation (anecdotal records, running records, photos/videos, or samples of babies' work) or simply observed during the experience, take time to reflect afterward. Ask yourself a series of questions about the babies' experiences and your own.

Evaluation Questions to Ask Yourself:

About the babies' experiences:

1 What did the babies do?

2 What did they experience?

3 What skills did they practice?

4 What did they learn?

About your experience:

1 What did you do and say?

2 What was your experience? What surprised and delighted you?

3 What went well?

4 What did not go so well?

5 What might make the experience better for supporting babies' development?

If a change in the experience would provide a better learning opportunity, modify the written plan right away for next time. Sometimes you will identify additional skills the babies are developing and plan new experiences for them. In this case, your evaluation actually serves as the Document, Reflect, and Plan part of the cycle!

Planning for and responding to multiple babies with varying skills simultaneously (DVL-S7)

Because development is so rapid, the babies in any infant or toddler classroom have widely ranging skills. We must constantly adjust or scaffold experiences to either simplify them or extend them to challenge children. You will work with babies with disabilities and delays, and doing so will require the same flexibility you use in planning for and responding to typically developing infants and toddlers whose skills are months or a year apart.

The DR.PIE process individualizes curriculum for specific babies, but most educators work with infants and toddlers in groups. How do we take this process and make an experience that is relevant for a group of four or eight infants, or up to twelve toddlers?

Your skills in scaffolding (DVL-S4; figure 6.5) and flexible, responsive, spontaneous interactions (DVL-S5) will support babies with more- or less-advanced skills. But we must also be attentive to babies' range of skills when setting up the environment and selecting materials and when planning specific developmental experiences. To do this, we use **simplifications** and **extensions**. We simplify a material or experience so a baby with less advanced skills can participate in a way that supports the same domain, skill set, or learning objectives. We extend a material or experience to challenge the child to learn and practice new skills related to the same domain, skill set, or learning objective, often by adding to it or showing a child a more advanced use. Figure 6.8 shows open-ended toys and toys that have been modified by educators to offer simplifications.

Use simplifications and extensions so all babies can participate in all planned learning opportunities, even when they weren't planned specifically for them. When planning an experience, carefully compare the skills it requires with the range of your class's skills. If you are supporting sensory and motor skills through art, a three-month-old may not use paint to make marks on paper, but he could feel it on his fingers or feet. Meanwhile, extend art experiences for more skilled infants by providing a variety of materials and tools for practicing motor skills. Moving to rhythm, a six-month-old can't dance on her feet, but she can wave her hands and bounce her torso as her caregiver holds her and dances. You could extend this experience by providing instruments to play along or scarves to wave.

Planning experiences across babies, domains, and time (DVL-S8)

How do we take this process and make a curricular plan for a group of babies for a week or a month? We suggest making a grid to use each week that represents the days of the week (as the columns) and the domains of development (as the rows). Here are some principles involved in taking these individualized, responsive supports for development and learning and turning them into a curriculum for a group of babies:

1. Each domain every day: Different programs and curricula have different names for developmental domains, and some include additional domains such as art, music, math, and science. This book reflects development across six domains that should be supported every day:

❋ Health, safety, and self-care

❋ Emotion and self-expression

❋ Sensorimotor: fine and gross motor

❋ Cognitive

❋ Language, including emergent literacy

❋ Social

Simplify by adding materials to make the same behavior easier to do for less skilled babies.

The educator added canning rings to the beads and pegs so that babies with less advanced motor control and hand-eye coordination could practice placing the rings around the peg, even if they couldn't yet fit the beads on.

Simplify by altering materials to make them easier, or create other ways to use them.

The educator cut the elastic band off one end of the shape sorter so that babies can place the shapes in the center hole even if they cannot put them through the shape-specific holes.

Open-ended materials that can be used in multiple ways offer natural extensions and simplifications.

These cups can be stacked on top of or placed inside one another, banged against one another, placed upside down to hide smaller objects, or spoken into to hear the echo of a voice.

The natural peg shape sorters can be banged together, square ones can be stacked, round ones can be rolled, and they can all be fitted inside their slots. Having two shapes presents a challenge for older infants who can discover that round shapes will fit only into the round holes, and square ones into the square holes.

Figure 6.8. Choose or Modify Toys to Offer Natural Extensions and Simplifications

www.redleafpress.org/wwb/6-6.pdf

2. Each child every week: Each week, there should be an experience that has been planned intentionally for a specific child, based on your observations of and reflections on the child's current and emerging skills.

3. Each experience for every child: Each experience should be developmentally supportive for any baby in the group through simplifications and extensions, even if it was planned for a specific child. Thus, when you are gathering your materials and planning how you will present them to the babies, consider the babies' skills and plan scaffolding. Handout 6.6, Curriculum Planning, provides an example weekly schedule of planned experiences.

After making sure each child is represented each week with focused support of an emerging skill or extension of an existing skill, fill in the remaining cells on the grid.

STRATEGIES

- Represent each child a second or even third time.

- Create experiences around a theme (for example, our bodies, our communities, nature, animals, seasons, our feelings and emotions, vehicles and transportation, places and geography).

- Follow children's interests you've observed (for example, digging, scooping and pouring, music making, playing with vehicles, cooking, caring for baby dolls).

- Use your state's Early Learning Experiences Standards documents to generate ideas.

- Use or refer to an existing curriculum for infants and toddlers.

Planning and implementing experiences that are consistent with the values and philosophy of the community of learners (DVL-S9)

At a minimum, the experiences you plan should be developmentally appropriate, following what educators believe to be best practices. But other qualities of these experiences are determined by the educators individually, in teaching teams, or as a whole-program philosophy.

Educators' philosophies or approaches to caring for and educating babies come from training, experience, and personal beliefs. These may be based on certain theories, such as attachment theory or Piaget's constructivism, or a particular approach such as Reggio Emilia or RIE. These approaches should also reflect the culture and values of the community of learners, such as an emphasis on inclusion of babies with additional support needs, multiculturalism and welcoming all, or social justice and antibias education. It could reflect cultural values regarding respect within the family or regarding community interdependence. It is important to recognize your own beliefs, as well as your colleagues' and community's, and how these beliefs influence your approach to caring for and educating babies. As you develop your **professional identity**, you may incorporate your community's values into your approach to care and education, teaching these values to the next generation.

Evaluating available materials and curricula from developmental and theoretical perspectives (DVL-S10)

One advantage to using an existing curriculum is that it provides a systematic approach to developing learning opportunities for children. However, not all curricula or preplanned learning opportunities are equal in terms of their developmental value, and not all will fit with your own philosophy. Further, existing curricula may not offer enough flexibility for the children in your group.

www.redleafpress.org/wwb/6-7.pdf

Once you have identified curricular resources for infants and toddlers (DVL-K7), you can apply your understanding of developmentally supportive experiences (DVL-K5) to evaluate whether a resource is right for you. Handout 6.7, Evaluate Curriculum Resources, contains a list of sample questions you might ask based on different values and criteria; these questions can be used to evaluate materials you are considering adding to your classroom, experiences you are planning, and curricula you might use. Add your own questions as you develop your own philosophy for your classroom or program with your community of learners.

Reflect Back, Think Ahead

Look back at figure 6.1 at the beginning of this chapter, which shows the competencies involved in supporting development and learning. Which of these competencies did you have when you began this chapter? Which competencies did you develop? Which competencies will you intentionally work on building next? Use the Supporting Development and Learning chapter of the Professional Learning Guide (PLG [see page 11]) that accompanies this book to support your own professional growth in this domain.

Selected References

Center for Early Childhood Mental Health Consultation. 2020. "Infant Toddler Temperament Tool (IT³): Supporting a 'Goodness of Fit.'" Georgetown University Center for Child and Human Development. Accessed December 29. www.ecmhc.org/temperament.

Chazan-Cohen, Rachel, Martha Zaslow, Helen H. Raikes, James Elicker, Diane Paulsell, Allyson Dean, and Kerry Kriener-Althen. 2017. *Working toward a Definition of Infant/Toddler Curricula: Intentionally Furthering the Development of Individual Children within Responsive Relationships*. OPRE Report #2017-15. Washington, DC: Office of Planning, Research and Evaluation, Administration for Children & Families, US Department of Health and Human Services.

Gopnik, Alison, Andrew N. Meltzoff, and Patricia K. Kuhl. 1999. *The Scientist in the Crib: What Early Learning Tells Us about the Mind*. New York: William Morrow.

Martin, Anne, Rachel Razza, and Jeanne Brooks-Gunn. 2012. "Specifying the Links between Household Chaos and Preschool Children's Development." *Early Child Development and Care* 182 (10): 1247–63.

Meltzoff, Andrew N., Joni N. Saby, and Peter J. Marshall. 2018. "Neural Representations of the Body in 60-Day-Old Human Infants." *Developmental Science* 22 (1): 1–9.

Mindes, Gayle. 2011. *Assessing Young Children*. 4th ed. Boston: Pearson.

NAEYC (National Association for the Education of Young Children). 2009. "Developmentally Appropriate Practice in Early Childhood Programs Serving Children from Birth through Age 8." www.naeyc.org/sites/default/files/globally-shared/downloads/PDFs/resources/position-statements/PSDAP.pdf.

Scarr, Sandra, and Kathleen McCartney. 1983. "How People Make Their Own Environments: A Theory of Genotype Greater Than Environment Effects." *Child Development* 54 (2): 424–35.

Super, Charles M., and Sara Harkness. 1986. "The Developmental Niche: A Conceptualization at the Interface of Child and Culture." *International Journal of Behavioral Development* 9 (4): 545–69.

CHAPTER 7

Assessing Behavior, Development, and Environments

This competency focuses on systematically collecting information about babies' behavior and development to individualize and adapt supports and screen for developmental delays. We refer to this skill as *assessment*. Assessment also includes evaluating babies' care and learning environments. In this chapter, you will learn terminology for different types of assessment, the purposes of assessment, common assessment tools used with infants and toddlers and their families, and what makes an assessment high quality. In figure 7.1, the key dispositions, knowledge, and skills that promote high-quality, reflective practices in assessing behavior, development, and environments are summarized.

Why is assessment an important competency? Observing behavior and development is your primary source of knowledge about individual babies. Your observations provide key input in how you build relationships, guide behavior, and support development. Assessment takes observation further, making it systematic and using it for a variety of purposes. Screening is critical for identifying children who need extra support or might be eligible for early intervention or other services. Assessment is essential for monitoring children's developmental progress and creating and maintaining high-quality learning environments.

How are observation and assessment related to other competencies? Observations are the cornerstone of assessment for infants and toddlers and should be incorporated into everyday activities and interactions. You learned observation skills in chapter 2, which highlighted the role of observation in reflective practice. Then you learned how these observations and your reflections on them help you build relationships with babies and support development and learning. In this chapter, we build from these essential observation skills to make those observations systematic. Then they can guide your planning as you set learning objectives, create

Knowledge

ABD-K1: Understanding of key terms related to assessment

ABD-K2: Awareness of the purposes of assessment related to the goals of educators, families, and programs

ABD-K3: Awareness of how assessments relate to broader systems, early intervention, and quality initiatives

ABD-K4: Awareness of what makes assessment high-quality and meaningful

ABD-K5: Awareness of factors that influence assessment results

ABD-K6: Knowledge of methods for documenting behavior and development in authentic ways

ABD-K7: Knowledge of functional assessments for determining reasons for behaviors

ABD-K8: Awareness of standardized tools for screening and assessing babies' development, interactions, and environments

Skills

ABD-S1: Skills to identify and select useful assessment tools

ABD-S2: Skills to observe and describe behaviors clearly, objectively, and in detail

ABD-S3: Skills to interpret observations to understand behavior and development

ABD-S4: Skills for effective communication of observation and assessment results

ABD-S5: Skills to utilize assessment information to advance your work

ABD-S6: Skills to use ongoing observation systems to update plans and track progress

Reflective, Relationship-Based Practices

PROMOTED BY Knowledge, Dispositions, Skills, and Facilitating Conditions

Dispositions

ABD-D1: Curiosity about babies' development and individuality

ABD-D2: Openness to new information about babies, families, curriculum, environment, and self

ABD-D3: Willingness to reflect on beliefs about behavior and development that influence observation

ABD-D4: Willingness to communicate difficult information

ABD-D5: Belief in a collaborative approach to assessment practices

Facilitating Conditions

ABD-FC1: Paid time to observe babies and reflect on observations and development

ABD-FC2: Availability of and training in an observation system

ABD-FC3: Support for communicating assessment information with families

Figure 7.1. Competencies for Assessing Behavior, Development, and Environments

responsive learning experiences, and monitor developmental progress. We also assess care and learning environments and interactions—both in the home and in group care settings—to determine how we can improve them to better meet babies' needs. We use screening to identify babies who may be at risk of delays or disorders so that we can best include and support babies with additional support needs. Finally, our own work with babies may be assessed as part of our commitment to continually improving our work and to advancing our practices as professionals.

Facilitating conditions. Using assessment systematically is resource intensive and requires program-level support and commitment. Program policies must support educators' assessment practices or this work will not be effective in supporting children's development. Educators need paid time to observe babies and reflect on their observations (ABD-FC1). This may mean having another person take an active role with the children while they observe, reflect, or make plans. There must be organizational support (including paid time) for training in the assessment tools or observational methods (ABD-FC2). Program policies should include families in the assessment process and reflect a commitment to ongoing two-way communication, such as through regular parent-educator conferences (ABD-FC3). Finding time to conduct observations, reflect, and share results with families can be especially challenging for family child care providers, who are less likely to have extra help. Some family child care networks have temporary assistance for providers to give them release time to do this type of work. Other family child care providers take professional development days, but that creates hardship for families who rely on consistent care.

Knowledge

To assess infant and toddler behavior and development, educators must first understand key terms, such as *screening, testing, measuring, evaluating,* and *assessing* (ABD-K1). Educators must understand how assessments relate to their own goals as professionals, families' goals for their babies' care and education, and programs' goals (ABD-K2), as well as to broader systems, early intervention services, and quality initiatives, such as state rating systems for identifying the quality of early childhood programs (ABD-K3). Educators require knowledge of what makes assessment high quality and meaningful (ABD-K4), the factors that may influence assessment results (ABD-K5), and methods for documenting behavior and development in authentic ways (ABD-K6). Finally, educators need knowledge of functional assessment to determine the reasons behind behaviors (ABD-K7), and they need an awareness of **standardized assessment tools** for screening and assessing babies' development, classroom interactions, and classroom environments (ABD-K8).

Understanding key terms related to assessment (ABD-K1)

Many terms associated with the assessment process have overlapping definitions; here we try to disentangle the common terms.

The terms *screening*, *testing*, *measuring*, *evaluating*, and *assessing* all refer to collecting comprehensive information about each baby's developmental strengths, skills, interests, preferences, and other individual characteristics. The terms *testing*, *measuring*, and *evaluating* usually indicate more **formal assessment tools**. Broadly speaking, *tools* refer to specific methods for testing, measuring, and evaluating. Sometimes the term *tool* refers to specific materials used to collect information, such as developmental checklists or anecdotal records.

The methods for collecting information on babies are termed observational when you observe a baby's behavior to understand something about their development; these observations may be either **qualitative** (describing in words what a baby did or said, for example, using an anecdotal record or running record) or **quantitative** (using a checklist to indicate whether they did a particular behavior, making a rating on a scale to indicate how well or how much they do something, or tallying to indicate how many times per day a baby does a particular behavior). Another method is to collect information via **parent report**, where parents make ratings or complete a checklist, or you can directly test a baby one-on-one as they interact with materials in a scripted manner (which is called standardization), to see how they compare with other babies their age (**norm-referenced**).

Tools can also refer to formal, standardized assessments, such as the Bayley Scales of Infant Development. Formal assessment refers to longer, often more involved tools that are standardized to measure specific domains or skills; these assessments can be used to guide treatment and to individualize the child's learning experiences. A formal **evaluation** is a comprehensive assessment (or set of assessments) used to diagnose and identify whether a child has met the qualification for receiving early intervention services, as well as to learn about the baby's strengths, needs, and contexts to develop a plan for intervention. In most states, babies need to be substantially developmentally delayed in at least one domain to be eligible for early intervention services, but states vary in how far below the average children need to be. When using a formal assessment tool, you want to be sure it has **reliability** and **validity**. We will discuss these terms further in qualities of assessment.

Stakeholders in assessment include anyone who has a stake—something to gain or lose—in the use of assessment results, and thus should be involved in making decisions in the assessment process. Stakeholders can include families, educators, program staff, and community members (for example, in health and education sectors), as well as policy makers.

Awareness of the purposes of assessment (ABD-K2) and how these are related to broader systems (ABD-K3)

Assessing babies, their caregivers, and their environments is not an end in itself but rather a critical part of advancing the broader goals that support children's development. Families are invested in their babies' well-being and have goals for their children's development and education. They are key stakeholders in assessments of their babies, their parent-child relationships, and their home environments. Educators also have learning and developmental goals for the babies they work with, as well as their own professional development. On a broader level, programs have goals for the well-being, development, and education of the children and families they serve, as well as for their staff and the programs themselves. Programs are also accountable to their funders, and sometimes to state- or national-level policies. Assessment plays a supporting role to all of these broader goals.

Screening to identify possible delays or disabilities. Screening is a brief, narrow assessment process used to detect whether babies are meeting expected developmental milestones. See appendixes A (see page 126) and B (see page 128) for the developmental milestones and possible red flags that might warrant screening and further assessment. Typically **screening tools** do not require too much training to use and are quick to administer. For example, screening tools might include brief developmental checklists with criteria for "missed" skills that suggest the need for a more in-depth assessment. Once screening tools have identified a possible developmental delay, further testing is needed to identify specific disabilities that would enable children and families to access early intervention services. The sooner a baby is identified and begins receiving services, the better their long-term outcomes.

Programs that receive state or federal funding are often required to screen babies' development. The largest federally funded early childhood program, Head Start, requires developmental screening to identify concerns in any area of well-being or development. This Head Start Program Performance Standard (HSPPS) requires that screening be done in collaboration with parents and with parental consent. Screenings should be used to identify concerns with children's development in all domains soon after the child enters the program. Chapter 8 provides details on steps to take if you identify that a child has an indicator of a disability or delay.

Planning and individualizing supports. Planning is the most frequent reason for performing observations and other assessments. Knowing about child abilities and interests, as well as family well-being, culture, and goals for their babies, allows educators to plan truly individualized goals and supports, based on the child's current developmental stage and needs.

Monitoring development in the context of intervention. When a baby has an identified delay or disability and is receiving state-funded early intervention services, they will have an individualized family service plan with specific developmental goals. These goals, usually framed as specific skills or behaviors, are reassessed after a certain period of time. Assessments and observations track development over time to determine whether the educational supports that we (and others) are providing for them are helping them meet goals.

Evaluating effectiveness. When assessments of individual babies or families are brought together (aggregated) at the program level, the information can indicate how effective services are or point out where improvements are needed. True learning communities seek information to guide their continuous quality improvement. Program stakeholders decide together what their desired outcomes are for babies or families, choose and use assessment tools to measure the outcomes, and study the results of their assessments. Such program evaluation can help staff determine how effective the program is (how do babies or families change while they are in the program?) and whether they need to make changes (for example, identifying a curriculum that needs to be revised or areas in which staff need additional professional development or support).

Accountability. Assessment information about babies, families, educators, and programs can be used for accountability purposes. Some funders simply require that assessments be done, and programs are accountable to do them if they want to keep receiving funds. Other funders require that program assessments show effectiveness or meet a certain standard of quality on the assessment ratings. Professional organizations also use assessments to certify or rate programs. For example, assessments can inform ratings on state Quality Rating and Improvement Systems (QRIS), which can be tied to funding or other support.

Awareness of what makes assessments high quality and meaningful (ABD-K4)

To ensure the assessments you conduct are meaningful, you must follow a high-quality process for conducting them, and the tools themselves must be adequate for the purpose and implemented in a high-quality way. The following are principles that make an assessment process high quality:

Strength-based. Strength-based approaches focus on identifying the child's current skill levels in all areas of development, as well as what helps them learn and grow. Focusing on strengths and resources that the individual, the parent-child dyad, and the family bring assists educators in promoting development, including in areas the child and family find challenging. Identifying strengths can help practitioners understand the contexts in which the child learns best and use that to support them where they need the most help. When you know what strengths the child brings to their learning and development, you can use those strengths to help the child learn in other areas. For example, for a young infant who enjoys eye contact and smiling with others but has a motor delay, an educator could engage the infant in face-to-face interactions to motivate the infant to stay in tummy time longer, which could support motor strength and development. For a toddler who gravitates toward blocks and construction but does not have the social skills to play with other children, an educator could invite other children to join the child in parallel play while modeling how to make these invitations. In short, a strength-based approach helps practitioners learn about the whole child, rather than just focusing on areas of weakness or challenge, and to respectfully support the child in ways that are likely to be most effective.

Collaborative. Collaborate with families to observe and assess babies, together deciding what is important to assess. Gather information from families in addition to your own observations. Periodically check in with parents to share your assessments and see whether they are similar to the parents' view of their baby. In this approach, you are not the expert telling the family about their child. Rather, you are coming together to share perspectives. Parents and educators see babies in a very different environment and thus may see different things. Seeing how a baby's behavior differs with their parents can give you insights into setting up the classroom for the child.

Ongoing versus snapshot. One assessment provides just one snapshot of a baby's skills, but babies change rapidly. Assessments are most useful when they are conducted over time. In chapter 6 on supporting development and learning, we talk about a process of observing, reflecting, planning, and implementing, then evaluating and reassessing. This provides a fuller picture of the baby and supports educators to continually adapt the ways they support development.

Used versus filed. Finally, you must use your observations! Sometimes assessments are done because you must check a box on a form indicating you have done the assessment. But resist the temptation just to do the assessment and file it away to be seen by the funder, evaluator, or monitoring team. Assessments, both observations and formal assessments, must be used to inform practice—otherwise they are a waste of everyone's time and resources.

Some assessment tools are better than others, some people are more skilled at conducting assessments than others, and some situations are more conducive to assessments than others. Consider the following aspects of quality when choosing and using individual assessment tools:

Validity means that the tool measures what it says it does or is capable of providing the information you need. There are many ways of making sure a tool is valid. Face validity means that the items on the tool "look like" they are measuring a specific skill or developmental area. For example, if you looked at a set of items asking about words a toddler can say, words a toddler can understand, and pointing and gesturing by a toddler, you would likely conclude that the tool assesses toddler language and communication. For your purposes, it may be the most important form of validity because it ensures that it is useful in your work. You can also see how the tool is associated with other tools that assess the same thing and whether it predicts outcomes in the expected way. You must also make sure that the tools are valid for your purpose and your population and that they are **sensitive** and **specific** enough. Sometimes familiar or readily available tools are not valid or appropriate for your current purpose. For instance, if you are assessing a toddler's language skills, you must ensure that the tool is available in the languages the child speaks, or you may need to rely on your observations of how the child understands and communicates with others or ask others to observe with you.

When screening to identify possible delays or disabilities, you need a screener that is specific, that does not have too many false positives (saying that there is a problem when there is not). It must also be sensitive enough to identify delays with few false negatives (saying that there is no problem when there is an issue). Sometimes you may detect a delay very early based on your knowledge of development before a screening tool indicates an issue. You may need to readminister the screener over time.

Reliability means the tool is dependable. If two people use the tool with the same baby in the same situation, they should get very similar results. Or if one person uses the same tool with the same baby twice, a day or a week apart, they should get similar results. Conducting an assessment requires training, and some measures are easier to learn than others. Most measures have standard ways they should be used so the child can be compared to a standard for their age. However, sometimes you want to know what a child is capable of rather than how they compare to others. In those cases, you can adapt what you do or say to see what the child can do. However, if you adapt the tool, you cannot compare the scores of your baby or group of babies to all other children on whom the assessment was normed.

Awareness of factors that influence assessment results (ABD-K5)

The reliability of an assessment tool isn't just about the assessment tool itself, but about the way individuals use it. The accuracy of results might be influenced by the assessor, the child, or the context. We must be vigilant about getting accurate results and recognize when the accuracy might be compromised.

When assessors are not reliable. Even after learning to use the tool in a standardized way, assessors' perspectives can drift or they may forget subtle aspects of the tool over time, and thus do not implement it with **fidelity**. Fidelity means that you use a tool in the same way with all children. Standardization is closely linked with fidelity. Bias also harms fidelity, so you must reflect on your own possible biases, especially when conducting observations. For instance, if you have a particularly close relationship with a child in your room, you may interpret their behaviors as more skilled or more positive than others'. You can help avoid bias by learning to describe behaviors in objective detail and to separate that from your interpretation of the behavior's meaning. The same social biases that exist in our culture show up in assessments, such as certain expectations based on children's gender and race. For example, research has shown that teachers rate African American children as having more school adjustment problems and fewer academic competencies than children who are white (Pigot and Cowan 2000). However, seeing your own biases can be difficult or impossible. Thus, it can be helpful to have multiple practitioners assess each child and compare their ratings, as well as to have parents observe and assess their own children, then thoughtfully consider how your views differ.

When babies are not reliable. Babies themselves are not reliable. They don't do the same things or show the same skills every day, and their behaviors are highly influenced by their context and how they feel. A single assessment is only a snapshot of the baby's behavior. Consider what could be influencing the child's behavior at that moment. Is the baby tired or hungry or overwhelmed? Is that baby in a new and unfamiliar setting? Are they with strangers or with trusted caregivers? Repeating an observation is often helpful if you are uncertain that you have gotten a true sense of what the child is capable of doing. And always compare the results of your assessment to what you observe in the baby's behavior from day to day.

Knowledge of methods for documenting behavior and development in authentic ways (ABD-K6)

The most common form of assessing babies is observation. Observation allows you to see the baby as they are in their natural setting, does not require extensive training, and is easy to communicate with families. However, it can be hard to know if you are seeing the extent of what the child can do or if they could do more in other circumstances. It can help to do several observations before summarizing and interpreting what you have learned, then share the information with parents and colleagues to get their input as well.

Observations serve many purposes: to get to know a new baby by watching them interact with materials and people, to learn about a baby's interests and skills, or to answer a specific question about their behavior or development. Clarify the purpose for your observation to help you determine which method to use. Below we describe several methods for observing and documenting behavior objectively; refer to Resources and Further Readings online for more extensive information about observation methods.

Anecdotal records are short accounts of behavior in a specific context and time, written shortly after the event. They can compare babies' behaviors, skills, and interests across domains and track how skills develop over time. Anecdotal records are useful in gathering data about a specific skill, such as observing and recording emerging social skills during play alongside peers in the house area. Anecdotal notes capture the objective details of developmentally significant events; see examples in chapter 6. They are factual in nature and describe where the event occurred and what happened. Use vivid vocabulary to paint a picture of what happened, but your comments should be as objective as possible. Describe the behaviors but not your interpretations or assumptions about the meaning of the behavior, the child's internal state, or your own emotional response. If you do want to record your interpretations of the baby's state of mind (or your own), write those separately, using one column for your observations and another for interpretations.

Running records are similar to anecdotal records in that they detail a sequence of a baby's behavior. However, while anecdotal records typically capture one event, running records are longer, following the baby's behavior across settings to capture a broader array of developmental skills. In conducting a ten-minute observation on the playground, you might observe emerging gross-motor skills as the toddler pushes a scooter, cognitive and motor-planning skills as she navigates an obstacle, and communication skills as she interacts with peers and other adults. The intent is to capture everything the baby does and says, including actions, gestures, and facial expressions, being as objective as possible. Running records are helpful in identifying growth in skills over time and in seeing patterns of growth across a variety of developmental skills in multiple contexts (areas of the indoor classroom, outdoors on the playground, during routines and transitions).

Checklists can record specific behaviors or skills you are interested in. They can help you gather a lot of information quickly. Create columns for each skill and rows for each baby, and mark them off as you see each baby use each type of skill. For instance, you could track fine-motor skills in your room by looking at how babies get objects, such as swiping at objects with their whole arm, using a palmar grasp with the whole hand, or making a pincer grasp with thumb and finger. This is a useful technique when you are watching for specific developmental milestones. You can use this method for observing an individual child or a group of children. The traditional checklist has several variations:

- **Tally-event sampling** records how many times a behavior occurs. It is like a checklist, but you make a check mark every time you see the behavior.

- With **time sampling,** you create regular time intervals (depending on the behavior, it might be one minute or one hour) and indicate whether the behavior occurs in each time interval.

- **Rating scales** allow you to rate how often you see a behavior or something about its quality. This method often uses a table with behaviors in rows and ratings in columns labeled something like *usually*, *frequently*, *rarely*, or *never*.

Knowledge of functional assessments for determining reasons for behaviors (ABD-K7)

Functional assessment is used to understand why a specific behavior—usually problematic or challenging—is occurring. It helps you figure out the function of the behavior. The ABC method is a common functional assessment that organizes information from several observations. The *A* refers to the *antecedent*, the event or activity that immediately precedes a problem behavior. The *B* is the observed *behavior*. And the *C* is the *consequence*, or the event that immediately follows. Performed over time, functional assessments can help determine whether a behavior is being elicited by the antecedent (for example, whenever Kalli is in a group of children in a tight space, she hits another child), or whether the consequence is reinforcing it (for example, whenever Kalli hits another child, the others leave and Kalli plays by herself). The functional assessment does not tell you how to address the behavior, but it can give insights into why it happens. This can help you find alternative ways to meet the child's needs so the behavior becomes less likely (such as rearranging the classroom so that there are fewer tight spaces or stationing an educator nearby whenever Kalli is in a group in a tight space).

Awareness of standardized tools for screening and assessing babies' development, interactions, and environments (ABD-K8)

In elementary school and beyond, state requirements determine which standardized assessment tools are used. Many preschool programs that receive state or federal funding (including Head Start programs) are required to use assessments, but they can choose which are appropriate for their program. In work with infants and toddlers, program directors or individual educators often control these decisions. Many programs rely solely on the observational methods described above.

Formal assessments can gather information about (a) infants' and toddlers' well-being and development, (b) parenting, family needs, and the home environment, and (c) educator-child interactions and the quality of the group care environment. Refer to the online document Resources and Further Readings for useful assessment tools and methods for conducting meaningful observations.

Screening and assessing development. Both screening and assessment tools are based on developmental norms or milestones—skills that develop in a predictable sequence in many children across countries, cultures, and languages (such as those described in appendix A [see page 126]). These assessment tools measure a baby's development relative to other babies the same age.

As described above, screening tools are generally used to identify possible delays. The Ages and Stages Questionnaire (ASQ) is a multidomain screener that can be completed with parents. The Devereux Early Childhood Assessment (DECA) and the ASQ: Social-Emotional assessment cover the social-emotional domain. The Child Behavior Checklist looks at babies' challenging behaviors to assess emotional health.

Formal assessments take longer to administer than screeners. They are more detailed and give a fuller picture of a child's development in one or more domains, as opposed to screeners that just indicate whether there might be a problem. Assessment tools highlight emerging skills, so you can use the results to plan intentional supports. Formal assessments also determine eligibility for early intervention services. Two cross-domain measures are the Battelle Developmental Inventory, third edition (BDI-3) and the Bayley Scales of Infant Development, third edition (BSID-III). The MacArthur-Bates Communicative Development Inventory (CDI) is a parent- or educator-reported measure of babies' language comprehension and expression; both parents and educators complete the CDI because babies learn and use different words at homes and at school.

Assessing learning. Assessments can also measure learning, the change over time in what babies know and can do. Assessments of abilities (such as tool use or speech articulation) and knowledge (such as vocabulary

Ms. Diaz uses a standardized play-based measure to complete a developmental screening.

or basic concepts) are useful in measuring the success of planned experiences and determining whether a curriculum is working. Are children learning what they are expected to know in their schools, community, and culture?

Because learning objectives are tied to the curriculum, there are fewer standardized measures. Thus, learning assessment tools are typically associated with a particular established curriculum. Examples include Teaching Strategies Gold, which is associated with Creative Curriculum, and High-Scope COR Advantage, which is related to the HighScope Curriculum. These assessments must be done repeatedly over time to track learning.

Assessing practitioner interactions and group care environments. Assessing service quality can steer efforts to improve the program as well as your choice of professional development opportunities. Quality measures are also used for accountability purposes, like state-based QRIS systems or the Head Start monitoring system. Educators should become comfortable videotaping their practice so they can review it alone, with peers, or with supervisors. All of these **observational tools** can be complex, and some require attending formal training to be certified.

All measures of quality are based on particular values or theoretical perspectives. Select a measure for program improvement that captures the things you think are important, the qualities you think really make a difference for children and families. Make sure you agree with the tool's underlying values. Measures of classroom quality for infants and toddlers include the following:

- Infant/Toddler Environment Rating Scale-Revised (ITERS-R) measures quality as related to space and furnishings, care routines, listening and talking, planned activities, interaction, program structure, and the needs of parents and staff. The similar Family Child Care Environment Rating Scale-Revised (FCCERS-R) is used in home-based child care settings.

- Toddler Classroom Assessment Scoring System (CLASS) measures interactions and relationships in the classroom, including the emotional climate, behavior guidance, practitioners' sensitivity to children, and how practitioners facilitate learning and development, give feedback to children, and model language. The CLASS is only used in center-based settings.

- Quality of Caregiver-Child Interactions for Infants and Toddlers (QCCIIT) focuses on educators' behaviors that support babies' social-emotional, language and literacy, and cognitive development, as well as discerning red flags in safety and well-being. The QCCIIT can be used in both family- and center-based settings.

✳ Program Quality Assessment (PQA) Infant/Toddler version, associated with the HighScope Curriculum, assesses schedules and routines, adult-child interactions, curriculum planning and child observation, and babies' and families' experiences in the learning environment.

Dispositions

Many of the dispositions that help you become reflective and use your reflections to make changes will also aid you in your assessment work, including curiosity (ABD-D1), openness to new information (ABD-D2), and willingness to reflect on what you have learned (ABD-D3). Dispositions that support your partnerships with families in the assessment process include the willingness to communicate difficult information (ABD-D4) and to take a collaborative approach to assessment (ABD-D5).

Curiosity (ABD-D1)

Curiosity about babies' development in general and an interest in how each child grows can help you in this work. Your desire to understand each baby's and family's strengths, challenges, needs, preferences, and interests can guide your assessments.

Openness to new information (ABD-D2)

It is critical to keep an open mind through the assessment process so you can learn about the babies and families, the curriculum and environment, and yourself. If you think you know the answer before you conduct an assessment, you may look for information that confirms your preexisting belief and ignore contradictory information.

Willingness to reflect (ABD-D3)

Complete the cycle by reflecting on your assessment and allowing it to inform changes in your work. Be willing to reflect on how your own beliefs could be influencing your objectivity; this will go a long way toward helping you conduct accurate, valid, and reliable assessments.

Willingness to communicate difficult information (ABD-D4)

Nobody likes to be the bearer of difficult news. After conducting assessments and observations, you will need to talk with families about their child's strengths, weakness, and needs. Sometimes you will help the family decide whether to pursue formal assessment of a possible developmental delay. This is not easy, but practitioners must be willing to do it because it is in the best interest of the baby.

Collaborative approach to assessment (ABD-D5)

Avoid falling into an expert model, where you are seen as the expert. Rather, as professionals, we support the family as experts on their own baby. Thus they participate in the information-gathering part of assessment as well as in interpreting and understanding the results.

Skills

Educators need the skills to identify and select useful assessment tools (ABD-S1), to use those tools to observe and describe behaviors clearly (ABD-S2), and then accurately interpret their observations (ABD-S3). Next, educators need effective communication skills to share their observations and assessment results with families and other educators (ABD-S4). Finally, educators must be able to utilize assessment results to inform their work with infants and toddlers (ABD-S5) and to embed and utilize ongoing observation systems to continually update their curriculum planning and track babies' progress (ABD-S6).

Identifying and selecting useful assessment tools (ABD-S1)

The first step in the assessment process is identifying the purpose of the assessment and who should be involved; your answers guide your choice of assessment tools and procedures. For instance, if your questions relate to planning and curriculum, you will probably use an observation method or one of the knowledge or learning assessments. If you are determining whether the baby has a possible developmental delay, use a formal screening tool. Ensure that your tool is valid for the people and contexts you are working in. Handout 7.1, Choose Tools, provides examples of matching the purpose to the type of assessment tool and shows how to compare specific assessment tools to select one. Below are questions to ask yourself, and the other stakeholders, to develop your assessment process.

www.redleafpress.org/wwb/7-1.pdf

- ❊ What is the purpose of the assessment? What question(s) will it answer?

- ❊ Who are the stakeholders? Who should have input?

* What will be assessed (for example, babies' development, educator-child interaction quality)?

* Who will be assessed, and in what context (for example, babies in their homes, educators in their classrooms)?

* Is observation sufficient to answer your question? If so . . .

  • which method of observation is best suited to answer the question?

  • who should be the observer?

  • when and where will observations take place?

  • how many observations should be done?

* If you need to use a standardized screener or formal assessment tool . . .

  • are you qualified or trained to use the tool?

  • does the tool have sufficient validity and reliability?

  • is it appropriate for your population?

  • how quickly and easily can it be completed and scored?

Once you know what method to use (screener, formal assessment, informal observation), you will need to choose the specific tool. When choosing among formal standardized screeners or assessment tools, compare their qualities to each other to find the one best suited to your purpose and population.

Observing and describing behaviors clearly, objectively, and in detail (ABD-S2)

Before starting, define the purpose of your observation and lay out the behaviors you will document. Remember that even subtle, nonverbal behaviors are critical cues to babies' and adults' internal states and developmental needs. When using a checklist, make sure the behaviors are defined clearly so that anyone using the tool understands what you are looking for. For ideas of what to observe, look at the sequences of developmental skills in each domain in appendix A (see page 126) or refer to documents such as state early learning guidelines.

Over time, your observations and ratings may drift. It is good to look back at previous observations and ask yourself whether you still see things the way you did before. If not, why? Have you become a more sophisticated observer? Are you getting to know the babies better? Or have you become more generous in your ratings? Check in with other educators to see if you agree on how to describe a behavior to determine how reliable your observations are.

Consider how you are an actor in your observation. Are you sitting back to do the observation? Is this different from the way you usually interact with babies, and does this affect their behavior? If you have unfamiliar people coming into your setting to do observations, how does this affect your behavior and that of the babies? These can all affect high-quality observations.

STRATEGIES

* **Be objective and positive.** Let go of preexisting expectations and become aware of possible bias. Focus on what the child does, how they do it, when they do it—not on what they don't do, what they do wrong or poorly, or why they are doing it.

* **Be vivid.** When writing anecdotal records or running records, describe behavior clearly and in sufficient detail to make sure that a reader can imagine what you observed.

Ms. Rachel takes a running record of what the children say and do as she watches them play.

✳ **Be intentional.** Watch with a question in mind. What can this baby do with objects? Is this child reaching the milestones typical of their age group? How does this toddler move and explore? How does this child interact with others? How does this baby respond during transitions? How does this child's classroom or home support development?

✳ **Keep interpretation separate.** Make sure to keep your interpretations of someone's internal states separate from your descriptions of the indicative behaviors. For example, "Observation: Her brows were furrowed as she watched Mr. Brendan walk through the door"; "Interpretation: She seemed wary of the new person in the room."

Interpreting observations to understand behavior and development (ABD-S3)

Bring your observations together with your knowledge of how babies' behaviors are affected by context (chapter 5) and of developmental sequences and red flags (chapter 6) to interpret your data. Ask yourself the following questions:

✳ What has this observation or assessment added to what I know about this baby's development, learning, strengths, needs, preferences, and interests? Or about this family's goals and expectations?

✳ How does what I learned take into account other information I know about the individual (child, parent, educator) and their current and larger context? How might these factors have influenced the results?

In many cases, it is useful to ask parents or colleagues to compare their observations of the same behaviors or interpret your observations with you. This adds an incentive to be very objective in your descriptions. Working together helps reflect a collaborative approach to assessment and ultimately provides richer information.

Effectively communicating observation and assessment results (ABD-S4)

After your interpretation, the next step is to communicate your findings with families and colleagues. The following are qualities that will help you effectively communicate assessment results:

Confidentiality. Ensure that you have permission from parents to share information about them or their children with other professionals (also see ethics of data collection in chapter 9).

Accuracy. Be as accurate as possible in sharing results. Keep careful and organized notes, avoid overgeneralizing or being too broad, and avoid sugarcoating difficult information.

Clarity. Finding the language to simply convey what you have learned is not always easy. Your knowledge of development is steeped in jargon that families may not know. Check in often when sharing results to ensure that you are being understood.

Respect and sensitivity. Convey respect and sensitivity when sharing results and possible next steps with family members. You are evaluating their babies, and maybe the entire family. Consider how it would feel to hear such things about yourself or your child. Check with parents to see if your view of their child is consistent with theirs. Do they see the same things at home? Is what you are saying a surprise?

Strength-based. When you need to talk with parents (or others) about problems with a baby's behavior or development, it is helpful to focus on what the child *can* do and what *can* be done to help the child make gains in the future. This does not mean that you ignore or sugarcoat weaknesses in a child's skills or challenges in their behavior. It means you start with what they can do well and find ways to use those things to build and support additional skills.

Some families have a hard time accepting assessment results that indicate a baby may have a delay or other behavioral or developmental challenge. It can be hard for practitioners to be present with families as they react, but you are in a unique position to help families in this process because of your deep knowledge of the baby, the family, and development.

STRATEGIES

* Follow the system or protocol in your program for communicating assessment information to families. This can help you be more comfortable and make this process easier. It also assures you that you have the support of your program.

* Talk with your supervisor or with colleagues about your plan for the conversation with the family, and try role-playing the conversation, pretending they are the family members.

Utilizing assessment information to advance your work (ABD-S5)

We have talked about how to choose assessment tools and how to conduct objective observations and interpret observations and assessments. Applying your interpretations to curriculum planning and to individualizing activities (see chapter 6) is critical in implementing high-quality programming.

Ms. Denise and her assistant teachers review anecdotes and children's work samples to plan the developmental experiences for the coming week.

We use this skill during daily interactions when we vary our approach based on the baby's reactions and when we alter or plan experiences based on what we have observed about each baby's developmental needs as well as what our observations have told us about the group's developmental needs and interests.

Using ongoing observation systems to update plans and track progress (ABD-S6)

The final skill in conducting assessments is to keep going! Assessments should be done in an ongoing and systematic way. The goal is to have an observational system in place where information can be gathered and stored in systematic ways. That way you can continually track the progress of individual children and families, as well as changes in your own practices. Over time, ongoing assessments of children and families can help determine whether additional services should be added to your program, such as broader social supports, health services, or early intervention. Observations on program quality can determine areas for enhancing services, such as planning professional development.

Embedding ongoing observation systems in your classroom practice and program structure becomes a dynamic and responsive way to continually modify and improve services. This requires buy-in at every level, from parents, program staff, and management to ensure the assessment system is maintained over time (ABD-FC2).

Reflect Back, Think Ahead

Look back at the figure at the beginning of this chapter that shows the knowledge, disposition, and skill competencies involved in assessing behavior, development, and environments. Which of these competencies did you have when you began this chapter? Which competencies did you develop? Which competencies will you intentionally work on building for yourself next? Use the Assessing Behavior, Development, and Environments chapter of the Professional Learning Guide (PLG [see page 11]) that accompanies this book to support your own professional growth in this domain.

Selected References

Centers for Disease Control and Prevention (CDC). 2020. "Developmental Monitoring and Screening for Health Professionals." CDC (website). www.cdc.gov /ncbddd/childdevelopment/screening-hcp.html.

Clark, Patricia, and Gayle McDowel. 2006. *The Developing Child Observation Guidebook*. Woodland Hills, CA: McGraw Hill. http://glencoe.mheducation .com/sites/dl/free/0078883601/680442/DC_ObsGuideBook.pdf.

Department of Education and Early Childhood Development of Victoria, Australia. 2012. *Strength-Based Approach: A Guide to Writing Transition Learning and Development Statements*. www.education.vic.gov.au/documents /childhood/professionals/learning/strengthbappr.pdf.

Head Start Early Childhood Learning & Knowledge Center. 2018. *Measuring What Matters*. https://eclkc.ohs.acf.hhs.gov/data-ongoing-monitoring/article /measuring-what-matters-using-data-support-family-progress.

Kisker, Ellen Eliason, et al. 2011. *Resources for Measuring Services and Outcomes in Head Start Programs Serving Infants and Toddlers*. Washington, DC: US Department of Health and Human Services, Administration for Children and Families. www.acf.hhs.gov/sites/default/files/documents/opre/resources _for_measuring_services_and_outcomes.pdf.

Meisels, Samuel J. 2018. "Readiness and Relationships: Issues in Assessing Young Children, Families, and Caregivers." Washington, DC: Head Start Early Childhood Learning & Knowledge Center. https://eclkc.ohs.acf.hhs .gov/child-screening-assessment/article/readiness-relationships-issues -assessing-young-children-families.

Mindes, Gayle, and Lee Ann Jung. 2014. *Assessing Young Children.* 5th ed. Boston: Pearson.

National Center on Parent, Family, and Community Engagement. *Tracking Progress in Early Care and Education: Program, Staff, and Family Measurement Tools.* Washington, DC: Office of Head Start. https://eclkc.ohs.acf.hhs.gov/sites /default/files/pdf/tracking-progress-early-care-education-long-version.pdf.

National Infant & Toddler Child Care Initiative. 2010. *Infant/Toddler Development, Screening, and Assessment.* Washington, DC: US Department of Health and Human Services, Office of Child Care Administration for Children and Families. www.zerotothree.org/resources/72-infant-and-toddler-development -screening-and-assessment.

Pigot, Rowan, L., and Emory L. Cowan. 2000. "Teacher Race, Child Race, Racial Congruence, and Teacher Ratings of Children's School Adjustment." *Journal of School Psychology* 38 (2): 177–95.

CHAPTER 8

Including Infants and Toddlers with Additional Support Needs and Their Families

—with Carla Peterson

About 14 percent of babies across early childhood settings have additional support needs. The term *additional support needs* refers to many types of needs, but here we focus on babies with delays or disabilities that qualify them for services under the Individuals with Disabilities Education Improvement Act (IDEA), Part C. Although a common term is *special needs*, the term *additional support needs* better characterizes a respectful description of children's developmental needs. Some babies have risks for developing a delay or disability because of their health history (such as premature birth), experiences (such as chronic stress), or environments (such as poverty).

You will use strength-based, collaborative, **family-centered practices** to support these infants and toddlers and their families. We have summarized the key dispositions, knowledge, and skills that promote these practices in figure 8.1. Part C of the IDEA describes requirements for services such as early identification, screening and referrals, direct services, and professional collaborations to identify and implement the most appropriate and meaningful supports for babies with additional support needs and their families. As an educator working with a baby with an identified disability and their family, you are likely to be involved in these professional collaborations.

You will learn about the child's diagnosis and sometimes need to use special materials or adapt the environment. You will find new ways to support the baby's interactions with you, their parents, other caregivers, and peers. You may see red flags or early signs of a delay or disability in babies

Knowledge

INC-K1: Knowledge of policies, legislation, and local processes related to babies with disabilities

INC-K2: Awareness of diagnosis processes for delays and disabilities

INC-K3: Awareness of red flag for developmental delays and disabilities and common false alarms

INC-K4: Awareness of characteristics and trajectories of common disabilities

INC-K5: Awareness of early intervention service models and Individualized Family Service Plans

INC-K6: Awareness of roles and responsibilities in identification, evaluation, and treatment processes

INC-K7: Knowledge of local, regional, and state services for babies with delays or disabilities and their families

INC-K8: Awareness of how families may respond to information about a baby's delay or disability

Skills

INC-S1: Skills to create an inclusive and accessible environment

INC-S2: Skills to use strength-based practices to adapt to specific learning needs

INC-S3: Skills to provide supports each baby needs to interact with and learn from the environment

INC-S4: Skills to use family-centered practices to help families support babies with special needs

INC-S5: Skills for communication about inclusion, assessment, individualization, and related topics

Figure 8.1. Competencies for Including Infants and Toddlers with Special Needs and Their Families

Reflective, Relationship-Based Practices

PROMOTED BY Knowledge, Dispositions, Skills, and Facilitating Conditions

Dispositions

INC-D1: Commitment to a strengths-based approach to working with babies with special needs

INC-D2: Commitment to a family-centered approach to working with families of babies with special needs

INC-D3: Openness to learning from others to meet babies' needs

Facilitating Conditions

INC-FC1 Systematic approach for screening and assessment across the program

INC-FC2: Systematic approach for referrals to additional services

INC-FC3: Support for communicating with families about assessments and intervention services

INC-FC4: Program model or curriculum adaptable to family-centered practice in natural environments

INC-FC5: Access to a variety of books, toys, and materials that reflect babies' diverse abilities and can be adapted to meet babies needs

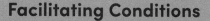

who have not had a disability diagnosed. You may refer that baby for additional assessment, an important first step in getting early intervention services for the child.

Why is this competency important? Everyone working with infants and toddlers will work with some babies who have additional support needs. Inclusive practices in which programs serve all babies, those typically developing and those with additional support needs, is best for the babies, their families, and the professionals who serve them. First, federal law mandates that all infants and toddlers eligible for services under Part C receive free and appropriate services in the same environments where typically developing children receive services. Second, the professional ethics of the National Association for the Education of Young children (NAEYC) and the Division for Early Childhood of the Council for Exceptional Children (DEC-CEC) as well as the policies of the US Departments of Health and Human Services and of Education (DHHS, ED) all advocate inclusive environments for infants and children with and without disabilities. You will enhance your professional skills as you learn about specific disabilities, collaborate with interdisciplinary teams, help parents navigate the system of services, and support others' competence and confidence in working with babies with additional support needs and their families.

How is this competency related to other competencies? Babies with additional support needs are babies, always. All babies need care, respect, and learning opportunities. Babies develop in individual ways, but some patterns may indicate a delay or a problem needing particular kinds of support for development. You will use all the same knowledge and skills for working with babies with additional support needs as with babies who are typically developing. But you may need additional knowledge, dispositions, and skills to ensure your work is effective for babies with additional support needs and their families.

Facilitating conditions. Programs are more likely to support effective services for babies with additional support needs if they use a systematic approach to screening and assessment across the program (INC-FC1). This requires identifying a set of screening and assessment tools for regular use and providing staff training to use these tools. Effective programs develop a systematic approach for referring children to additional services (INC-FC2) and provide support to educators or other staff for communicating with families about assessment and intervention services (INC-FC3). Finally, effective programs use strength-based and family-centered service models and curricula (INC-FC4).

To work with infants and toddlers with additional support needs, you need to know the laws and policies regarding services for babies with additional support needs (INC-K1), the process to assess and diagnose a disability (INC-K2), early signs of a delay or disability (INC-K3), characteristics of common disabilities (INC-K4), and various service models and plans (INC-K5). You need to understand your own role and responsibilities (INC-K6), what resources are available for you and the family (INC-K7), and how families may respond to all of this (INC-K8).

Knowledge of policies, legislation, and local processes related to babies with disabilities (INC-K1)

> **Inclusion** is defined by DEC and NAEYC (2009) as "the values, policies, and practices that support the right of every infant and young child and his or her family, regardless of ability, to participate in a broad range of activities and contexts as full members of families, communities, and society." The DHHS and ED (2015) clarify: "All young children with disabilities should have access to inclusive high-quality early childhood programs, where they are provided with individualized and appropriate support in meeting high expectations. . . . 'All' means all eligible infants, toddlers, and children with disabilities in the State and includes those who are English learners, immigrants (regardless of immigration status), homeless, and in foster care as well as those who reside on Indian reservations" (1, 4).

The Individuals with Disabilities Education Act (IDEA) is a federal law. The law makes free, appropriate, and individualized public education available to all eligible children with disabilities. Part C of the IDEA describes the requirements for early intervention services for infants and toddlers (birth through age three). Early intervention provides services to enable young children with disabilities to participate fully in a variety of natural settings (such as homes and community-based early childhood programs). Early intervention provides supports and resources to strengthen families' and caregivers' abilities to help children develop.

Each state administers Part C services. All states must meet the minimum requirements of the IDEA, but services vary by state. A designated state lead agency (education, health, or human services) administers state Part C programs, and an Interagency Coordinating Council ensures collaboration among all relevant agencies and service providers.

Awareness of diagnosis processes for delays and disabilities (INC-K2)

Part C requires each state to identify children eligible for services and to provide appropriate services to these children and their families. Each state's Child Find system must include public awareness campaigns, provide information about child development and services to parents, coordinate screenings and assessments across agencies and providers, and determine procedures for referring children to service providers. Each state sets its own criteria for developmental delays and diagnosed conditions that qualify children for services. Babies with developmental delays, measured with appropriate diagnostic tools and procedures, may qualify for services based on the size of the delay and the number of areas with delays (cognition, communication, social-emotional functioning, physical development, adaptive development). Babies may also qualify for services if they have a diagnosed physical or mental condition with a high probability of developmental delay: chromosomal abnormalities, genetic or congenital disorders, sensory impairments, inborn errors of metabolism, nervous system disorders, congenital infections, severe attachment disorders, or toxicity disorders such as fetal alcohol syndrome.

Awareness of red flags for developmental delays and disabilities and common false alarms (INC-K3)

As an early childhood professional, you will play a key role in identifying babies who are eligible for Part C services. You must be aware of the indicators of delays and disabilities as well as the characteristics of the disabilities often identified in the first three years.

Pay attention to developmental milestones that help identify developmental delays or disabilities (see appendix A [via QR code on page 126]). Children vary in their patterns of development, so some signs are false alarms, but waiting to see can lead to lost opportunities. Missing milestones are red flags for a possible delay or disability and should never be ignored.

Red flags in multiple domains are especially concerning. Delays in both language understanding (comprehension) and talking (expression) may signal a cognitive delay, and delays in both language and social interactions may indicate an autism spectrum disorder (ASD). A quiet baby demanding little attention may lack curiosity and exploration, leading to delays in problem-solving or cognitive skills.

False alarms make it important not to jump to conclusions. To decide what missing milestones mean and what to do about them, think about multiple factors that could influence the baby's behavior and development. For example, learning multiple languages (while associated with positive outcomes) can be associated with delays in early expressive language. Learn the red flags and false alarms in appendix B (see page 128).

Even if you suspect a concern is a false alarm, don't ignore it. Get more information from parents, other caregivers or colleagues, developmental specialists, standardized screenings, or additional assessments. Outcomes are almost always better if a delay or disability is identified and intervention begins early. Some delays or disabilities can be prevented.

Awareness of characteristics and trajectories of common disabilities (INC-K4)

Developmental disabilities are more common than many people realize. According to the Centers for Disease Control and Prevention (CDC 2018), 17 percent of children between the ages of three and seventeen have one or more developmental disabilities, and developmental disabilities occur across all ethnic and sociodemographic groups. Research done by Carla Peterson and colleagues (2004) at Iowa State University showed that among a group of babies in Early Head Start, most from low-income families, more than 80 percent had a health or developmental condition that is usually associated with a developmental disability, and 19 percent of these children went on to receive special education services at preschool age. But according to another study by Peterson and colleagues (2013), only 15 percent of children who receive special education services during their school years also received early intervention services (through IDEA Part C) as infants and toddlers. Early identification of developmental disabilities begins the intervention process as early as possible, but identification in the first three years is challenging for many reasons. As a practitioner who is knowledgeable about child development, you have a unique opportunity to help identify babies who may be eligible for early intervention.

Some developmental disabilities are likely to be identified at birth. For example, Down syndrome and spina bifida, both of which affect fewer than 1 percent of infants, are sometimes identified even before birth. Newborn screenings that test for certain genetic, endocrine, and metabolic disorders, as well as for hearing loss and critical congenital heart defects, are provided for millions of US babies prior to hospital discharge each year. Low birthweight, premature birth, multiple births, and infections during pregnancy, all factors known at birth, put babies at higher risk for developmental disabilities.

Some developmental disabilities will become evident later. Some toddlers will not develop language fluency, which is a sign of possible developmental disorders, but this is usually identified only after age two.

Children with autism spectrum disorders (ASD) have significant impairments in both language and social skills that may not be identified until later toddlerhood or even after age three.

You will see many developmental differences among babies, including those listed below. Some babies will show some of these characteristics even if they do not have a specific diagnosis. Keep these issues in mind so you are prepared to meet a diverse range of babies' needs and possibly help family members get their baby a diagnosis.

Late-talking toddlers (9 percent of young children) talk substantially later than their peers but eventually catch up. Their language delays can leave toddlers frustrated when they try to communicate, holding back their social skills, interactions with peers, and emotion and behavior regulation. It is often impossible to tell whether a toddler's language delay is temporary or a sign of a more pervasive disorder, so seek additional support.

Flat head syndrome or deformational plagiocephaly (22 percent of babies at seven weeks; 3 percent at two years) occurs when babies spend too much time lying in the same position (before or after birth), putting uneven pressure on their head. To prevent it after birth, make sure nonmobile infants switch positions regularly, get carried, and spend time lying on their tummies. To treat it, infants wear a corrective helmet or headband for three to six months.

Sensory processing disorder (5 percent of young children) is either over- or undersensitivity to sensations that gets in the way of a baby's functioning. Symptoms include extreme sensitivity and reactions to loud sounds (a leaf blower or blender), textures of food or clothes, or bright colors or lights. Symptoms can also involve *not* responding to sensations such as extreme heat or cold. Babies with sensory processing disorders often have difficulties with change or anything that's unpredictable. They may respond with loud and persistent crying or tantrums. These babies may seem fussy, but if their needs are not met, their sensitivities can lead to more anxiety later in life. Work with parents to identify a baby's unique sensitivities to maximize their comfort and minimize their stress.

Hearing impairment (1.4 percent of screened babies; 5 percent of children over age three) includes temporary loss from frequent ear infections, called otitis media, that inflame the middle ear. Signs of ear infections include fussiness, intense crying, pulling the ear, wincing in pain, losing balance, ear drainage, and poor hearing. Identifying a baby's hearing loss and understanding whether it is permanent or temporary enables family and educators to get help from pediatricians or other specialists, such as audiologists, in supporting the baby's language development. Decisions should be made early about using speech or signing so babies can start receiving language input as soon as possible.

Visual impairment (3 percent of children) includes vision loss, amblyopia (lazy eye) and other vision problems. When vision problems aren't corrected, opportunities for important neural connections may be lost. If a baby shows signs of not seeing well, help the family get a professional visual assessment.

Autism spectrum disorder (ASD; 1 to 2 percent of children) is a developmental disorder that affects social and communication skills. The effects can include difficulty communicating and interacting with others, having a restricted range of interests (such as only playing with one type of toy), and exhibiting repetitive behaviors. The signs of ASD, often delays in language or communication, usually become clearer in the second year of life. You may see early signs in atypical interactions (lack of joint attention, reluctance to look at others' faces, lack of response to one's name) and eating (extreme sensitivity to food textures, limited food options).

Fetal alcohol syndrome disorder (FAS; 1 percent of babies) encompasses a range of developmental problems related to prenatal alcohol exposure. Specific problems may include facial deformities, developmental delays, learning disabilities, neurological problems, and emotional or behavioral problems. No level of prenatal alcohol exposure is known to be safe.

Down syndrome (under 1 percent) is a chromosomal abnormality more common in babies of older mothers. Babies with Down syndrome often have low muscle tone that affects their overall physical development and may make eating and speaking difficult. Down syndrome is associated with cognitive delays, though these may not be apparent in young infants.

Cerebral palsy (under 1 percent) is the most common developmental motor disability. Signs include problems with movement, balance, posture, and muscle tone. Risks include prematurity, birth complications, or maternal infection.

Cleft palate (under 1 percent) is a split in a baby's upper lip and sometimes the roof of the mouth (palate) that can create problems with swallowing, latching on to the bottle or breast, and speech development.

Cystic fibrosis (under 1 percent) is a genetic disorder that impacts the respiratory, digestive, and excretory systems and includes an enlarged heart, increased chance of clubbed fingers and toes, asthma-like symptoms, excessive sweating, excessive mucus in the lungs, and foul-smelling bowel movements.

Brachial plexus (under 1 percent) is paralysis or weakness of the shoulder, forearm, hand, and finger muscles, often due to birth complications. By a few months of age, if the nerves are still damaged, the collarbone on the injured side will grow forward, making the two shoulders look lopsided.

Spina bifida (under 1 percent) is a neural tube defect that happens during pregnancy, exposing the spine and resulting in excessive fluid in the brain, lower extremity paralysis or weakness, and learning disabilities. Maternal obesity and low folic acid are risks for spina bifida.

Awareness of early intervention service models and Individualized Family Services Plans (INC-K5)

Developmentally supportive interactions with families and **developmental generalists** (who understand all domains of development and learning processes), within a natural and inclusive environment, are the most effective early intervention for most babies with developmental delays. Of course, some babies also need specialized support, such as those with sensory or motor impairments. Babies with visual impairments may have an orientation and mobility specialist. Babies with cerebral palsy may have a physical therapist or occupational therapist, teaching everyone involved how to best position and handle the baby. Families and generalists work together to understand the baby's overall development and incorporate specific recommendations from other professionals (such as a physical therapist) into daily activities.

Early intervention services are planned by a multidisciplinary team, including the family, that develops an **Individualized Family Service Plan (IFSP)**. This team could include an audiologist, family therapist, nurse, occupational therapist, orientation and mobility specialist, physical therapist, psychologist, registered dietician, social worker, special educator, speech and language pathologist, or vision specialist. One team member, often the developmental generalist, may be appointed as the service coordinator to manage service implementation. An IFSP is developed for each eligible child and their family, and family members are involved each step of the way, from initial assessment through program implementation and transition planning. Parental consent is necessary before any assessment or service can be provided.

The IFSP describes the baby's current strengths and needs; services that will be provided; and major outcomes expected; as well as dates for the initiation, length, frequency, and duration of services. Developing and implementing an IFSP is an ongoing process. Plans for transitioning the child, at age three, from early intervention to preschool services must be made at least six months before the toddler's third birthday.

Each child's IFSP is required to include the following:

⁖ **People and organizations involved:** who provides services, who pays, where services occur

* **Current levels of functioning:** medical, sensory, and developmental assessments

* **Family information:** priorities, concerns, strengths, needs

* **Services:** type and frequency recommended, how they'll be evaluated

* **Outcomes:** developmental goals that are short-term, relevant, specific, measurable

Awareness of roles and responsibilities in identification, evaluation, and treatment processes (INC-K6)

As part of the intervention team, you remain responsible for providing high-quality care and education services. As more assessment data become available and, possibly, a specific diagnosis is made, you will be part of the team that designs the IFSP. You may need to find information about specific practices that will be most effective for this baby, arrange times to collaborate with other service providers, and make adjustments to the physical space or daily schedule of activities to accommodate special interventions. You will need to communicate with family members and service providers to implement the IFSP and monitor the baby's progress.

You are not alone in this process. Start learning about local and state resources and service providers even before you meet an individual child with a disability. Find out who administers early intervention programs in your state and community, who performs initial assessments and delivers services, and what is entailed in local procedures for information exchange and ensuring confidentiality. When you become part of an IFSP team, you will need to learn about specific services the child and family are receiving, who is responsible for each, and who is the service coordinator monitoring the IFSP.

Your competencies for partnering with and supporting families are crucial to working effectively with babies with delays or disabilities. You need to understand the roles, responsibilities, and rights of families, caregivers, and others on the IFSP team so you can guide families through the process of screening, referral, assessment, evaluation, IFSP planning, and monitoring IFSP implementation and child progress. The steps in the diagnosis and treatment process are summarized in table 8.1.

Table 8.1 Diagnosis and Treatment Process: Family Rights, Practitioner Responsibilities

	Goal	Family rights	Professional's role
Step 1: Screening	To identify babies with signs of possible delay or disability and refer them for further assessment.	To be notified in writing a reasonable amount of time before any evaluation is conducted on their child.	To explain the purpose and process of screening and its results.
Step 2: Referral	To have a child with a suspected delay or disability assessed by appropriate professional(s) for a diagnosis.	To be fully informed of family rights under early intervention in their own language in a way they understand.	To explain the process, explain the family's rights, and ensure that they understand.
Step 3: Assessment	To determine whether a child meets the criteria for the diagnosis of a specific disability or current developmental functioning.	To understand the available information and consent in writing before the initial evaluation and assessment of their child, and to understand that their child will not be able to receive the evaluation and assessment without consent.	To explain the family's rights and guide their decision about consent.
Step 4: Evaluation	To determine eligibility for Part C services in the state where the child lives.	To receive a written explanation of why the child is considered eligible for disability services, the family's right to dispute eligibility, and the process for disputing the child's eligibility.	To explain the family's rights and guide their decision about disputing the determination.
Step 5: IFSP	To describe recommended plans for early intervention services appropriate for the child's delay or disability.	To have an IFSP within 45 days of referral, to understand the IFSP and consent to recommended services, to understand the services available, to understand that parent consent is required to receive services, and to fully participate in and invite others to all IFSP meetings.	To explain family's rights, guide their decision about services for their child, and provide information for the IFSP planning process.
Step 6: Monitoring	To monitor the child's and family's progress, strengths, and needs, and review the IFSP at least every six months.	To have the child receive services in the natural environment of home or community settings, to examine all IFSP documents and relevant records, and to have all identifying information remain confidential.	To implement aspects of the IFSP, explain the family's rights, and inform their decisions.

Knowledge of local, regional, and state services for babies with delays or disabilities and their families (INC-K7)

Each state is different. Learn about the agencies in your state that serve families of babies with additional support needs and the resources in your community. Answers to these questions may help you feel more prepared and confident:

* What state entity implements IDEA Part C?

* Which agencies do comprehensive evaluations to identify disabilities?

* Who monitors Individual Family Service Plans?

* What are local support groups for families of children with disabilities?

* Which parks have playground equipment for children with physical disabilities?

* Which theaters have sensory-friendly movie events for children with autism spectrum disorders or sensory processing disorders?

Awareness of how families may respond to information about a baby's delay or disability (INC-K8)

You may be the first professional to identify a developmental concern; this means you may be the first to communicate these concerns to the baby's family. You will need to support family members throughout the identification and intervention process. It is not unusual for a parent to react negatively when hearing concerns about their baby's development. Each family has a dream for their child, for who they will become as they grow. This dream must often be adjusted as families learn about a baby's diagnosis and grapple with a new reality.

Some parents may display negative emotions, deny the information, or question your knowledge and judgment. Other parents may feel reassured that a professional confirms their own concerns. Some may seek to understand why their child has a disability, or blame themselves or others. Some families engage in a prolonged search for the *right* diagnosis. Whatever the reaction, your role is to help them fully understand their baby's development, find information and resources, and plan for next steps. Keeping the focus on planning for the future is key. You can help families develop and reach new dreams for their children.

Dispositions

Certain ways of thinking about babies with additional support needs will help you be more effective in your work with them. These include positive attitudes focused on the strengths of the child and family (INC-D1), respect for the family (INC-D2), and a collaborative approach to working with families and with other professionals (INC-D3). These dispositions are based on professional ethics and values regarding diversity and inclusion, including those from NAEYC and DEC-CEC.

Commitment to a strength-based approach to working with babies with additional support needs (INC-D1)

Remember that a baby with additional support needs is first and foremost a baby, which is why early childhood professionals use person-first language, such as "a child with a disability" instead of "a disabled child." A strength-based approach respects every baby as a competent and eager learner who has the right to education and community engagement. We value the unique potential of each child to contribute meaning and richness to family life and a community of learning. Families always have strengths, and effective educators build on those strengths. Your competencies in guiding and supporting infants and toddlers are valuable strengths for helping families understand their babies' behaviors, develop realistic expectations, and support development.

Commitment to a family-centered approach to working with families of babies with additional support needs (INC-D2)

Value the strengths each family has to support their child's development and learning. Respect that the family is the prime influence on the baby and most responsible for their development. Demonstrate that you value families as experts on their own babies by asking questions about their baby, as well as their concerns, ideas, and values. Then use the information to engage families as collaborators in supporting the baby's development.

Openness to learning from others to meet babies' needs (INC-D3)

Being open to new information and new collaborations is critical. You cannot learn everything about all disabilities ahead of time, so you must keep learning from others as you go. You need to reflect on and acknowledge your own fears, uncertainties, and biases about interacting with and supporting babies with additional support needs and their families. Be willing to seek resources and work together with parents, who may know more than you do about their child's disability.

To work effectively with babies with additional support needs, practitioners must first be able to create an inclusive and accessible environment (INC-S1). They must use strength-based practices to adapt to specific learning needs (INC-S2) and to provide the supports each baby needs in the environment (INC-S3). Practitioners will use family-centered practices to help families support babies with additional support needs (INC-S4), which includes communicating to families about inclusion, assessment, individualization, and other related topics (INC-S5).

Creating an inclusive and accessible environment (INC-S1)

You are legally required to provide services in the **least restrictive environment**, meaning the environment must be as much as possible just like the environment for any other baby. To meet to the needs of babies with delays or disabilities, you may need to choose different materials and make adaptations to the environment to support and encourage their exploration and interactions.

STRATEGIES

Dolls with additional support needs

Books with braille and signs

※ Adapt the environment or remove barriers, such as securing rugs with loose edges, so each child can explore and interact with others. Adapt materials to make manipulation easier; for example, add larger wooden knobs or extended handles to toddler puzzle pieces or add extenders to board book pages to make page turning more accessible. Add supports that help a baby sit up or move around. Consider consulting with physical therapists or occupational therapists about adapting existing toys and materials to increase accessibility.

※ Reflect positive images of diverse babies and families—in posters, photos, books, toys, and other materials—including children and adults with additional support needs.

※ Plan ahead to include everyone in classroom activities. The concept of universal design means that educators use materials and create experiences that are the most accessible for the most children (Center for Universal Design 1997). Educators select materials and experiences that can be experienced in multiple ways. For example, toys and materials should include multiple types of sensory information (visual, sounds, textures) that can be used in different ways. Experiences such as singing together can include both auditory and visual information, such as a song with picture cards.

Using strength-based practices to adapt to specific learning needs (INC-S2)

Strength-based, person-centered practices begin with remembering to speak about a child as a baby, a toddler, or a child and not as a label for their diagnosis or condition. While many individuals prefer person-first language (for example, a child with autism spectrum disorder rather than an autistic child), it is best not to make assumptions. For example, some individuals with disabilities prefer identity-first language as they view their disability as an important part of their identity as a person and as part of a wider group of people. A strength-based approach also means setting **functional goals** that are useful in the baby's everyday life (for example, communicating using gestures is a more functional goal than building a tower with blocks). Observe what babies *can* do, and build on those strengths to help them reach the next step toward their functional goals. You can use strength-based strategies to support development and learning for babies with and without disabilities.

Two babies with the same diagnosis will still look, act, and interact in different ways. Some may have mild impairments, while others' may be more severe. You are probably already working with babies who have a wide range of developmental skills, from babies who cannot yet roll over or hold a bottle to young toddlers who can walk and feed themselves. Adapting to the additional support needs of a baby with a delay or disability requires the same careful observation, flexible planning, and individual attention that you already use with babies who are typically developing. But the need for individualization is especially critical; you must precisely know the skills and needs of each baby with a delay or disibility.

STRATEGIES

❋ Use the child's name when talking with families. Ask parents about their preferences for person-first or identity-first language. Ask parents about what they see and what works for them at home and what skills would make family routines easier.

❋ Join in play to observe the skills that work for this baby and the kinds of interactions and materials they seem most interested in. Ask their parents what they are most interested in at home. Adapt materials and activities to these skills and interests.

Supporting each baby to interact with and learn from the environment (INC-S3)

You already have skills for observing and reflecting on development, then planning, implementing, and evaluating supports through environments, materials, and interactions (chapter 6). You use the same strategies to support babies with additional support needs. Each step of the DR. PIE process of curriculum planning may be modified to provide specialized supports for babies with additional support needs.

STRATEGIES

Document: Watch closely to identify patterns in babies' nonverbal behaviors.

* Pay close attention to quiet babies and those who don't move around on their own; they may need the most support.

* Pay attention to how a baby shows their desire to interact or to move their body.

* Watch for clues of intentional communication—does a toddler with a severe delay show recognition of objects or people in any way, through a sound, movement, or gesture?

* Take careful notes about the contexts, people, and events that babies with delays respond to most.

Reflect: Understand babies' current and emerging skills in context.

* Focus on what the baby *can* do in each domain; identify their current and emerging skills without paying attention to the typical ages these skills emerge.

* Review your notes to make sure you observe quiet babies as often as others.

* Review your notes to find times when the baby seems most engaged and consider ways to increase these opportunities.

Plan: Create developmental and learning opportunities for functional goals.

* Focus on functional goals relevant to the baby's home and classroom contexts. Set goals by following these steps:

  • Ask about the family's goals for the baby and together choose one you can support at school.

  • Learn about the daily routines (at home or school) when opportunities for these behaviors would naturally occur.

- Conduct a **task analysis** by listing each small step and the specific behaviors and skills the baby would need to meet each step toward the goal.

- Identify the baby's current and emerging skills related to each step of the task analysis.

- Establish a series of learning objectives that would build the skills for the goal.

Implement: Flexibly and intentionally engage in developmentally supportive interactions.

❋ Work within the baby's daily routines as much as possible; create additional learning opportunities as needed.

❋ Actively initiate and sustain interactions with the baby, and between the baby and others. There is a balance to be learned over time—giving more directions might be necessary, but being too intrusive or forceful may overwhelm the child.

❋ Wait even longer than usual for a response from babies who need time to process sensory or communication input.

❋ Be as responsive as possible to every cue from the baby, with help from others as needed.

❋ Help other children and caregivers understand the baby's communication cues, language comprehension, and physical abilities, and demonstrate any effective strategies you have for interacting.

Evaluate: Identify small changes that indicate progress.

❋ Be realistic; it can take longer for babies with disabilities to reach goals.

❋ Celebrate small changes along the way.

❋ Communicate small successes with families and help them understand their significance.

Handout 8.1, Support Communication, gives information about planning interactions to support the communication skills of babies with delays.

www.redleafpress.org/wwb/8-1.pdf

Using family-centered practices to help families support babies with additional support needs (INC-S4)

Family-centered practices recommended for working with families of babies with disabilities are the same practices you should be using with all families,

Conlin's educators learn a lot about his communication and social skills as they watch Conlin interact with his family.

but they are even more crucial with these families. In early intervention, family-centered practice means putting the family literally at the center of interactions with the baby and figuratively at the heart of the intervention strategy. Focus on helping parents do their best for their babies. Your skills in family-centered practices will prepare you to help families understand their rights, assess their needs and goals, respond to families' priorities, collaborate to set functional goals for babies, and involve families in supporting their babies' development in the home and community. You are likely the professional who knows the baby and family best. You can help other professionals understand the baby's and family's strengths and what works for them.

STRATEGIES

✳ Show respect for parents (or other primary caregivers) by asking about their experience with their baby and what they have learned about their child's disability. Use this information to better adapt your classroom and curriculum for the baby.

✳ Avoid giving advice that is not requested.

✳ Observe parents' interactions with their babies and how they adapt to the baby's needs. Encourage their positive interactions and notice which interactions calm the baby or help the baby learn.

✳ Keep parents' needs in mind so that you support functional goals for the baby that are the most important to the family.

Communicating about inclusion, assessment, individualization, and related topics (INC-S5)

Your knowledge of assessing behavior, development, and learning environments is crucial for establishing eligibility, monitoring developmental progress, and modifying plans. When you are communicating with parents and other caregivers about these assessments, be both direct and empathic. Include time to learn what parents already know about their baby's behavior, prior assessments, or diagnoses. Help them understand new assessment results, next steps in the process, and their rights at each step. You will be partnering with parents, coordinating with early intervention specialists, and advocating for the child and family.

✳ Look up information so you can clearly explain assessment results, the IFSP process, available resources, and other helpful information for parents.

✳ Explain jargon words like *functional goals*, *inclusion*, or *task analysis*. Access the Key Terms via the QR code on page 11, and look up any other words as needed. These words may be familiar to you, but you are likely to need a clear way to explain them to parents.

Reflect Back, Think Ahead

Look back at the figure at the beginning of this chapter with the knowledge, disposition, and skill competencies involved in including infants and toddlers with additional support needs. Which of these competencies did you have when you began this chapter? Which competencies did you develop? Which competencies will you intentionally work on building for yourself next? Use the Including Infants and Toddlers with Special Needs chapter of the Professional Learning Guide (PLG [see page 11]) that accompanies this book to support your own professional growth in this domain.

Selected References

CDC (Centers for Disease Control and Prevention). 2019. "Increase in Developmental Disabilities among Children in the United States." CDC website. www.cdc.gov/ncbddd/developmentaldisabilities/features/increase-in-developmental-disabilities.html.

CDC (Centers for Disease Control and Prevention). 2020. "Facts about Developmental Disabilities." CDC website. www.cdc.gov/ncbddd/developmentaldisabilities/facts.html.

CDC (Centers for Disease Control and Prevention). 2020. "Newborn Screening Portal." CDC website. www.cdc.gov/newbornscreening.

Center for Universal Design. 1997. "The Principles of Universal Design." Version 2.0. Raleigh: North Carolina State University. https://projects.ncsu.edu/ncsu/design/cud/about_ud/udprinciplestext.htm.

DEC (Division for Early Childhood) and NAEYC (National Association for the Education of Young Children). 2009. "Early Childhood Inclusion: A Summary." A joint position statement of the Division for Early Childhood (DEC) and the National Association for the Education of Young Children (NAEYC). Chapel Hill: University of North Carolina, FPG Child Development Institute.

DEC (Division for Early Childhood). 2014. "DEC Recommended Practices in Early Intervention/Early Childhood Special Education 2014." DEC website. www.dec-sped.org/recommendedpractices.

Deiner, Penny Low. 2013. *Inclusive Early Childhood Education: Development, Resources and Practice*. 6th ed. Belmont, CA: Wadsworth Cengage Learning.

DHHS (US Department of Health and Human Services) and ED (US Department of Education). 2015. *Policy Statement on Inclusion of Children with Disabilities in Early Childhood Programs*. Washington, DC: US Departments of Health and Human Services and Education. www2.ed.gov/policy/speced/guid/early learning/joint-statement-full-text.pdf.

Peterson, Carla A., Shavaun Wall, Hyun-Joo Jeon, Mark E. Swanson, Judith J. Carta, Gayle J. Luze, and Elaine Eshbaugh. 2013. "Identification of Disabilities and Service Receipt among Preschool Children Living in Poverty." *Journal of Special Education* 47 (1): 28–40.

Peterson, Carla A., Shavaun Wall, Helen A. Raikes, Ellen E. Kisker, Mark E. Swanson, Judith Jerald, Jane B. Atwater, Wei Qiao. 2004. "Early Head Start: Identifying and Serving Children with Disabilities." *Topics in Early Childhood Special Education* 24 (2): 76–88.

Wolery, Mark, and Donald B. Bailey Jr. 2002. "Early Childhood Special Education Research." *Journal of Early Intervention* 25 (2): 88–99.

CHAPTER 9

Leadership, Mentoring, and Coaching

—with Julia Torquati

If you work with babies, you are working with other caregivers, including parents. In these professional relationships, you can provide leadership, mentoring, and coaching to help others develop competencies to support infant-toddler development. Together, you can reflect on the work you do, sharing clear communication and goals. Supervisors can use leadership, mentoring, and coaching to support the professional development of infant-toddler educators. Mentors and coaches who are not supervisors can sometimes be even more effective in supporting professional development. Leadership, mentoring, and coaching help ensure effectiveness, continuity, and ongoing improvement in services for babies and their families. The competencies for providing leadership, mentoring, and coaching are summarized in figure 9.1.

Why is this competency important? With this competency we *all* support others to develop and use the other eight competencies for working with babies. Supervisors, mentors, and coaches guide the professional development of practitioners. Educators and caregivers learn from each other, reflect together on their experiences, and encourage each other in working with babies and families. Educators can use coaching, mentoring, or parent workshops to build parents' competencies in supporting their babies' early development. Leadership—in many roles—contributes to a thriving organization of people who help each other do their best. Leaders promote others' recognition of the importance of the early years and the value and emotional labor of infant-toddler care. Every practitioner can be a leader in the field, whatever professional role they play, and they can often mentor others, including other practitioners and parents. In this chapter, we will use the term *leader* to mean someone who is working within an organization, often a supervisor, to support both the program and the competencies of those who implement it. Some leaders are mentors and coaches, inside or outside of the organization, with specific roles focused on

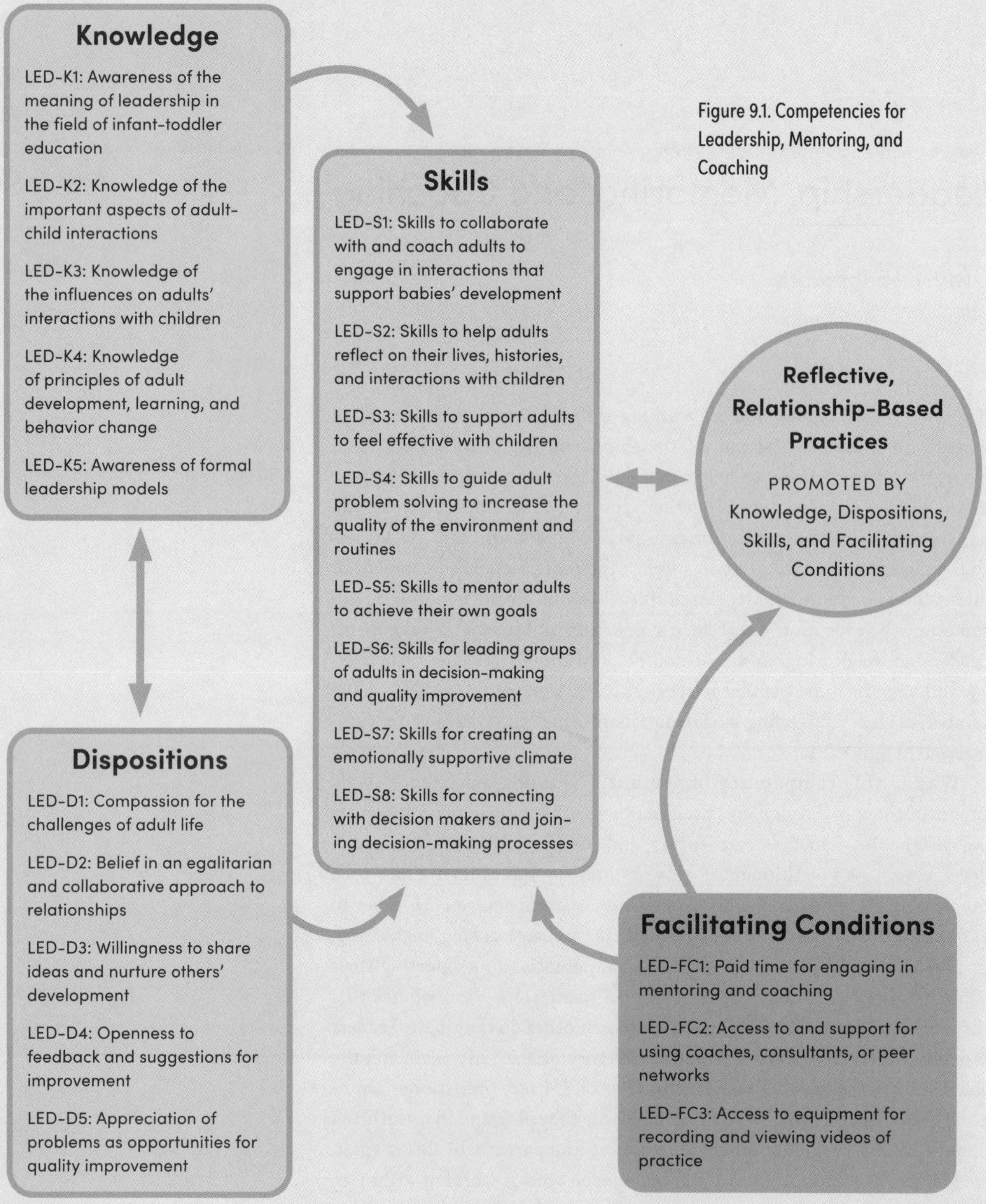

Knowledge

LED-K1: Awareness of the meaning of leadership in the field of infant-toddler education

LED-K2: Knowledge of the important aspects of adult-child interactions

LED-K3: Knowledge of the influences on adults' interactions with children

LED-K4: Knowledge of principles of adult development, learning, and behavior change

LED-K5: Awareness of formal leadership models

Skills

LED-S1: Skills to collaborate with and coach adults to engage in interactions that support babies' development

LED-S2: Skills to help adults reflect on their lives, histories, and interactions with children

LED-S3: Skills to support adults to feel effective with children

LED-S4: Skills to guide adult problem solving to increase the quality of the environment and routines

LED-S5: Skills to mentor adults to achieve their own goals

LED-S6: Skills for leading groups of adults in decision-making and quality improvement

LED-S7: Skills for creating an emotionally supportive climate

LED-S8: Skills for connecting with decision makers and joining decision-making processes

Figure 9.1. Competencies for Leadership, Mentoring, and Coaching

Reflective, Relationship-Based Practices

PROMOTED BY Knowledge, Dispositions, Skills, and Facilitating Conditions

Dispositions

LED-D1: Compassion for the challenges of adult life

LED-D2: Belief in an egalitarian and collaborative approach to relationships

LED-D3: Willingness to share ideas and nurture others' development

LED-D4: Openness to feedback and suggestions for improvement

LED-D5: Appreciation of problems as opportunities for quality improvement

Facilitating Conditions

LED-FC1: Paid time for engaging in mentoring and coaching

LED-FC2: Access to and support for using coaches, consultants, or peer networks

LED-FC3: Access to equipment for recording and viewing videos of practice

promoting the competencies of other adults. As you read this chapter, ask yourself these questions:

❋ How do I help other adults develop their skills in supporting babies' development?

❋ What do I look for in leaders, mentors, and coaches?

How are leadership, mentoring, and coaching related to other competencies? In this book, you have learned about knowledge, dispositions, and skills that promote high-quality reflective practices with babies and their families. As you will learn in the final chapter of this book, the professionalization of the field and the quality of reflective practices depend heavily on the leadership, mentoring, and coaching efforts that promote the knowledge, dispositions, and skills of educators. Leaders, mentors, and coaches inspire, guide, and skillfully support the development of educators in a variety of ways, such as creating a positive climate for growth and helping educators develop and meet goals in their work. And educators become leaders—formally or informally—as they master competencies and begin to mentor other adults in those competencies.

Facilitating conditions. Programs must provide resources for any leadership model to work, including paid time for engaging in mentoring and coaching (LED-FC1), access to and support for using coaches, consultants, or peer networks (LED-FC2), and access to equipment and support for recording and viewing videos of practice (LED-FC3).

Knowledge

To be an effective leader of your peers and other adults, you need to understand the meaning of leadership in infant-toddler education (LED-K1). You need to know which adult-child interactions are best for babies' development (LED-K2), what influences adults as they interact with babies (LED-K3), and how adults can learn to work well with babies (LED-K4). You will want to become familiar with models for supporting competencies in adults (LED-K5).

Awareness of the meaning of leadership in the field of infant-toddler education (LED-K1)

Leadership is influence. It is a way of inspiring and motivating others to do their best work. Leaders set the tone for open and creative conversations about best practices and practical solutions to common problems. Leaders facilitate learning and development and recognize ways to collaborate and learn from others to improve the quality of care. A leader is a vision holder who can see a theory of change—the goals we are aiming for, the strategies for getting there, and the reasons we believe we will be effective—in the details of everyday work. Leaders point out connections between what we believe is important for babies and what we are *actually* doing and why. Leaders create positive working environments by being responsive to diverse languages and cultures among workers and families, providing information and guidance to people inside and outside the program, and connecting with other organizations and systems. What does it mean to show leadership, regardless of which position you are in professionally? Here are seven characteristics of leadership:

* **Share the vision:** A leader helps you "keep your eye on the prize," focused on what is important. Ultimately the development and well-being of babies is the prize for our work. Reminding each other can help us keep our focus.

* **Set clear goals:** Goals should be specific and concrete, or we won't know if we are close to reaching them. Leaders clarify goals, help us track progress, and tell us when we are getting closer.

* **Adapt and innovate:** Regulations, health concerns, safety issues, nutrition, technology, and our everyday lives all keep changing. Leaders help us adapt and explore new ways to move toward our goals. At the same time, remember that babies need continuity and consistency more than ever when things are changing.

* **Coordinate systems:** Leaders help people solve problems together across levels within an organization and between organizations in the community.

* **Know who the decision makers are:** Leaders keep track of the people who make decisions on policies, practices, and priorities. Inside programs, we are all decision makers. If those who must implement a decision do not agree with it, the decision is unlikely to lead to positive change. Strong leaders convince and inspire us to make good decisions.

* **Share achievements:** Leaders talk about *us* instead of *me*. They know that important accomplishments take more than one person. They share their pride and are quick to point to the contributions of others.

* **Support others:** Leaders use reflective practice to help others develop their competencies to work with babies. They recognize how adults learn and how life experiences and mental health influence their interactions with babies and with other adults.

Knowledge of the important aspects of adult-child interactions (LED-K2)

Adult-child interactions are critical for early development, so leaders find ways to support positive adult-child relationships. You need to know best practices for *how* adults should interact with babies and *why* those things are important so that you can explain them to others. It helps if you can frame these aspects and your feedback positively—what *to* do, rather than what *not* to do. This knowledge is reflected in the other chapters of this book. Leaders must be sensitive to the fact that working with babies can be emotionally challenging for both educators and parents. Leaders create a way of talking about babies and families reflectively, positively, empathetically, and developmentally, using words reflecting the competencies in this book. Further, leaders talk about other adults (colleagues, parents) in strength-based ways, just like they talk about babies.

The tools that assess program quality provide a framework for understanding what quality adult-child interactions should look like; these are tools such as the Toddler CLASS, Program Quality Assessment (PQA), The Pyramid Infant-Toddler Observation Scale (TPITOS), or the Quality of Caregiver-Child Interactions for Infants and Toddlers (Q-CCIIT). Each tool has its own focus and framework for understanding what quality is, but each includes the important aspects of interactions that we know affect babies' well-being and development.

Knowledge of the influences on adults' interactions with children (LED-K3)

When you are supporting other adults in their work with babies, consider what might be influencing their interactions, including their histories and current stresses. You may not be aware of a colleague's or parent's personal history or everything going on in their life. Being aware of the types of things that might influence them can help you pause before making assumptions or judgments. You may take a more empathic and supportive perspective.

Early life experiences affect caregiving. Critical things happen in our early years, and even if we don't remember them, they can influence us for the rest of our lives. Influences on babies' behavior and development continue to have an impact as they become children, teenagers, and eventually, parents and educators of another generation. When babies experience trauma, loss, chronic stress, or maltreatment, they are more likely to have lifelong health, developmental, behavioral, and social problems. Early trauma or erratic caregiving can lead to problems in relationships, difficulty trusting or taking care of others, difficulty establishing and maintaining long-term relationships, or difficulty caring for a baby. Babies can be irritating and frustrating for anyone, but for some, the piercing cry of a colicky baby can bring up strong negative emotions tied to our past experiences and current state of mind. Those with a history of adversity or mental health challenges may find it especially difficult to handle the emotional demands of infants and toddlers.

Current stressors and mental health influence adult-child interactions. Factors that affect a family's life and parents' stress, well-being, and mental health (such as not having enough money, housing instability, or changes in family structure) influence how they interact with their children, and these same things influence how practitioners interact with babies. Depression and anxiety can reduce empathy, sensitivity, and warmth and interfere with an adult's ability to regulate their emotions and respond positively to a baby.

Babies influence their own care! Babies' temperaments, communication skills, needs, and other characteristics all influence the way adults interact with them. This can be good when adults are sensitive and responsive to babies' differences, because they adjust their caregiving to each baby's needs. But when adults are stressed, these individual differences can pose an added challenge, and some adult-baby dyads (pairs) may struggle more than others with their goodness of fit. While we never blame babies for adults' caregiving challenges, and we want every baby to be cared for in the best way for him or her, we should still be sympathetic to parents or practitioners who struggle with the needs or personalities of certain babies.

Supports and resources. Everyone who cares for babies sometimes finds it difficult to regulate their emotions. Support from leaders, mentors, and coaches can help caregivers reflect on their emotions, learn skills for self-regulation, practice mindfulness, and increase their empathy. These skills help people with current stresses or a history of adversity care for babies more responsively and engage in positive relationships with families and with other professionals.

Knowledge of principles of adult development, learning, and behavior change (LED-K4)

Learning is lifelong. As an educator, you are constantly expanding your knowledge and skills to improve your work with babies and their families. You are always learning from children, and from families and colleagues too. Many infant-toddler programs are **two-generation programs** that support both parent development and child development. As you read these principles of adult learning in figure 9.2, remember how these also apply to babies.

Adults learn best when we can help them do the following:

Set their own goals. Adults learn best by exploring what they find interesting and using what they know to learn more. Self-selected learning goals connect to adults' real problems in their everyday lives. Some adults need guidance to learn to set their own goals. However, adults learn better when their goals are their own.

Link their learning to what they know. We need to see how new concepts relate to the knowledge and skills we already have. One tool is **advance organizers**, such as a list previewing the main ideas to be learned, a chart showing the parts of the information to come, or a short story or example from a familiar situation. Advance organizers provide an adult learner with a framework for understanding what they are about to hear, which helps them link it to what they already know. For example, when teaching about infant temperament, we might start by asking educators to describe what they have noticed about babies' personalities and then reflect on patterns across babies and across contexts (for example, common patterns in how babies respond to daily transitions in the classroom). This sets up a framework for thinking about ways educators might adapt the environment to support different temperament styles.

Figure 9.2. Principles of Adult Learning Guide How Leaders Support Them

Adults . . .		So we . . .
. . . have a lifetime of learning and experience	→	. . . link new knowledge to what they already know . . . link new skills to what they can already do
. . . have knowledge and skills about their child, family, and parenting	→	. . . respect their expertise by adapting information to their knowledge, skills, and interests
. . . develop in multiple domains that influence each other	→	. . . provide open-ended materials in multiple formats, including visual, auditory, sensory modes that allow exploration of ideas in many ways
. . . are motivated to actively explore and learn about things relevant to their lives	→	. . . follow their lead to adapt to their interests and motivation . . . encourage them to set goals and try new things . . . support their autonomy in learning
. . . learn in social contexts where they feel respected	→	. . . collaborate and learn together, reflecting on our shared experiences with babies
. . . learn from all of their experiences, but some experiences are better than others	→	. . . engage together as collaborative partners in activities that support adult development and increase self-efficacy

Engage with materials and process. Just like babies, adults learn best from hands-on experiences that apply to their everyday lives. For example, playing with playdough while discussing ways to use it to support language and fine-motor skills in a toddler classroom is more engaging and more effective than hearing a lecture about it.

Apply their learning in their everyday lives. Adults want to use what they learn today for something useful tomorrow. They want to know when and where they will be able to use what they learn. They want to solve a problem. They may need guidance for planning the actions steps to use what they have learned.

Get support to apply their learning in their work. Adults need support to integrate what they learn into working with babies. They may need reminders, encouragement, coaching, and time to reflect so they can apply what they learned.

Support one another. Adult learners can help one another learn and apply what they are learning. Collaborative learning helps make learning more meaningful and sustainable. It establishes a culture of working together that improves the quality of care and support for babies and families.

Get feedback from observations of their work with babies. Educators can review and reflect on their work with a leader, supervisor, or coach, or observe themselves by watching a video showing them applying what they have learned. To make this a supportive experience, practitioners can take the lead in seeking feedback; specifically they can describe their goals (things they are working to improve) and invite their colleagues or leaders to give them feedback and ideas. In chapter 7 on assessing behavior and development, we talked about the importance of using a strength-based approach in assessing babies and communicating with parents. A strength-based approach is also vital when mentoring adult learners. Focusing on the positive and building from there helps build confidence and also makes it more likely that the person will hear what you are saying. A strength-based approach is more effective than a critical stance, talking about what the person is not doing well.

Awareness of formal leadership models (LED-K5)

Professionals in the early childhood field use several leadership models to support one another. Each model works well in certain situations or for certain individuals. Educators may experience one or more of these leadership models as practitioners, and as you develop as a professional, you may be drawn to become a mentor, supervisor, or coach yourself.

Reflective supervision is a process of collaborative reflection that occurs regularly between one or more practitioners and a supervisor. The process of reflective supervision involves three things:

* Reflection—trust, listening, asking, empathy

* Collaboration—open, bi-directional, sharing power

* Regularity—time, availability, dependability, flexibility

Reflective supervision requires time for reflection, to think about our experiences with babies and their families and our feelings. With time, we understand our emotions better, practice strategies for better regulating strong negative emotions, and see a broader perspective that includes other people's experiences and emotions. Reflective practice can buffer some of the stress of working with babies. Educators who become mentors, leaders, and coaches also benefit from reflective supervision, as they too need a space in which to reflect on their work. When leaders, mentors, and coaches receive reflective supervision, they are better able to use relationship-based practices with educators, who can then better support babies and families through reflective practice (see chapter 2). Working with educators in the same relationship-based manner we want them to use with babies and families is called *parallel process*. We want caregivers to interact with babies warmly, sensitively, and encouragingly, parallel to how we want caregivers to interact with each other and leaders, mentors, and coaches to interact with educators.

Mentoring is a one-on-one, long-term relationship that supports a person's development. Mentoring relationships offer ongoing support by encouraging, informing, coaching, guiding, inspiring, and collaborating. Usually a mentor has more experience but not always more authority. Particularly in the infant-toddler workforce, where there is little consistency in the education and experience one needs to be a lead teacher, two individuals with vastly different training and experience may work together in the same role. Effective mentoring relationships have the following qualities:

* **Relationship-based.** Trust and openness are necessary for mentoring. A mentor with no authority over raises or promotions may offer a more comfortable relationship.

* **Ongoing.** Mentoring relationships continue with regular, dependable meeting times. Goals and topics change over time as the mentee develops professionally.

* **Reflective.** Mentoring relationships usually include self-assessment and self-observation that can be discussed openly and reflectively with the mentor.

* **Goal-oriented.** The mentor and mentee collaborate to identify goals, plan steps to reach those goals, and watch for signs of progress.

* **Informed by observation.** Observation and descriptive feedback guide reflective discussions. These discussions are a key aspect of coaching often incorporated into mentoring relationships.

Coaching is a specific strategy, often part of mentoring, that follows a cycle. Coaches facilitate adult learning by observing skills, providing descriptive feedback, guiding goal setting, providing information, and encouraging practice. Coaching helps adult learners, including peers or parents, develop competence and confidence in supporting babies' development. Coaching adult learners is experiential, practical, and based on current skill and expertise. A coach observes carefully to identify current strengths that can be expanded, describing positive adult-child interactions, guiding educators to see why quality interactions matter to the baby's development, or discussing ways to expand on those strengths. For example, a caregiver who talks well with toddlers but not with nonverbal babies can be coached to observe, recognize, and respond out loud to a baby's body language.

Dispositions

Leaders, mentors, and coaches—whether in formal or informal positions—must have compassion for the life challenges educators have experienced (LED-D1). They take an egalitarian and collaborative approach to relationships, rather than seeing themselves as superior in their abilities (LED-D2). Likewise, they are willing to share their own ideas (LED-D3) and are open to suggestions to improve their work as leaders (LED-D4). Finally, effective leaders, mentors, and coaches view problems as opportunities for their own development (LED-D5). Growing in these dispositions as a practitioner is a way to become a leader in the field, whether or not you have an official title or role as a leader, mentor, or coach.

Compassion for the challenges of adult life (LED-D1)

It can be hard to feel compassion for adults, especially if they act in ways that might hurt or fail to support a child. But caregiving is more difficult when an adult is experiencing depression or anxiety or coping with the influences of earlier life experiences. When we reflect with compassion, we can consider reasons why adults react the way they do. For example, a struggle at pickup might conclude with the mother carrying out her screaming child, perhaps because the mother is stressed, in a hurry, overwhelmed with responsibilities, or embarrassed. By wondering about the mother's thoughts and feelings, we can find ways to be supportive without being critical.

Belief in an egalitarian and collaborative approach to relationships (LED-D2)

Practitioners, parents, and other caregivers learn best when they collaborate and feel respected as equals. They develop more knowledge and skills when everyone is equally welcome to share ideas and reflections. This assumption of **mutual competence**—that each person has something valuable to offer to the relationship—is a foundation for strong leadership, mentoring, and coaching.

Willingness to share ideas and nurture others' development (LED-D3)

Sharing your ideas will help you build collaborative professional relationships. New educators have ideas, reflections, and insights to share with more experienced educators. Ask other educators to share their thoughts about a situation and to reflect with you on possible responses. Listen well and connect their ideas to your own reflections. A willingness to share as equal partners is valuable no matter how much experience you have or whether you are a leader, mentor, or coach or an educator.

Openness to feedback and suggestions for improvement (LED-D4)

It takes openness and reflective skills to be able to hear feedback and not get defensive or feel criticized. Listen to feedback with curiosity and an open mind, imagining what it would be like if you did things a little differently. When you find yourself becoming defensive or resisting change, ask yourself why you feel that way.

Appreciation of problems as opportunities for quality improvement (LED-D5)

When something is not working and babies are fussing and caregivers are stressed, it is a time to reflect on what might be going on. Ask an educator, caregiver, or parent their ideas about what is happening and what you can do about it. What might be going on? Is it a problem with the timing or pace of routines, with group dynamics, or with something related to family stress? Think of these problems as opportunities in disguise for improving quality of care.

You need leadership skills when mentoring or coaching, engaging in group decision-making with small groups (for example, two coeducators figuring out what to do in their classroom) or in larger groups, inside or outside of a single program or organization. Leaders, mentors, and coaches must have the skills to effectively collaborate with and coach educators in their work (LED-S1). They must skillfully help adults to reflect on their lives, histories, and interactions that promote babies' development (LED-S2), to feel effective in their work with children (LED-S3), and to problem solve to increase classroom quality (LED-S4). And they need skills to actively promote professional development. Specifically, leaders, mentors, and coaches mentor adults in setting and achieving their goals (LED-S5), lead groups of adults in decision-making and ongoing quality improvement (LED-S6), and create an emotionally supportive climate (LED-S7). Leaders, mentors, and coaches have opportunities to impact the field beyond any one program. Hence, they need the skills to connect with decision makers in the program, the community, and at the state level (LED-S8).

Mr. Jung supports Lily's development through pretend play while his coach observes to give feedback on the skills Mr. Jung wants to develop.

Collaborating with and coaching adults to engage in interactions that support babies' development (LED-S1)

Leadership, mentoring, and coaching require collaboration skills, working with others as equals and sharing your ideas while giving equal attention and credit to others' ideas. Coaching requires specific collaboration skills to set goals together, observe strengths, give feedback, share reflections, offer encouragement, provide information, and update goals as needed.

These skills are parallel to those used to support babies in the cycle of documenting, reflecting, planning, implementing, and evaluating. Likewise, it is important to take a strength-based approach to this process. However, in this case, you are including the adult (a colleague or the baby's parent) in your reflections together, and they will implement the plans. Let the adult being observed determine when you will observe, what kinds of behaviors or practices you will focus on, and how they like to get feedback. Frame your feedback around babies' needs and interests, rather than adults' behaviors and practices, to take the pressure off. For example, instead of asking, "What do you want to improve?" ask, "What are babies doing and learning that you would like to be able to support?"

STRATEGIES

- Work with the person being coached to identify meaningful, achievable, specific goals. For example, a goal could be to respond more quickly to infant communication cues or to use more descriptive words when talking with toddlers.

- Observe the practitioner carefully, using an assessment of skills for working with babies, to identify their strengths and challenges.

- Provide detailed positive feedback, describing what the educator did, how the child or children responded, and how it matters to children's development.

- Encourage the person being coached to expand specific strengths to more situations and more babies, more of the time.

- Provide individualized information about similar strategies and their links to child development and well-being.

- Reflect together on how the coaching and observation experience went.

- Update goals together in a continuous coaching cycle.

Helping adults reflect on their lives, histories, and interactions with children (LED-S2)

When you have engaged in reflective practice and gained an understanding of your own reactions (see chapter 2), you can expand these skills by inviting others to reflect with you. By asking good questions, listening well, and reflecting back what you hear, you can help adults engage in reflective practice. When adults hear their own messages summarized and reflected back to them, they can clarify for themselves how they feel about a situation. It also helps them feel understood, which can make it easier for them to gain insights.

STRATEGIES

* Ask about adults' mental state behind their behaviors ("What was going through your mind during that situation?" or "What were you feeling in your body during that interaction?").

* Ask open-ended questions or use "I wonder" statements ("It seems like that was a really hard transition. I wonder what was going on for you").

* Listen carefully and follow up with related questions to get more information ("You used the word 'tough.' What does that word mean to you?").

* Use **active listening** skills to summarize the other person's words, reflecting back what you heard ("So it sounds like you felt nervous because it seemed like you lost control of the situation, and it was hard to get back into being playful").

Supporting adults so they feel effective with children (LED-S3)

Feeling competent (self-efficacy) in caring for and educating babies is important for both educators and parents. It helps them remain calm and open, and they respond to babies more authentically. Promote self-efficacy in educators and parents by increasing their confidence in caring for and teaching babies.

STRATEGIES

* Describe others' positive interactions with babies. For example, comment on a baby's positive reaction to something new an educator is trying.

* Acknowledge others' knowledge and abilities with appreciation.

* Offer opportunities for others to use their strong skills. For example, an educator who is particularly skilled in a certain area could be invited to help other educators with this skill or lead a discussion about the skill during a professional development event.

Guiding adult problem solving to increase the quality of the environment and routines (LED-S4)

Guide problem solving and encourage creative ideas. For example, when discussing a problem of toddlers running through a classroom, one educator said jokingly that they should put up road barriers, spurring a coeducator to add that it could be an obstacle course. These ideas sounded silly at first, but they led the educators to rearrange their room to block the runway with obstacles. The effect was to slow down the toddlers, leading them to engage in more social interaction.

STRATEGIES

* When problem solving with another adult, first define the problem together, then generate as many possible solutions as you can. Only then should you talk about the strengths and limitations of each idea.

* Discuss each idea in detail. Consider reasons why an idea may not work and think of ways it could work. Engage together with curiosity ("I really wonder if this could work!").

* When a possible solution seems like it could be useful, decide together when and how to try it out, how long to try it, how to tell if it is working, and when to decide whether to keep using it.

* Try out the idea and see if it works. Whether or not the initial idea is fully successful, consider what you learned. Then decide whether to continue with that idea, make adjustments, or try another idea altogether.

Mentoring adults to achieve their own goals (LED-S5)

Focus on the educator's or parent's own goals for their work with babies, because adults learn best when they are self-directed and their goals are self-selected. Effective mentors help another adult choose goals that are achievable—things they can change or learn in a fairly short time, such as helping a baby sleep—but linked to their long-term professional or personal goals, such as becoming a child care consultant or reducing family stress. Whether you are a mentor or mentee, paid time for engaging in mentoring and coaching supports this skill (LED-FC1).

❊ Work with an educator or parent to reflect on what is important for them to learn.

❊ Help them define their goal in an achievable way. A goal of being better at working with babies is too broad, a goal of supporting early language development is too general, but a goal of using more words to label what a baby is touching or looking at is specific, observable, and achievable.

Leading groups of adults in decision-making and quality improvement (LED-S6)

Good leaders help groups make good decisions and do high-quality work, giving and receiving feedback and engaging others in open, collaborative discussions. Everyone is invited to share with open-ended questions and follow-ups. Leaders guide problem solving and decision-making that involves all stakeholders. This entails involving everyone who has a stake in the decision and making sure that everyone has a chance to share their ideas. It is easy for a few enthusiastic voices to dominate the conversation, but it is important that everyone has a chance to contribute and be heard. Leaders clarify who is accountable for carrying out the decisions.

❊ Invite everyone in the group to share. Keep asking questions until everyone has a chance to contribute ideas and concerns.

❊ Try to engage everyone who will be affected by the decision, especially anyone who will have to carry it out. This may include parents and administrators.

❊ Be clear about everyone's responsibilities and tasks, the steps to take, and the documentation needed.

Creating an emotionally supportive climate (LED-S7)

Good leaders create a safe, accepting environment for practitioners, babies, and their families with regular reflective supervision. Leaders recognize the importance of adults' well-being in their work with babies and encourage caregivers (colleagues, parents) to take care of themselves, to get rest and exercise, and to build social connections and support. They promote relationships of trust, respect, and support at every level—between caregivers and babies, caregivers and parents, caregivers and other staff—by being transparent and open while respecting others' needs for confidentiality and taking a strength-based approach to each individual.

Connecting with decision makers and joining decision-making processes (LED-S8)

Infant-toddler services are often provided by multiple organizations focused on education, social services, health, or nutrition, whose leaders must collaborate to make sure services get to the babies and families who need them. These groups of decision makers may work within a single large organization or intersect at the community, regional, or state level. Leaders connect with other decision makers and work to make decisions collaboratively, serving as a voice for babies and families.

STRATEGIES

* Identify leaders in your community, region, and state who make decisions that affect services for babies.

* Contact decision makers and other stakeholders to get to know them and learn more about their perspective and goals for babies in your community.

* Attend community events that decision makers and other stakeholders also attend so they become familiar with you.

* Invite decision makers and other stakeholders to events that highlight your program's strengths or directly address policy issues about working with babies.

Reflect Back, Think Ahead

Look back at figure 9.1 at the beginning of this chapter that shows the knowledge, disposition, and skill competencies involved in leadership, mentoring, and coaching. Which of these competencies did you have when you began this chapter? Which competencies did you develop? Which competencies will you intentionally work on building for yourself next? Use the chapter on Leadership, Mentoring, and Coaching in the Professional Learning Guide (PLG [see page 11]) that accompanies this book to support your own professional growth in this domain.

Selected References

Ambrose, Susan A., Michael W. Bridges, Michele DiPietro, Marsha C. Lovett, and Marie K. Norman. 2010. *How Learning Works: 7 Research-Based Principles for Smart Teaching*. Hoboken, NJ: Wiley.

Donegan-Ritter, M., and B. Van Meeteren. 2018. "Using Practice-Based Coaching to Increase Use of Language Facilitation Strategies in Early Head Start and Community Partners." *Infants & Young Children* 31 (3): 215–30.

Heffron, Mary Claire, and Trudi Murch. 2012. *Finding the Words, Finding the Ways: Exploring Reflective Supervision and Facilitation*. DVD. Sacramento, CA: WestEd.

LeMoine, Sarah. 2008. *Workforce Designs: A Policy Blueprint for State Early Childhood Professional Development Systems*. NAEYC public policy report. Washington, DC: National Association for the Education of Young Children. www.naeyc.org/sites/default/files/wysiwyg/user-74/workforce_designs.pdf.

McLeod, R., K. Artman-Meeker, and J. K. Hardy. 2017. "Preparing Yourself for Coaching." *Young Children*, 72 (3): 75–81.

Parlakian, Rebecca. 2001. *Look, Listen, and Learn: Reflective Supervision and Relationship-Based Work*. Washington, DC: Zero to Three.

Roggman, Lori A., Lisa K. Boyce, and Mark S. Innocenti. 2008. *Developmental Parenting: A Guide for Early Childhood Practitioners*. Baltimore: Paul H. Brookes.

Tomlin, Angela M., Lynne Sturm, and Steven M. Koch. 2009. "Observe, Listen, Wonder, and Respond: A Preliminary Exploration of Reflective Function Skills in Early Care Providers." *Infant Mental Health Journal* 30 (6): 634–47.

Tschannen-Moran, B., and M. Tschannen-Moran. 2011. "The Coach and the Evaluator." *Educational Leadership* 69 (2): 10–16.

CHAPTER 10

Becoming an Infant-Toddler Professional

Much of this book has detailed the knowledge, dispositions, and skills that you need to provide high-quality child care and education to babies and their families. This chapter encompasses how you see yourself as an early childhood professional and how that affects your work and advancement in your career (see the summarized competencies for professionalism in figure 10.1). Professionalism is about finding your voice, knowing who you are as a practitioner within your program, and communicating that outside of your program. Professionalism also includes the ethical and legal requirements of working with babies and their families.

Why is this competency important? Having a sense of professionalism gives direction to your career. Your professional identity can help you identify where you want to work and guide you as you improve your practice and take on new challenges. Professionalism also gives a deeper meaning to your work, which can be sustaining when the work is challenging and demanding. Fostering a sense of professionalism in yourself and others also helps develop the broader infant-toddler field. Ultimately, increased professionalization will improve conditions for the workforce, the quality of care provided, and eventually the outcomes for babies and their families.

How is this competency related to other competencies? Professionalism is strongly related to reflective practice, which enables you to develop competencies in a conscious and intentional way. This lifelong learning is a central aspect of being a professional. Professionalism is also connected to leadership. Although professionalism can be seen in your everyday actions with babies, families, colleagues, and supervisors, it is also about your interactions with decision makers at the local, state, and national levels.

Facilitating conditions. All program staff should have access to training and understand professional codes of conduct, as well as state and local

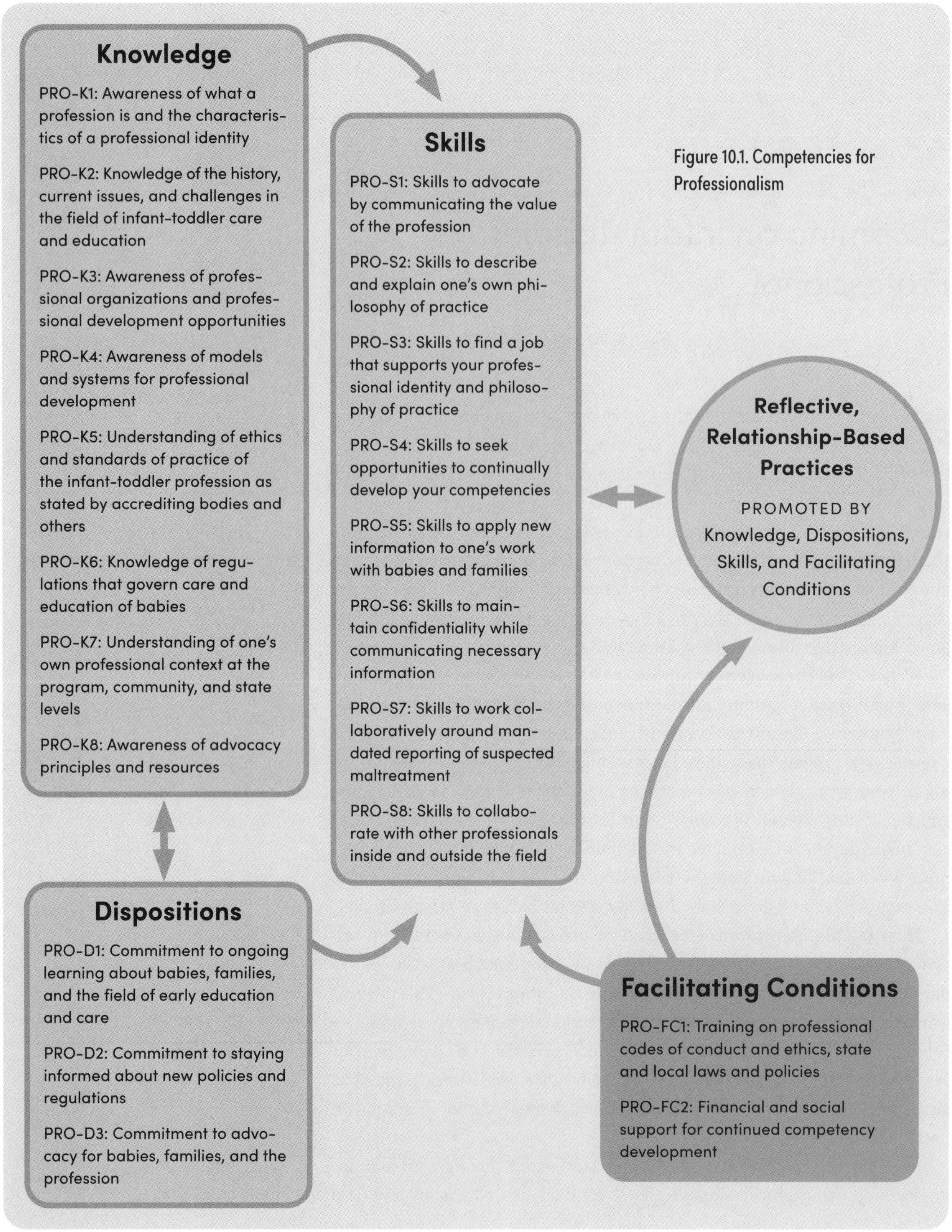

Knowledge

PRO-K1: Awareness of what a profession is and the characteristics of a professional identity

PRO-K2: Knowledge of the history, current issues, and challenges in the field of infant-toddler care and education

PRO-K3: Awareness of professional organizations and professional development opportunities

PRO-K4: Awareness of models and systems for professional development

PRO-K5: Understanding of ethics and standards of practice of the infant-toddler profession as stated by accrediting bodies and others

PRO-K6: Knowledge of regulations that govern care and education of babies

PRO-K7: Understanding of one's own professional context at the program, community, and state levels

PRO-K8: Awareness of advocacy principles and resources

Skills

PRO-S1: Skills to advocate by communicating the value of the profession

PRO-S2: Skills to describe and explain one's own philosophy of practice

PRO-S3: Skills to find a job that supports your professional identity and philosophy of practice

PRO-S4: Skills to seek opportunities to continually develop your competencies

PRO-S5: Skills to apply new information to one's work with babies and families

PRO-S6: Skills to maintain confidentiality while communicating necessary information

PRO-S7: Skills to work collaboratively around mandated reporting of suspected maltreatment

PRO-S8: Skills to collaborate with other professionals inside and outside the field

Figure 10.1. Competencies for Professionalism

Reflective, Relationship-Based Practices

PROMOTED BY Knowledge, Dispositions, Skills, and Facilitating Conditions

Dispositions

PRO-D1: Commitment to ongoing learning about babies, families, and the field of early education and care

PRO-D2: Commitment to staying informed about new policies and regulations

PRO-D3: Commitment to advocacy for babies, families, and the profession

Facilitating Conditions

PRO-FC1: Training on professional codes of conduct and ethics, state and local laws and policies

PRO-FC2: Financial and social support for continued competency development

laws (PRO-FC1). Regular workshops can address changes in regulations and how they affect the work. Further, programs must provide financial and social support for continued competency development (PRO-FC2) through policies and a culture of learning. Supervisors should help each professional articulate their own philosophy of practice. They should outline a professional development plan indicating where the professional needs or wants to work on knowledge or skills. Program leadership should allocate training resources (paid staff time, money for trainings) to address professional development needs for the staff as a whole and to support individuals' own growth. This may mean sending some staff to a conference or enrolling them in online or in-person classes. Supervisors must help staff apply the knowledge they gain through training in their own real-world practice. Mentors, coaches, consultants, and peer networks can help practitioners turn their knowledge into skills and professional growth.

Knowledge

The foundation of professionalism includes being aware of what a profession is and the characteristics of a professional identity (PRO-K1). Knowledge of the history, current issues, and challenges in the field of infant-toddler care and education (PRO-K2) helps educators better advocate for their profession and move the field toward more optimal infant-toddler care and education. Educators should be aware of professional tools and resources, specifically professional organizations and professional development opportunities within and outside of their programs (PRO-K4). Understanding the ethics and standards of practice (PRO-K5) and state regulations that govern the care and education of babies (PRO-K6) are critical to high-quality, professional care. While administrators are responsible for setting the general practices and procedures that align with state child care licensing guidelines, educators implement caregiving, health and safety procedures, and daily experiences at the classroom level. Professional educators understand the unique characteristics of the programs, communities, and states in which they live, such as program policies on professional development, community supports for families that affect babies, and state regulations and guidelines on early care and education (PRO-K7). Finally, educators are advocates for the field, thus becoming aware of advocacy tools and resources that aid educators in their work (PRO-K8).

Awareness of what a profession is and the characteristics of a professional identity (PRO-K1)

A *profession* is a group of individuals who share a common purpose and identity. The members of the profession agree upon a set of responsibilities and characteristics. Often this means sharing agreements on the following:

* distinct responsibilities, including what practitioners can and cannot be expected to do

* a code of ethics, including shared values and standards for conduct

* expected competencies (knowledge, skills) for beginning and advanced professionals

* standards for practice, defining what lower- and higher-quality practice looks like

* education and training requirements, including what is required to enter the profession, maintain professional standing, and advance to higher responsibilities

* certifications or licenses, which likely vary by state but may share common requirements that are defined at the national level

* legal and professional consequences for negligent practices

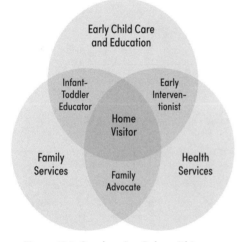

Figure 10.2. Overlapping Roles within the Field

Infant and toddler care and education has a special role within the broader field of early child care and education, with its imperative need to individualize practices for each baby as well as the need to work closely with families (though these practices are also good for children of all age groups). As we describe in figure 10.2, infant-toddler educators, early interventionists, home visitors, and family advocates engage in intersecting roles. For example, infant-toddler educators are providing family services when they offer parenting education workshops or help parents identify needed services in the community.

Forming your professional identity means linking your own identity as a practitioner with that of the profession you have chosen. Your professional identity is about connecting with others who do similar work while understanding what makes your work unique. It is about both fitting in and standing out. Understanding your own practice—how you do what you do and why you do it that way—is an integral part of developing your identity. Developing your professional identity will also help you become more active in your career. When you've developed self-awareness, including a sense of your own competencies, you can consider whether this profession is a good fit for you. And if it is, you may learn more about the type of setting you want to work in, such as a program that has policies that reflect your values and promotes the kind of work you want to do. Your identity can also help you select among continual learning and professional growth options as you attend conferences or fulfill annual professional training requirements.

Professionalism is about finding your voice, knowing who you are as an individual practitioner in your program or agency, and communicating that outside of your program. You can use this voice in many arenas, sharing your knowledge and practice with others.

Knowledge of the history, current issues, and challenges in the field of infant-toddler care and education (PRO-K2)

For much of history, there has been a belief that caring for infants and toddlers is just babysitting—easy work that is mostly custodial caregiving without long-lasting effects on children. Infant-toddler care and education has been thought of as low-skilled work and women's work. However, this belief has been challenged by the growing science of child development, recognizing (a) the importance of the first three years of brain development, (b) the unique needs of infants and toddlers, and (c) the tremendous competencies it takes to provide optimal support during this time of rapid and vulnerable development. These advances are pushing forward political support for infant and toddler services as well as the professionalism of the workforce, and the immense value of this profession is starting to be recognized. While infant-toddler educators are still the lowest-paid members of the educational workforce, there is a move toward the professionalization of the workforce, including calls for increased educational requirements and quality standards as well as increased pay to go along with these new requirements.

National policies play a role in how many infants and toddlers are in early care, whether the policies encourage working families to stay at home with babies or go to work. In the United States, most primary caregivers of infants and toddlers work at least part-time out of the home. With so many babies in early care and education at the most vulnerable and influential time in their lives, organizations are paying new attention to the quality of babies' experiences and the qualifications of the educators at state and national levels. For example, the Administration on Children and Families in the US Department of Health and Human Services and other federal organizations, including Head Start, have emphasized the importance of professionalizing the early care and education field, including work with infants and toddlers. We are in a time of great change in the early childhood workforce, and there are many forces pushing for increased professionalism. Through this push, however, it is important that the workforce remain diverse and that avenues for professionalization are available to the providers who are currently doing the work. During this time of rapid social and professional change, affiliating with professional organizations can help you stay connected to current issues in the field.

Awareness of professional organizations and professional development opportunities (PRO-K3)

You will learn about the standards of practice and ethical guidelines set out by professional organizations, as well as laws and licensing as determined by the local, state, or federal government. Professional organizations can be a source of *professional development* as well as information about the broader profession and your place in it. If you choose to become affiliated with professional organizations, they can help you become an active learner and advocate for the profession and the children and families you work with. Professional organizations such as Zero to Three and the National Association for the Education of Young Children (NAEYC) provide many free or low-cost resources, covering topics such as antibias approaches in caregiving, developmental guidance, and advocacy "tool kits" with easy actions educators can take to promote higher-quality care. Other organizations partner with state organizations to oversee credentialing. For example, the Michigan Association for Infant Mental Health and the Alliance for the Advancement of Infant Mental Health partner with many states to implement infant and early childhood mental health credentials, including an endorsement designed for early childhood educators.

The Resources and Further Readings document that accompanies this book lists organizations providing professional development and advocacy opportunities, practice guidelines, and resources and networks for infant-toddler educators, including standards and best practices, codes of ethical conduct, and licensing regulations. However, it is always best to ask around where you live and work to see which organizations are most active in your area.

Awareness of models and systems for professional development (PRO-K4)

As explained by NAEYC, a professional development system (PDS) refers to a broad set of tools and resources in integrated frameworks designed to support the ongoing development of early childhood professionals. Professional development should be offered in multiple modes and adapted to educators' specific needs. A PDS can encompass the following:

❋ **Credentialing for the infant-toddler workforce:** Credentials (such as the Child Development Associate Infant-Toddler credential) ensure quality when all practitioners are expected to have them.

* **Certifications and endorsements:** Certifications and endorsements build and verify specialized knowledge and skills beyond a credential; examples are the Infant Mental Health endorsements in Michigan and California.

* **Competencies for infant-toddler workforce:** Many states have defined sets of competencies for early child educators, and some have separate competencies for infant-toddler educators. States should ensure that there are professional development opportunities framed around each set of competencies.

* **Individualized professional development plans:** Educators need an individualized professional development plan adapted to their strengths, knowledge, and goals. Some states have registry systems where practitioners can track their growing competencies as they attend conferences and workshops aligned with specific topics. Communicating your professional development plan with a supervisor can help them become a resource for you. Let them know what you want feedback on, and seek their help in identifying opportunities that can help you advance your skills and career.

* **Individualized coaching:** You can increase your knowledge by reading a book or attending a workshop. But to change your skills and practices, you need feedback over time provided by a trusted person in the work setting. Effective coaching involves collaboratively deciding goals, observing practice, providing feedback, reflecting together, and planning together.

* **Communities of practice (CoP):** CoPs involve people doing similar work who meet regularly to share ideas and challenges, set goals, engage in training to meet those goals, and track progress.

* **Collaboration:** Professionals can work together to identify goals and take action steps to accomplish these goals. This collaboration is most productive with colleagues who share your values and have overlapping experience and expertise to help you reflect on your work. Observing others can highlight where you want to focus in your own practice.

States vary in their efforts and progress toward developing a PDS for the infant-toddler workforce, or even the early childhood profession in general. There is movement nationally toward increasing the professionalization of the workforce, perhaps eventually requiring either a two-year associate's degree or a four-year bachelor's degree. Many practitioners are already pursuing higher education while they gain work experience with infants and toddlers. As it stands currently, most professional development in the infant-toddler workforce is not organized into a system but offered piece by piece. Often the individual educator must determine what they need and seek opportunities to meet those needs. You can use the competencies in this book to understand your own strengths, as well as areas where you need more support, so that you can systematically pursue education opportunities and do your best work.

Understanding of ethics and standards of practice of the infant-toddler profession as stated by accrediting bodies and others (PRO-K5)

Ethical guidelines. The ethics of the early childhood profession guide how practitioners work with babies and families, as well as how they interact with colleagues. Our professional ethics guide how we include and involve diverse families, guide babies' behavior, support learning, assess development, include babies with additional support needs, and support our colleagues. Internationally, the United Nations Convention on the Rights of the Child has defined the international standard for how children have a right to be treated, including aspects of their care and education. In the United States, the NAEYC Code of Ethical Conduct and Statement of Commitment (2011) "offers guidelines for responsible behavior and sets forth a common basis for resolving the principal ethical dilemmas encountered in early childhood care and education" (1). The NAEYC Code of Ethical Conduct is the basis for most ethical frameworks in early education. The code includes our ethical responsibilities to children, families, colleagues, communities, and society.

The first principles of the NAEYC Code of Ethical Conduct (2011) provide general guidance and apply to all of our work with babies and families: "Above all, we shall not harm children. We shall not participate in practices that are emotionally damaging, physically harmful, disrespectful, degrading, dangerous, exploitative, or intimidating to children" (3). NAEYC provides specific ethical guidance on how we include all families and show respect for family diversity, how we guide babies' behavior, how we support learning and development, how we conduct and use assessments, and how we include babies with additional support needs.

Standards of best practice. In the United States, national professional organizations, states, and the federal government provide standards that guide practices in early child care and education. Links and additional organizations are provided in the Resources and Further Readings document:

※ *Head Start Program Performance Standards*—for quality requirements for Head Start programs

※ *Head Start Parent Family and Community Engagement Framework*—for intended program outcomes

❊ *Build Initiative State Quality Rating and Improvement Systems*—for QRIS standards

❊ *NAEYC Early Childhood Program Standards*—for characteristics of high-quality programs

❊ *Division of Early Childhood of the Council for Exceptional Children (DEC-CEC)*—for recommended practices for working with babies with delays or disabilities

❊ *National Center on Early Childhood Quality Assurance Early Learning Guidelines*—for state-by-state information on standards for the educational experiences infants and toddlers should have

Knowledge of regulations that govern care and education of babies (PRO-K6)

You must know your legal obligations to babies and families, which typically come from state licensing regulations. In addition, local, state, or national organizations, including NAEYC and DEC-CEC may describe sets of "best practices." These reflect the field's current scientific understandings for supporting well-being, development, and learning during early childhood, as well as the organization's values and philosophies.

Each state has its own environmental safety standards and licensing regulations for child care and education programs, often with particular items for infants and toddlers. These follow recommendations from the American Academy of Pediatrics (AAP) and the American Public Health Association (APHA). To find your state's regulations, visit the National Database of Child Care Licensing Regulation website. A comprehensive and detailed Health and Safety Screener checklist is also available from the Office of Head Start's Early Childhood Learning & Knowledge Center. For nationally relevant standards of care for health, safety, and stimulation, see *Caring for our Children: National Health and Safety Performance Standards; Guidelines for Early Care and Education Programs*, fourth edition, jointly written by the AAP, the APHA, and the National Resource Center for Health and Safety in Child Care and Early Education.

Child maltreatment and your role as a mandated reporter. While each state has its own laws related to reporting child abuse, early childhood caregivers and educators are *always* mandated reporters. A mandated reporter is someone who, because of their job or role in children's lives, is required by law to report any indication that a child is being maltreated. The program or agency you work for may have its own protocol for making reports, and discussing your concerns about a child or family with a supervisor is usually a good idea, but this does not change your legal obligation to report suspected abuse to the state-appointed agency. You must make sure

www.redleafpress.org/wwb/10-1.pdf

the report is made or you may face a criminal penalty for neglecting your legal responsibility. See appendix B (via QR code on page 128) for signs of maltreatment in infants and toddlers; see handout 10.1, Mandated Reporting, for information on how to make a report of suspected child maltreatment and what happens when you do. Visit the website of the Child Welfare Information Gateway to learn more.

Understanding your professional context at the program, community, and state levels (PRO-K7)

Developing your own professional identity involves learning about your unique context, including the state and community in which you work, the children and families you serve, and the specific program you work in. To learn about your own professional context, ask yourself the following questions:

- ❋ What state agencies govern early intervention, home visiting, and child care? How do those entities collaborate?

- ❋ What are your state's regulations surrounding early childhood licensing and certifications?

- ❋ Does your state have early learning guidelines for infants and toddlers? Get a copy of them.

- ❋ What are the elements in the state Quality Rating and Improvement System? Which assessments are used to evaluate programs in the system? Get a copy of them.

- ❋ What are your state's criteria for early intervention eligibility?

- ❋ What are strengths in your community? What public and private institutions support families, including faith-based centers, community centers, and informal community groups? What employment opportunities are there?

- ❋ What are common challenges many families face, such as homelessness, unemployment, mental health issues, teen parenting, addiction, isolation, or lack of community cohesion?

- ❋ What are the cultural backgrounds of the families you work with? Do families live in segregated or integrated communities? Do families from cultural or ethnic minorities live near others from their culture, or do they experience isolation?

- ❋ What are community events that influence families' need for child care and education (for example, the influx of new jobs with a new plant opening, seasonal migrant workers).

Awareness of advocacy principles and resources (PRO-K8)

The importance of the first years of life and babies' relationships with adults implies a need for local, state, and federal policies and resources that support families with young children, increase the availability of high-quality care and education programs, and increase the number of competent infant-toddler professionals. With your expertise as an infant-toddler professional, you are uniquely qualified to advocate for babies and their families and for the early childhood profession as a whole.

Who are the decision makers? Learn who the decision makers are at every level so you know who to call or visit. Your expertise and knowledge are valuable to policy makers. Over time, if you develop relationships with them, they may come to you with questions about policies. You can show them your high-quality program in action and talk about the importance of early childhood. Such decision makers include executive (mayors, governors, or people who work in the Department of Education or Department of Public Health) and legislative officials (members of local boards, councils, and committees as well as state-level legislature or general assembly).

What are the issues and decisions being made? At the local level, you might push to expand disability or mental health services for children and families. At the state level, it may be issues of professional certification or resource distribution. At the national level, you might advocate for tax credits for young children, family leave policies, or funding for federal early childhood services. The lack of pay equity for the early childhood workforce affects well-being. To learn more about each state's policies that affect pay and support for the early childhood workforce, see the website of the Center for the Study of Child Care Employment.

Choose the issue that is most meaningful for you and where you think you can make a difference.

* NAEYC has materials for building your advocacy skills; their initiative Power to the Profession aims to professionalize the early childhood workforce.

* Zero to Three resources include advocacy tools and state-by-state facts for advocating for babies and families.

* the National Child Care Association is devoted to supporting policies that are beneficial to children.

* the Center for the Study of Child Care Employment has information on policies related to the workforce.

Connect and collaborate. Gathering a group of child care professionals can send a powerful message to decision makers. Enlisting families can be especially effective. When the national Head Start program was threatened, busloads of families and professionals came to hearings in Washington, DC, to protect these resources.

Dispositions

Educators' dispositions about supporting professionalism reflect their commitments to ongoing learning (PRO-D1), staying informed about new policies and regulations (PRO-D2), and advocating for the well-being of babies, families, and the profession (PRO-D3). Collectively, these commitments promote professionalization of the field as they call educators to strive for their optimal development and support of the field.

Commitment to ongoing learning about babies, families, and the field of early education and care (PRO-D1)

A commitment to ongoing learning is a critical characteristic of your professional identity, and being a lifelong learner means being willing to change based on what you learn. Commit to staying informed about new assessment tools, curricula, and professional standards. Find ways to learn about new research on children's development. Continually refine your practice and discover new ways families and practitioners can support children.

Commitment to staying informed about new policies and regulations (PRO-D2)

You also have an ethical and legal obligation to stay current on policies and regulations dictating your practice. Your commitment to ongoing learning and adapting your practices to new policies is foundational to being an early childhood professional.

Commitment to advocacy for babies, families, and the profession (PRO-D3)

As an early childhood expert and professional, you can help to generate support among the general public. You can make your case to local, state, and national decision makers on behalf of the profession as well as calling for services and policies to support young children and their families. You can make a difference to the profession and to children and families nationwide through your advocacy.

Professionalism begins with building advocacy skills to communicate the value of the field (PRO-S1) and to explain your philosophy of practice to colleagues, families, and the community (PRO-S2), which helps others understand how vital your work is to the well-being of society's youngest members. Make a place for yourself within the profession by finding a job that aligns with your professional identity and your philosophy of practice (PRO-S3), seeking ongoing professional development (PRO-S4), and applying new information to your work (PRO-S5). Finally, professionalism includes maintaining confidentiality with children and families (PRO-S6), working collaboratively in mandated reporting (PRO-S7), and working with other professionals (PRO-S8) to serve babies and their families.

Being an advocate by communicating the value of the profession (PRO-S1)

You are learning the importance of the first three years of life and how we as adults can best support children's development. Many people may not understand what your work as an infant-toddler practitioner really means. Sharing what you do and the effects of your work on babies and their families (and society in general) can generate support for the profession. You can describe the complexity of the competencies needed for working with infants and toddlers. Some opportunities for educating others come in offhand remarks from people who are not knowledgeable. You might hear comments such as these:

- "Infant-toddler educators are just babysitters. You don't need a degree to do that."

- "All you do is play with babies all day. How is that a profession?"

- "Infants and toddlers are not learning things that will matter later— they won't even remember it—so it doesn't really matter what you do with them."

Figure 10.3 illustrates a simple four-step pattern for communicating in a way that educates others about the value and importance of the profession, as well as what practitioners need in order to do their best work with babies and families.

To develop this communication skill, think about the most important aspects of how babies develop and what they need; then consider how this knowledge guides your practices with them.

Babies develop. . .		
Babies develop faster in the first three years than they will at any other time in their lives.	Babies may experience delays in development that could affect them for years to come.	Babies must feel secure and connected with their caregivers to be able to focus on learning.

So babies need. . .		
So they need rich stimulation, as well as nurturing care.	If so, they need extra support for development of certain domains, and may be eligible for early intervention.	So they need to be cared for consistently by people they trust.

Thus, infant-toddler practitioners must. . .		
Thus, infant-toddler practitioners must be intentional about the ways they talk to, play with, and choose materials for babies to best support their development.	Thus, infant-toddler practitioners must watch babies closely to monitor their development and seek extra support if needed.	Thus, infant-toddler practitioners must establish strong relationships with babies and their families and try to work with each baby for as long as possible.

Therefore, infant-toddler practitioners need. . .		
Therefore, practitioners need in-depth knowledge of babies' development and access to high-quality materials.	Therefore, practitioners need training on and access to screening tools, and support for using these systematically with all babies.	Therefore, practitioners need support for their own well-being and mental health so they can be emotionally present with babies and families.

Figure 10.3. Steps for Communicating the Importance of the Infant-Toddler Workforce

Describing and explaining your own philosophy of practice (PRO-S2)

Beyond communicating the importance of the infant-toddler profession as a whole, part of developing your professional identity is articulating your own practice—how you do what you do and why you do it that way. Your philosophy is based on your knowledge of the research evidence and professional standards but also on your values and beliefs from your life experience. When you reflect on the factors that influence your beliefs, the process can lead to further exploration and growth. Explaining your philosophy to colleagues and families can facilitate collaboration and connection. Some educators write brief philosophy of practice statements that they provide to new families. Others express their philosophies spontaneously when they are discussing their practices with families or colleagues, particularly areas of disagreement or possible misunderstanding. Your professional philosophy can help prioritize your day-to-day work. It can steer your professional development choices.

Use a three-step model to explain your own philosophy of practice:

1 *I believe* . . . about babies/families.

2 *So I do* . . . in my practice.

3 *The effect of this* for babies/families is . . .

For example, *I believe that relationships motivate babies and provide them with the sense of security they need to explore and learn. So when I meet new babies, I first work on forming a strong relationship with them, connecting emotionally through interactions. In my experience, I have found that babies trust me quickly. They use me as a secure base when they explore and are excited to share with me what they discover.*

You may find it helpful to build a professional portfolio with pictures and stories that show others what you do, how you do it, and what effects it has on children and families.

Skills to find a job that supports your professional identity and philosophy of practice (PRO-S3)

Understanding how your own philosophy and identity fit the policies, procedures, and professional culture of a program can help you decide whether it is the correct professional setting for you. Does the job serve the population of children and families you want to work with? Does the program value what you do? Is there support to do the work you want to do? Of course, as a professional you can also work to change the setting by articulating your philosophy of practice and working with program management. If you are in a formal leadership role, you can ensure that policies and resource distribution reflect your values and those of others in the program.

STRATEGIES

When evaluating your current position or considering a new position, ask yourself these questions:

⁑ Who does this program serve?

⁑ What specific responsibilities would your role/job entail?

⁑ What is the leadership like? Is there shared decision-making?

⁑ Is supervision focused on compliance with regulations, or is there opportunity for reflection?

⁑ Are there opportunities for individualized professional development?

* What is the interaction between coworkers like? Is it competitive or collaborative?

* Do staff talk to and about babies and families in respectful and kind ways?

* Do you have paid time to meet with families, conduct and reflect on observations, and plan curriculum?

Seeking opportunities to continually develop your competencies (PRO-S4)

Your reading this book is an example of this competency. This is a good start, but you will need to keep learning about babies and families and what you can do for them throughout your career. This is a lifelong endeavor in continually refining and improving your practice, helping you grow into the professional you want to be. Learn who you are as a learner, as well as an educator. Do you like to go to conferences or workshops, participate in semester-long college courses or online courses, or visit other early childhood settings? Some people prefer reading or watching videos to learn, while others like listening to learn. Others learn by doing and desire movement. Most of us are a combination of the above. Through reflecting on your experiences as a learner, you will figure out what works best for you. Your peers and supervisors can be valuable sources of information on professional development opportunities.

STRATEGIES

Look for opportunities that are the following:

* relevant—directly related to your work

* goal oriented—help you achieve a professional goal

* practical—focused on how theory or research can be applied to real life

* collaborative—instructors consider the learners to be colleagues

* self-directed—learners can assume responsibility for their own learning and choices

* aimed at utilizing life experience—learners are encouraged to bring their experience, knowledge, and opinions to bear

Applying new information to your work with babies and families (PRO-S5)

Seek feedback from others to help you apply new knowledge or change specific practices. Having a peer, a supervisor, or a coach/mentor observe you and give feedback is helpful—but, if possible, filming yourself and reflecting on your behavior with a trusted colleague, mentor, or coach is invaluable. Communities of practice can improve practice program-wide by bringing colleagues together to work on the same skills. As you become more skilled yourself, you may become a mentor to junior colleagues, which improves your own practice as well as your leadership skills (chapter 9).

Maintaining confidentiality while communicating necessary information (PRO-S6)

Chapter 4 discussed communicating with families about potentially sensitive topics. This can include sharing information about program policies and licensing requirements as well as their baby's behavior and development. Part of professionalism is maintaining confidentiality regarding the information you share with and about families, which supports their trust in you and their relationships with each other. For example, when you must tell a family that another child has gone home because of a communicable illness, or that their baby was bit by another child, don't indicate which other child was involved. You can simply say, "Two children are out sick today. Watch for symptoms of . . . ," or "Your baby was bit by another child today while they were playing together. She cried but calmed quickly. You may see a small red mark on her arm." This same principle also works for communication with and about your colleagues.

Working collaboratively around mandated reporting of suspected maltreatment (PRO-S7)

Reporting a family for suspected maltreatment is probably the most difficult thing you will do as an early childhood professional. Your work has focused on making strong relationships with families and supporting them in caring for their child. Reporting a family to authorities can be painful. You may worry that it will disrupt your relationship with the family or cause them to leave the program, possibly ending your relationship with the child. While this sometimes happens, it is not always the case. It can help if you tell families when they enroll in the program that you are a mandated reporter and explain what that means. Being comfortable with your legal responsibilities as a mandated reporter and developing your skills in this area is important. Hopefully you will not be required to report suspected maltreatment often in your career, but it is critical that you are prepared to do so if you must.

Become comfortable and confident in fulfilling this essential professional responsibility by taking the following actions:

❋ Talk to your supervisor to make sure you know program policies surrounding reporting, including asking questions like these: Are you expected to call your supervisor before making the call to your local child protective services (CPS) agency? Should you make the call together with your supervisor? Is it common practice in your program to let families know that you are making the call (only in cases where you would not place the child or yourself in danger by doing so)? Does your program have a designated contact at the CPS program to call?

❋ Ask colleagues and supervisors about past calls and what the consequences were. This will help you plan in advance should you need to make a report.

❋ Practice how you might talk to a family with your colleagues.

❋ Make families aware of your role and responsibilities as a mandated reporter so you have set yourself up to have these hard conversations if necessary. For instance, if a family lives in an unsafe building, you can let the family know that you are required to make a report, and that if you make the call together, the CPS agency may be able to help the family find a safer place to live.

❋ Review the definitions and signs of maltreatment in appendix B (see page 128), and see handout 10.1, Mandated Reporting, to understand the information you should gather and the steps you should follow.

After making a report, take time to process your feelings with peers or a supervisor. What did you learn? What might you do the same or differently the next time? How do you feel about how the CPS agency treated the family?

Collaborating with other professionals inside and outside of the field (PRO-S8)

As an early childhood professional, you will collaborate with others in similar roles inside your program (like your coeducators) and with professionals from different fields (such as public health workers, family advocates, social workers, or therapists), who may work from either inside or outside your program. Collaborating with colleagues in your program contributes to a happier work environment and makes transitions within the program easier for children and families. Collaborating with other professionals within and outside of your program exposes you to additional viewpoints. It also can help you generate ideas for professional development and advocacy activities. When families have needs for health, educational, or social services, you will have a professional network to go to for referrals.

STRATEGIES

Collaborating effectively includes the following:

- finding out what you can learn from others

- listening deeply to what others have to say and suspending your own views momentarily if needed

- sharing your views clearly and positively, avoiding a defensive stance

- remembering others' roles and expertise so you can draw on them in the future

Reflect Back, Think Ahead

Look back at figure 10.1 at the beginning of this chapter, which shows the knowledge, disposition, and skill competencies involved in becoming an infant-toddler professional. Which of these competencies did you have when you began this chapter? Which competencies did you develop? Which competencies will you intentionally work on building next? Use the chapter Becoming an Infant-Toddler Professional in the Professional Learning Guide (PLG [see page 11]) that accompanies this book to support your own professional growth in this domain.

In this book, we have described the knowledge and dispositions that promote high-quality early care and education, and the skills needed to be the most effective infant-toddler practitioner you can be. We hope that reading this book and engaging in self-reflection have influenced your work as a practitioner who works with, or will someday work with, infants, toddlers, and their families. At the end of each chapter, we invited you to reflect on the competencies that you already had when you began reading this book, those you developed as you read and used the PLG, and those you want to build in the near future. Continuing to reflect on your knowledge, dispositions, and skills is important to maintain and improve the quality of early care and education you provide. As you reflect on your experiences and learning with this book, use table 10.1 to review the competencies you have developed with each chapter of this book and set goals for yourself based on who you want to become as an infant-toddler professional.

Table 10.1. Self-Reflection on New Competencies and Goals in Each Domain as an Infant-Toddler Professional

Competencies	New Competencies	New Goals
Reflective Practice		
Building and Supporting Relationships		
Partnering with and Supporting Diverse Families		
Guiding Infant-Toddler Behavior		
Supporting Development and Learning		
Assessing Behavior, Development, and Environments		
Including Infants and Toddlers with Additional Support Needs and their Families		
Leadership, Mentoring, and Coaching		
Professionalism		

* How has your understanding of infant and toddler curricula changed?

* How would you describe the role of relationships in infant and toddler care and education to others?

* What is one way you will continue to grow as an infant and toddler professional?

* What is one new goal you are setting as an infant and toddler professional?

Working with infants, toddlers, and their families is a noble profession in which practitioners are charged with supporting and promoting human development and growth during a developmental period unlike any other. The work you do with babies is absolutely essential to the health and well-being not only of babies and families but also of the larger society. We thank you for your dedication and wish you well in your work.

Selected References

Aikens, Nikki, Laura Akers, and Sally Atkins-Burnett. 2016. *Professional Development Tools to Improve the Quality of Infant and Toddler Care: A Review of the Literature.* OPRE Report 2016-96. Washington, DC: Office of Planning, Research and Evaluation, Administration for Children and Families, US Department of Health and Human Services.

Interlandi, Jeneen. 2018. "Why Are Our Most Important Teachers Paid the Least?" *New York Times Magazine*, January 9. www.nytimes.com/2018/01/09/magazine/why-are-our-most-important-teachers-paid-the-least.html.

NAEYC (National Association for the Education of Young Children). 2011. "Code of Ethical Conduct and Statement of Commitment." www.naeyc.org/sites/default/files/globally-shared/downloads/PDFs/resources/position-statements/Ethics%20Position%20Statement2011_09202013update.pdf.

NAEYC (National Association for the Education of Young Children). *Power to the Profession.* www.naeyc.org/our-work/initiatives/profession.

Professional Standards Councils. 2020. "What Is a Profession?" www.psc.gov.au/what-is-a-profession.

Whitebook, Marcy, Caitlin Mclean, Lea J. E. Austin, and Bethany Edwards. 2018. *The Early Childhood Workforce Index 2018.* Center for the Study of Child Care Employment. https://cscce.berkeley.edu/early-childhood-workforce-2018-index.